INSPIRE / PLAN / DISCOVER / EXPERIENCE

NAPLES
AND THE AMALFI COAST

NAPLES
AND THE AMALFI COAST

CONTENTS

DISCOVER 6

EXPERIENCE 50

NEED TO KNOW 204

Left: Colourful deckchairs on a Sorrento pier
Previous page: The Amalfi coastline at dusk
Cover: The majolica-tiled cupola of Santa Maria dell' Assunta in Positano

DISCOVER

Naples and Vesuvius seen at dusk

WELCOME TO
NAPLES AND THE
AMALFI COAST

One of the world's oldest cities, Naples has stood the test of time. Its majestic Baroque façades and colourful alleys contrast with the exquisite landscapes of the Amalfi Coast nearby. Whatever your dream trip to Naples and the Amalfi Coast entails, this DK Eyewitness travel guide is the perfect companion.

1 View of Mount Vesuvius from Naples.

2 *Sfogliatella*, a traditional pastry from the region.

3 Café in a colourful street in the Quartieri Spagnoli.

4 The colourful houses of Marina Corricella on Procida.

With a local proverb declaring that you can "see Naples and die," it's clear the locals hold their home in high esteem, and with good reason. Hundreds of churches and palazzos still dot this Baroque-era gem, whose architecture always seems to be in a state of enchanting disrepair. Wander through its grand piazzas and atmospheric alleys, or join the Neapolitans in sipping dark espressos and ordering margheritas in the city where pizza was born. Time seems to have stood still here, although looming Mount Vesuvius is a reminder that things can change in an instant – nearby Pompeii testifies both to the region's ancient history and to the volcano's awe-inspiring power.

Just beyond the city, the Amalfi Coast's breathtaking landscapes feature a chain of kaleidoscopic towns tumbling down the cliffs, with a palette mixing turquoise seas, verdant hillsides and bright yellow lemons. Short ferry rides link you to Capri's lively piazzas, Ischia's thermal spas and Procida's pastel houses.

Naples and the Amalfi Coast are so full of things to discover and experience that it can be hard to know where to start. We've broken the region down into easily navigable sections, with detailed itineraries, expert local knowledge and colourful, comprehensive maps to help you plan the perfect visit. Whether you're staying for a weekend, a week or longer, this DK Eyewitness guide will ensure that you see the very best this beautiful part of Italy has to offer. Sip a glass of *limoncello*, enjoy the book and enjoy Naples and the Amalfi Coast.

REASONS TO LOVE
NAPLES AND THE AMALFI COAST

Naples and the Amalfi Coast is a dazzling show whose sights, sounds and flavours have tantalized visitors for millennia. Here are some favourites that will make you want to be part of the production.

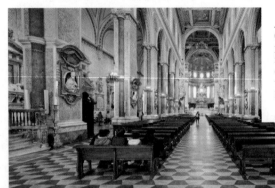

1 FAITH AND SPIRITUALITY

Come face to face with Naples' patron saint, San Gennaro, in churches on nearly every corner, or head to *presepi* shops to take home these traditional Neapolitan nativity scenes.

2 DRIVING THE AMALFI COAST

Prepare for sweeping vistas and sharp cliffs as you wind your way along the Amalfi Drive *(p176)*, the coastal road that reveals stunning towns seemingly rising from the sea.

3 LEMONS

This local speciality adds a delicious brightness to Neapolitan cooking. You can eat a Sorrento lemon with just a dusting of sugar, but make sure to try it in its most iconic form, *limoncello*, a liqueur made with lemon zest and grappa.

ANCIENT CIVILIZATIONS *4*

Walk in the footsteps of the ancients at Paestum's Greek temples (p174) or immerse yourself in the past at the Roman cities of Pompeii (p158) and Herculaneum (p174).

STREET LIFE *5*

Gesticulating grandmothers, honking scooterists, giggling children and chatting locals – a charming soap opera of everyday life unfolds in the streets of Naples. All you need to do is join in.

MUSEO ARCHEOLOGICO NAZIONALE *6*

Explore the long history of human civilization through the artworks at this museum (p96), but, most importantly, admire all of the artifacts that have been moved here from Pompeii and Herculaneum.

SOUND OF THE CITY 7

A street crooner singing in dialect, passionately yearning for his lover, is the soundtrack of Naples. Classical music lovers should also head to the world's oldest opera house *(p63)*.

A VOLCANIC VIEW 8

Mighty Mount Vesuvius *(p166)* looms over the region of Naples, its ever-fuming vents and smouldering sulphuric air suggesting that this giant is only sleeping, not dead.

9 ROYAL NAPLES

European rulers vied for Naples for centuries, and each left their mark. Walk in their footsteps through towering *castellos* and palaces like the glitteringly ornate Caserta *(p194)* and the grand Capodimonte *(p114)*.

10 ISLAND LIFE

Explore the colourful houses of Procida *(p192)*, soak at a thermal spa on Ischia *(p190)* or relax with an alfresco drink by the turquoise waters of Capri *(p186)*.

PIZZA 11

This irresistible food needs no introduction, especially in the city of its birth. Whether it's fried, folded to go or just a plain margherita, the world's best pizza can be found simply by strolling along Via dei Tribunali.

GHOULISH NAPLES 12

Beneath the city, awaiting those seeking to take a look at Naples's darker side, lies a world of catacombs and cemeteries where the Cult of the Dead makes offerings to the deceased, invoking their help.

EXPLORE
NAPLES AND THE
AMALFI COAST

This guide divides this area into seven colour-coded sightseeing areas: six city sections, as shown on this map, and Pompeii and the Amalfi Coast *(p154)*. Find out more about each area on the following pages.

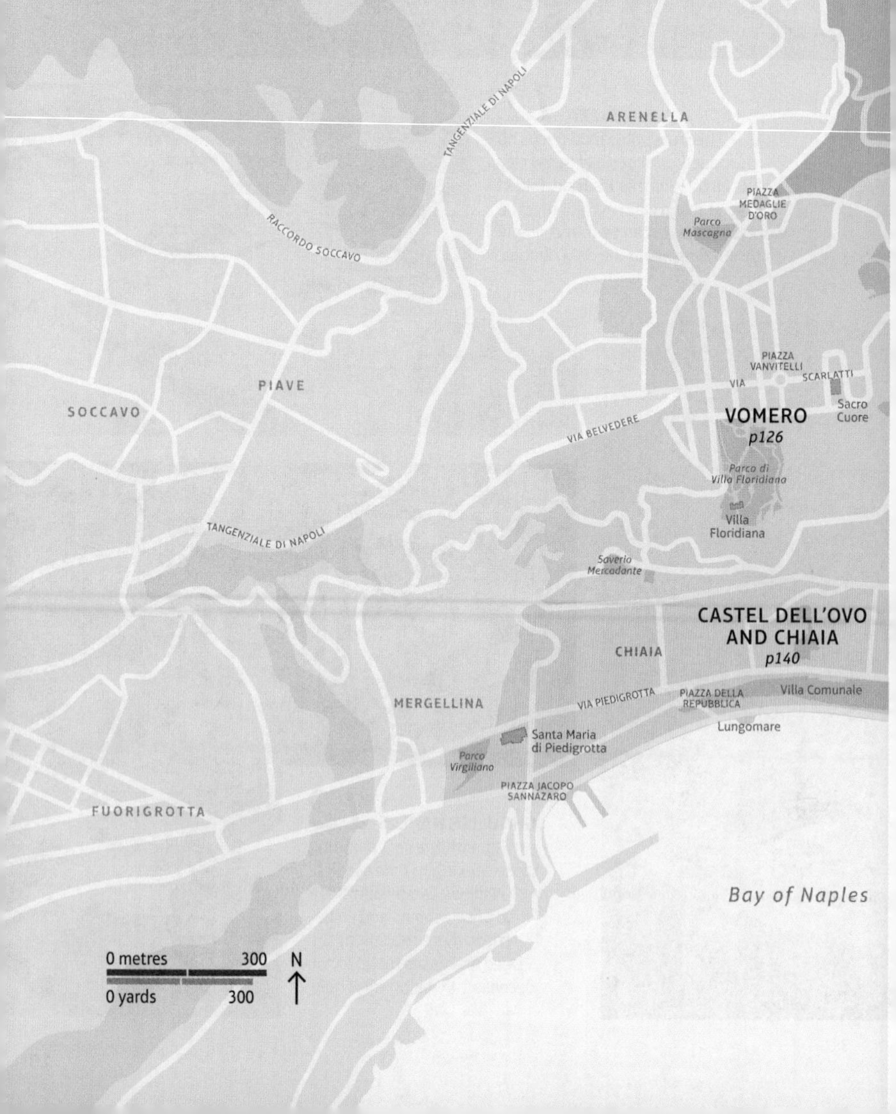

TANGENZIALE DI NAPOLI

ARENELLA

RACCORDO SOCCAVO

PIAZZA
MEDAGLIE
D'ORO

Parco
Mascagna

PIAVE

SOCCAVO

PIAZZA
VANVITELLI

VIA   SCARLATTI

Sacro
Cuore

VIA BELVEDERE

VOMERO
p126

Parco di
Villa Floridiana

TANGENZIALE DI NAPOLI

Villa
Floridiana

Saverio
Mercadante

**CASTEL DELL'OVO
AND CHIAIA**
p140

CHIAIA

MERGELLINA

VIA PIEDIGROTTA

PIAZZA DELLA
REPUBBLICA

Villa Comunale

Lungomare

Santa Maria
di Piedigrotta

Parco
Virgiliano

PIAZZA JACOPO
SANNAZARO

FUORIGROTTA

Bay of Naples

| 0 metres | 300 |
| 0 yards | 300 |

N
↑

SAN CARLO
ALL'ARENA

STELLA

Museo e Real
Bosco di Capodimonte

TANGENZIALE DI NAPOLI

Albergo
dei Poveri

San Gennaro
Catacombs

TANGENZIALE DI NAPOLI

Osservatorio
Astronomico

Orto
Botanico

CORSO GIUSEPPE GARIBALDI

VICARIA

Cimitero delle
Fontanelle

**CAPODIMONTE
AND I VERGINI**
p110

VIA FORIA

San Giovanni
a Carbonara

Stazione
Napoli
Centrale

Museo
Archeologico
Nazionale

Santa Maria di
Donnaregina
Nuova

Santa Caterina
a Formiello

PIAZZA
GARIBALDI

Duomo

**DECUMANO
MAGGIORE**
p90

Accademia di
Belle Arti
di Napoli

AVVOCATA

PIAZZA
DANTE

VIA SAN BIAGIO DEI LIBRAI

PENDINO

CORSO UMBERTO I

MERCATO

Parco
Viviani

V. PASQUALE SCURA

SPACCANAPOLI
p72

PIAZZA
NICOLA
AMORE

PIAZZA
MERCATO

Castel
Sant'Elmo

Santa
Chiara

PORTO

Musei
Interdipartimentali

Certosa di
San Martino

V. GUGLIELMO
SANFELICE

MONTE-
CALVARIO

TOLEDO AND CASTEL NUOVO
p52

Galleria
Umberto I

Castel
Nuovo

Stazione
Marittima

Basilica di
San Francesco
di Paola

Palazzo
Reale

PIAZZA
DEL
PLEBISCITO

RIVIERA
DI CHIAIA

Nunziatella

Santa
Lucia

SAN
FERDINANDO

VIA PARTENOPE

Isolotto
di Megaride

Castel
dell'Ovo

ITALY

GETTING TO KNOW
NAPLES AND THE
AMALFI COAST

One of the world's oldest surviving cities, Naples is a colourful collection of neighborhoods, each with its own character, while beyond the city are the Roman towns of Pompeii and Herculaneum and the stunning Amalfi Coast.

PAGE 52

TOLEDO AND CASTEL NUOVO

Via Toledo is the beating pulse of this lively district of shops and restaurants. It is also home to the Spanish Quarter, where you can still hear Neapolitan dialect being spoken. Soaring above all this is the opera house, which has attracted visitors for nearly 300 years.

Best for
Exploring the area's varied architecture, from the Spanish Quarter to the Galleria Umberto I

Home to
Palazzo Reale, Castel Nuovo

Experience
A bite of the local specialty, sfogliatella

PAGE 72

SPACCANAPOLI

A bit off the beaten path, Spaccanapoli has comparatively quieter streets and more rustic piazzas, but it's here you'll find Naples's best margherita pizza. A few major sights, such as Santa Chiara, draw in visitors, but its markets and churches are the realm of the locals.

Best for
The city's best pizza, authentic local outdoor markets and extraordinary nativity scenes

Home to
Santa Chiara

Experience
Queueing up with locals at Pizzeria Da Michele

PAGE 90

DECUMANO MAGGIORE

Being a hub of museums and eateries means the Decumano Maggiore district is impossible to miss. Greek and Roman history comes alive in Italy's most important archaeological museum, while countless churches stand in the labyrinthian alleys that always spill out onto some treasure or landmark. This area is the best place to try *graffe* (Neapolitan doughnuts) picked up at a local *friggitoria* (fried food place) in one of the many lively piazzas where locals congregate.

Best for
Exploring museums and galleries, and relaxing in piazzas with a leisurely limoncello

Home to
Duomo, Museo Archeologico Nazionale

Experience
Having an aperitivo on artsy Piazza Bellini while listening to a musician play at the nearby conservatory

PAGE 110

CAPODIMONTE AND I VERGINI

From underground attractions to the airy heights of bucolic Capodimonte, this district features some of Naples' oddest and biggest attractions. The plague-ridden skulls in the catacombs and cemeteries give way to the Renaissance masters in the museum and royal forest of Capodimonte atop the hill, while Europe's first astronomical observatory offers grand views and the botanic gardens a relaxing green retreat from the bustle.

Best for
Wandering the spine-chilling catacombs and Cimitero delle Fontanelle

Home to
Museo e Real Bosco di Capodimonte

Experience
Strolling around the verdant forest of Real Bosco di Capodimonte after admiring the art at the museum

→

VOMERO

This trendy district feels more put together than the rest of Naples. A relatively recent addition to the city, it's a light, airy neighbourhood with broader streets and fancier shops. Alongside its stores, there are fortresses and monasteries to explore. Vomero is also the best place to get your blood pumping and appreciate the pastel mosaic of Naples from above by walking up the Pedimentina, the stepped street leading to the Certosa di San Martino.

Best for

Breathtaking sea views and experiencing the trendier, less touristy side of Naples

Home to

Certosa di San Martino

Experience

Taking the funicular up to Vomero but descending through the stairways that snake through the neighborhood

CASTEL DELL'OVO AND CHIAIA

Naples is a city at one with the sea, birthed from it and always looking towards it. The pedestrianized seafront promenade, the Lungomare, with its bracing sea air and lovely sunset views of Posillipo and the Castel dell'Ovo, is a favourite spot of Neapolitans. A stroll here, followed by a meal at one of the waterfront restaurants, within earshot of crashing waves, are quintessential Naples experiences.

Best for

Nabbing a terrace seat for a sunset aperitivo and fresh seafood after a seaside stroll

Home to

Castel dell'Ovo, Lungomare

Experience

Sweating off some of that pizza by jogging along the Lungomare, or strolling through the gardens of the Villa Comunale

POMPEII AND THE AMALFI COAST

Each town along the Amalfi Coast will entrance you with its impossible beauty as you hike down steep stepped paths to the azure waters below. Further afield, ancient Greek and Roman ruins are scattered across the region, standing the test of time, while islands off the coast offer relaxing beaches and resorts with natural hot springs for spa treatments. Naples draws you in but the Amalfi Coast and its surroundings will make it hard to leave.

Best for
Exploring ancient Greek and Roman ruins and relaxing at thermal spas

Home to
Pompei, Herculaneum, Mount Vesuvius, Paestum, Amalfi Coast, Capri, Royal Palace of Caserta

Experience
Driving the stunning Amalfi Drive (State Road 163) along the Amalfi Coast

←

1 The Basilica di San
Francesco di Paola facing
Piazza del Plebiscito.

2 Colourful Via San Gregorio
Armeno in Spacconapoli.

3 Pizza from Di Matteo.

4 The clock tower of the
medieval Castel Sant'Elmo.

With its ravishing coastline, animated street life and ancient ruins, Naples and the Amalfi Coast is a feast for travellers. Whether you want spritz by the sea or pizza in a piazza, our itineraries will help you make the most of your visit.

3 DAYS
in Naples

Day 1

Morning Join the locals for a quick coffee at Gran Caffè Gambrinus *(p60)* then enjoy a wander around the grand Piazza del Plebiscito *(p60)*. Stroll through nearby Galleria Umberto I *(p60)* before taking in some regal history at Palazzo Reale *(p56)* and Castel Nuovo *(p58)*. To fuel up for the afternoon, grab a *pizza fritta* at Antica Pizza Fritta Zia Esterina Sorbillo *(p61)*.

Afternoon Walk along Lungomare *(p144)* to Castel dell'Ovo *(p144)* for sweeping vistas over the city and bay. If there's time, ride the Mergellina funicular to Via Manzoni for sunset views and gelato.

Evening Shop and dine in elegant Chiaia with seafood at Ristorante Dora *(p145)*.

Day 2

Morning Start your morning at the beautiful Santa Chiara *(p76)*, exploring the Roman ruins and colourfully tiled cloisters. Leaving the complex, venture through buzzing Spaccanapoli *(p72)*, experiencing the city's hectic streetlife, before retreating in the pious peace of the Duomo *(p94)* and Pio Monte di Misericordia *(Via dei Tribunali 253)*. Swing by Pizzeria di Matteo *(p100)* for one of the city's best margheritas.

Afternoon Pause for a drink at artsy Piazza Bellini *(p100)* then explore the old Greek city walls before getting a full dose of ancient history at the must-see Museo Archeologico Nazionale *(p96)*.

Evening Pop into Cammarota Spritz *(p63)* for a cheap and cheerful spritz then dine across the street at Trattoria Nella *(Vico Lungo Teatro Nuovo 103–105)*. End the evening with some late-night jazz at Bourbon Street *(Via Vincenzo Bellini 52–53)*.

Day 3

Morning Fuelled by more espresso, head uphill to spend a few hours gazing at the art in Museo Nazionale di Capodimonte *(p114)*. Afterwards, venture down to the spooky Cimitero delle Fontanelle *(p121)* to experience the darker side of Naples. Lunch nearby at local spot Cantina del Gallo for something simple *(p123)*.

Afternoon Take the funicular up to the trendy Vomero district *(p126)* and walk the famous ramparts of the Castel Sant' Elmo *(p135)* for some of the best views of the city. If you have time, duck into the marvellous Certosa di San Martino *(p130)*.

Evening End your trip with a spot of last-minute shopping and a bite to eat along leafy Via Scarlatti *(p137)*.

←

1 The rocky headland of Capo Miseno at Bacoli.

2 Picturesque Marina Corricella in Procida.

3 Spritz served at a café.

4 Watching the sunset from the coastal town of Forio.

5 DAYS

around the Phlegraean Fields and Islands

Day 1

Morning Start your morning with a short hike up Europe's youngest mountain in the Oasi Naturalistica di Montenuovo (*p201*), located in Pozzuoli (*p198*). After taking in the summit views, walk down to the city and reward yourself with tasty local food at Trattoria da Rita (*p198*).

Afternoon Set your sights on Baia (*p198*) and the archaeological museum at Bacoli (*p199*) nearby. After exploring the scenic coastal towns, follow the path of Pliny the Younger to the panoramic headland of Capo Miseno, where the Roman writer witnessed the eruption of Vesuvius.

Evening Dine seaside with a spritz at Baia Marinella (*p198*) and watch the water's colour change as the sun sets.

Day 2

Morning Walk in the footsteps of ancient civilizations at the archaeological site of Cumae (*p200*) and discover the origins of Sibyl's Cave, a tunnel described in the *Aeneid*. Lunch at one of the many restaurants surrounding the ampitheatre ruins.

Afternoon Head back to Pozzuoli's port to hop on a ferry to the vibrant island of Procida (*p192*), where you'll whisk away the next few days.

Evening After checking into your hotel wander the narrow lanes of island before settling into a local café at the port. Stay for an aperitivo and dinner as you watch the final ships go out to sea.

Day 3

Morning Rise with the sun and watch it climb over Ischia's Mont Epomeo from Marina Corricella (*p192*). Afterwards, head up to Terra Murata to see the Abbazia di San Michele Arcangelo and the fantastical exhibits used in the Good Friday procession. Wander back down to the colourful Marina Corricella for a seafood lunch.

Afternoon Leisurely tour the verdant hill behind Chiaiolella port for views over Vivara island, a protected Nature Reserve.

Evening Descend to Marina Chiaiolella for dinner and a stroll with sea views.

Day 4

Morning Ride the morning boat to Ischia (*p190*) and explore the main town of Ischia Porto. Delve into the island's history at the majestic Castello Aragonese, perched on a rocky islet, then return to town for another fill of seafood.

Afternoon Spend a tranquil afternoon pampering yourself at either the Poseidon spa (*p191*) or the thermal baths at Casamicciola Terme (*p191*).

Evening Dine in style at the Regina Isabella Hotel (*Piazza Santa Restituta 1*) and end your meal with some Rucolino, a dark local liqueur.

Day 5

Morning Wear some comfy shoes to hike Ischia's extinct volanco, Monte Epomeo, for the best view of the island. Lunch at Il Grotto (*Via Militare 24*), just before you reach the summit.

Afternoon Hike down and make your way to Sant' Angelo (*p191*), a quaint fishing village. Relax in the sun on Maronti beach then take the water taxi to Forio (*p190*).

Evening Wrap up your trip with dinner in one of Forio's atmospheric trattorias.

8 DAYS

on the Amalfi Coast and Capri

Day 1

Morning Begin your trip at Pompeii and meander through remarkable excavations at this ancient UNESCO World Heritage Site (p158). For lunch, have a picnic in the shade of the pine trees by the Great Gymnasium (p160).

Afternoon Hop on the Circumvesuviana train to ancient Roman Stabiae (p185). This town was destroyed in the same eruption as Pompeii.

Evening Dine at the Michelin-starred Ristorante Presidente (p159) in Pompeii.

Day 2

Morning Your next stop is Vico Equense (p185), a town famed for its 14th-century Gothic church Santissima Annunziata. After wandering around the church, have a snack in a trattoria on Piazza Umberto I.

Afternoon Travelling down the coast you'll soon reach Sorrento (p180). Make for nearby Bagno della Regina Giovanna (p182) to swim in the sheltered bathing spot under rocky ruins of a Roman villa.

Evening Sample traditional dishes and sip limoncello at L'Antica Trattoria (p180).

Day 3

Morning Take the ferry from Sorrento to Capri (p186) for a taste of glamourous island life. Ride the funicular up to Capri Town to explore lanes draped in flowers, before settling into a restaurant for lunch.

Afternoon Walk towards the lighthouse at Punta Tragara, which overlooks the rock formations of I Faraglioni. Unwind with an aperitivo in a restaurant nearby.

Evening While away the evening at Capri Rooftop with unbeatable sea views (p189).

Day 4

Morning Rise early for a swim at Marina Piccola (p188) or the far-flung lighthouse outpost of Faro; the former's tiny pebbly beach is backed by seafood restaurants, while the latter has a rocky shore and deeper waters popular with snorkellers.

Afternoon Board a bus to Anacapri (p186) and hold on tight as it negotiates the twisting, narrow roads. Explore Anacapri's lanes, and take the chairlift up to Monte Solaro for a breathtaking view.

Evening Head back into town for dinner at glitzy Da Paolino (p187).

1 Impressive ruins in Pompeii.

2 Busy restaurants spilling out into a square in Capri Town.

3 Lonely Faro Lighthouse standing watch over the sea.

4 Visitors enjoying spectacular views at Villa Cimbrone.

5 Boats moored in the tranquil harbour of Cetara at dusk.

Day 5

Morning After a cool *caffè shakerato* at the Piazzetta *(p186)*, stroll to the Certosa di San Giacomo *(p188)*. The monastery gardens offer a moment of serenity before the boat trip back to the mainland.

Afternoon Return to Sorrento to explore the Massa Lubrense coast *(p184)*. Adventurous types can scramble over the cliffs at Punta della Campanella to the ancient temple of Minerva *(p184)*.

Evening Enjoy an elegant fish supper at Michelin-starred Terrazza Bosquet *(p180)*, overlooking the Bay of Naples.

Day 6

Morning Cut across the coast to Positano to weave your way around the pastel-hued houses of this pretty town *(p176)*. Don't miss the Santa Maria dell'Assunta church with its majolica-tiled cupola. Lunch at famed Chez Black *(p177)*.

Afternoon Hire a car to sweep along the Amalfi Drive (State Road 163) to Praiano *(p177)*, pausing in scenic Vettica Maggiore.

Evening In Praiano, go to Marina di Praia for a dip, then dine on the sea's bounty.

Day 7

Morning Venture to busy Amalfi *(p178)* to admire the ornate tracery of the Duomo di Sant'Andrea. Take time to peek into the Museo della Carta.

Afternoon Travel inland to lofty Ravello *(p178)*. Have a picnic lunch in the shadow of the Duomo before ambling through the lush grounds of Villa Cimbrone.

Evening Linger over dinner at nearby Hotel Villa Maria and watch the sun set from the romantic terraced gardens *(www.villamaria.it)*.

Day 8

Morning Drive down the remaining stretch of the coast to visit Vietri sul Mare *(p177)*, known for its bright majolica tiles, and on to Cetara *(p179)*, home of *colatura di alici*, a piquant anchovy sauce.

Afternoon Head to the town of Cava de' Tirreni *(p179)* to stroll the porticoed streets and visit the Benedictine abbey Santissima Trinità.

Evening Have a bite to eat at Cetara's Falalella *(hotelcetus.com)* before making the short return drive to Naples.

Perfect Piazzas

Naples is dotted with lively, picturesque piazzas, public squares that both create throughways between neighbourhoods and serve as the nerve centre of Neapolitan social life. Amble into Piazza del Plebiscito *(p60)* for a royal view or wander into Piazza Bellini *(p100)* for a more intimate feel. To capture the perfect memory, book a photo tour with Personalized Italy *(personalizeditaly.com)*, whose expert guides will help you capture the best angles of each piazza.

→

Light and symmetry in a panoramic shot of Piazza del Plebiscito

AMAZING ARCHITECTURE

Naples and the Amalfi Coast brim with architectural wonders. Majestic ruins pepper the volcanic landscapes, the legacy of ancient master builders, while *castellos* soar along the coastline. Elsewhere, colossal palazzos, Baroque beauties and subterranean treasures reveal the city's exquisite engineering.

Subterranean Sights

The architectural wonders of Naples don't stop at ground level. About 40 m (130 ft) below the city's clamorous, bustling streets is a quiet, unexplored world of Roman roadways, aqueduct tunnels and cisterns, Greek tufa quarries and a Greco-Roman theatre, many converted into air-raid shelters during World War II *(p102)*. Take a tour with Napoli Sotterranea *(www. napolisotterranea.org)*, who will help bring this ancient hidden world to life.

←

A chapel created in one of the World War II air-raid shelters in Naples's tunnel system

TOP 5 BAROQUE ARCHITECTURE FEATURES

Grand Stairways
Broad, ornate stairways allow dramatic arrivals.

Soaring Domes
The domes bring light and add to the building's impressive height.

Quadratura
Stucco and trompe l'oeil art create 3D illusions.

Undulating and Colossal Columns
Soaring up, these huge spiral columns bring motion to buildings.

Unfinished Elements
Deliberate flaws and imperfections add to the building's uniqueness.

Beautiful Baroque

Take to the water for a grand introduction to the monumental *castellos* that tower over Naples's waterfront. The Naples to Ischia ferry *(www.omio.com)* drifts past the magnificent Palazzo Reale *(p56)*. Further afield, Caserta's *(p194)* dramatic Bourbon palace rivals any in Europe.

→

Palazzo Reale's grand staircase, intricately decorated with sculptures of the Muses

Ancient Architecture

Uncover traces of ancient civilizations wherever you go. Spot a section of the original wall of the Greek city of Neapolis underfoot in Piazza Bellini *(p100)*, venture out to Paestum *(p174)* to admire the perfect symmetry of 6th-century-BC Greek temples or take a tour of Pompeii *(p158)* to discover a treasure trove of ancient domestic architecture.

→

Ancient Greek temples glowing softly in the sun at Paestum

ARTEMISIA GENTILESCHI

Known for her brutal, haunting and strong depictions of women, as well as for her own struggle for justice after being raped, Artemisia Gentileschi was once one of the most successful artists in Naples. The first woman admitted to Florence's Accademia delle Arti e del Disegno, she moved to Naples in 1630, likely at the behest of the Spanish viceroy, the Duke of Alcalá, who owned three of her paintings. Her influence on the city's art echoes in the works of artists such as Massimo Stanzione. It is believed she died in Naples during the plague of 1656.

ARTFUL AESTHETICS

The streets of Naples, long blessed by the Muses, have been crisscrossed by artists seeking inspiration. From Caravaggio and the Great Masters to Banksy and surprising street art, Naples brims with centuries of artistic achievement.

Creative Collections

Vast collections of Italy's best art hang in the city's countless palazzos. But it's not all classical paintings and sculptures. Tucked inside the Castel Sant'Elmo *(p135)*, the Novecento a Napoli is a hidden gem displaying contemporary local artists, while the MADRE *(p104)* showcases emerging artists who are sweeping new energy into the Napoli art scene.

→

Daniel Buren's *Axer / Désaxer. Lavoro in situ* (2015) in MADRE

Simply Divine

Art has been intertwined with the Church for hundreds of years, and Naples's basilicas and churches are a vast repository for representations of Jesus and Mary, as well as other religious scenes. Demystify the complex history behind these impressive works with a docent from Context Travel *(www.context travel.com)*, whose enlightening walk, "Caravaggio and the Baroque", delves inside Pio Monte della Misericordia *(p105)* where, among other works, hangs an exquisite Caravaggio. If you don't fancy a tour, pop into the Duomo *(p67)*, Nunziatella *(p67)* and Gesù Nuovo *(p79)* to get your fill for free.

←

Divine art covering every surface in Naples's splendid Duomo, and *(inset)* a room in the Pio Monte della Misericordia

INSIDER TIP
Art For Free

In addition to free first Sundays during some months, the annual Museum Week opens the doors to select museums for free. Head online *(www.iovadoal museo.beniculturali.it)* to check out dates.

Urban Scrawl

San Gennaro, a photorealistic mural in Forcella *(p87)* by Neapolitan artist Jorit Agoch, is one of Naples's Instagram favourites, but it's not the only one of its kind. The city's crumbling walls have been transformed into canvases by world-class street artists. Even Banksy left his mark – find it at Piazza Gerolamini *(p103)*. A day out with Tour Angels *(www.tourangels napoli.it)* will reveal some of the best street art in places that you might not look.

↑ *San Gennaro* by Jorit Agoch, on Via Duomo in the Forcella neighborhood

Neapolitan Bestsellers

Make room in your suitcase – Elena Ferrante's wildly popular Neapolitan tetralogy is a riveting, if hefty, introduction to her hometown. Spot key landmarks on the Progetto Museo's Ferrante tour *(www. progettomuseo.com)*, then look out for them in the TV adaptation, *My Brilliant Friend*. Another Neapolitan megahit is *Gomorrah*, Roberto Saviano's jaw-dropping tale of the Naples underbelly. Heralded as one of the New Italian Epics, it'll take you to places you never knew existed.

→

The colourful houses of Forio, a key setting in Ferrante's tetralogy

READERS AND WRITERS

If you're a lover of words, you'll be a lover of Naples. Its bustling streets, lively cafés and serene coastal scenery offer an ideal retreat for writers and readers alike. From classic texts to 21st-century hits, read the stories on the pages or in the streets, whichever you choose.

To Naples, With Love

Writers from around the world have inked longing love letters to this region. Stroll along the Lungomare *(p144)*, which Henry James visited in the 1870s and 80s, to witness what he called "the merciless June beauty of Naples Bay at the sunset hour" in *Italian Hours*. Then cross town to Via Toledo *(p61)* to understand why French author Stendhal declared in his biography, *Rome, Naples et Florence*, that Naples "has no equal and is the most beautiful city in the universe".

←

The Lungomare's pleasant seafront, Via Partenope by night

Writer's Retreat

The Amalfi Coast is a perfect place to cloister yourself. Visit Villa San Michele *(p187)*, now a cultural center, where Swedish memoirist Axel Munthe gathered his life stories. Or echo Jean-Paul Sartre's lost hours pondering *granita* and existence at Naples's Gran Caffè Gambrinus *(p60)*.

← French philosopher Jean Paul Sarte in a state of contemplation

TOP 4 ELENA FERRANTE LOCATIONS

Rione Luzzatti
This working-class area likely inspired Lila's neighbourhood.

Pasticiello Bakery
Come here for Signor Spagnulo's favourite treats *(Via Vesuvio 3/C)*.

Piazza dei Martiri
Lila goes on spending sprees in this high-end piazza *(p145)*.

Forio
Ischia's second town features heavily as the characters' beloved island escape *(p190)*.

Pedro Berruguete and Justus van Gent's *Virgil* ↑

Classical Scribes

Writing from the edge of a volcano, Neapolitan scribes of the ancient world knew a thing or two about hellish landscapes. Visit the smouldering Phlegraean Fields *(p199)*, the basis of Virgil's depiction of the underworld in his epic poem *Aeneid*. Alternatively, delve into Pliny the Younger's *Epistulae* for his account of Vesuvius's eruption *(p166)* before visiting Pompeii *(p158)* and Herculaneum *(p164)* to see its effects for yourself.

Revel in Renaissance and Baroque Style

The artists and architects of Naples fuelled stylistic shifts from the Renaissance into the Baroque. Pop into Museo di Capodimonte *(p114)* to be inspired by the era's art. Then join Napoli That's Amore *(www.napolithatsamore.org)* to tour palazzos, Sanfelice's staircase *(p119)* and Gèsu Nuovo *(p79)* and uncover this history in the streets.

←

The Baroque majesty of Gèsu Nuovo, an exemplar of Neapolitan Baroque

UNEARTHING THE PAST

Home to beautifully preserved Roman ruins and majestic Baroque façades, Naples is just the beginning for history lovers. Venture into neighbouring towns and villages to uncover the region's long and lustrous history.

Enter the Macabre

When the 1656 plague swept through Naples it killed nearly half the population. Mass graves in nearby caves were developed to deposit the dead. Visit the Fontanelle Cemetery *(p121)* to commune with these lost souls. Then nod up to the column at Piazza San Domenico Maggiore *(p80)* to honour the saint credited with ending the epidemic.

→

Monumental gratitude at the centre of Piazza San Domenico Maggiore

Follow in French Footsteps

Like the ancients, the French left their mark. Visit the Royal Palace of Caserta *(p194)*, whose design pays homage to Versailles, and look for Parisian monuments stitched into cushions at the Museo di Capodimonte *(p114)*. If museums aren't your thing, get a taste of French inflections in *parigina* (puff-pastry pizza) or rum babas *(p37)*, sold in most local bakeries.

HIDDEN GEM
Museo di Paleontologia

Secreted away within a hidden courtyard, this surprising little museum *(Largo S Marcellino 10)*, owned and run by the University of Naples, brims with stones and fossilized bones. Kids will enjoy the massive Allosaurus fragilis.

↑ The exquisitely Rococo Reading Room of the Royal Palace of Caserta

Dig Into the Ancient World

The Greek and Roman ancient worlds are still alive in Naples today. Walk along the remnants of Greek walls, Roman tunnels and even Roman roads, then check out Castel dell'Ovo *(p144)*, a Roman stronghold that thrusts dramatically over the sea. Further afield, step into ancient daily life in the ancient towns of Pompeii *(p158)* and Herculaneum *(p164)*.

← Excavated walls of ancient Neapolis in Piazza Belini

Visit the Rebuilt City

The World Wars were brutal to Naples. It endured an estimated 200 bombing raids during 1940–44, and its archives and libraries were razed in 1943 by the German army's "scorched earth" policy. The harbour and Galleria Umberto I *(p60)* survived almost unscathed, but Museo Civico Filangieri *(p83)* and Santa Chiara church *(p76)* took longer to rebuild and are symbols of the city's rebirth.

→ The great glass skylights of Galleria Umberto I, which survived bombing raids

Lively Liqueurs

Innovative Italians have perfected the art of liqueur-making over centuries. Sunny Sorrento *(p180)* is home to the most famous – *limoncello* – a zingy nectar created from the bounty of the region's lemon groves. You'll find it filling chocolates and pastries, or drunk ice-cold with a slice of citrus. On Ischia *(p190)*, seek out bitter *rucolino*. Made from local rocket (arugula), it's a perfect digestif. Over on Procida *(p192)*, liqueur artisans go off-piste to craft local favourites *cantaloupecello*, *tangerinecello* and *pistachio-cello* – not to be missed.

→

Shelves of a Sorrento shop lined with tall, slim bottles of locally made *limoncello*

60

per cent of the lemons grown on the Amalfi Coast are used for *limoncello*.

RAISE A GLASS

Meet for a morning espresso at a café counter. Share an afternoon beer along a quiet seaside promenade. Chat over an evening aperitivo in a piazza. Neapolitan life marks time in empty glasses, and fortunately the locals have some of the greatest drinks to fill them with. *Salute!*

Going For Grape

Ribboned with vineyards, Campania has ideal growing conditions throughout, while micro-terroirs on Vesuvius add complexity to its earthy reds and crisp whites. Take a trip with Swirl the Glass *(www.swirltheglass.com)* to wineries around Positano *(p177)* for a tour with their experts. If there isn't time to leave the city, venture into Enoteca Belledonne *(www. enotecabelledonne.it)* to pick a well-chosen bottle. Look out for a DOC or DOCG label, which means it's a top quality wine from the specified region.

←

Bottles of wines lining the walls of one of Naples's *enotecas*

NOTICE for LIMONCELLO
CHECK for I.G.P. CERTIFICATION
the ORIGINAL with Sorrent...

COFFEE ETIQUETTE

Drinking coffee is an art form in Italy, and even more so in Naples. Many visitors know that Italians refuse milk in their afternoon coffee, but not many are aware that in Naples it is customary to drink a cup of water before your coffee. Neapolitans say it is meant to prepare the stomach. An older tradition, made popular after World War II and still going strong today, is to drink one coffee but pay for two, as a gesture for the next customer. Join in by telling your barista that you'd like a *caffè sospeso*, or a "suspended coffee".

→
Tiny shots of espresso *(inset)*, a perfect pick-me-up at the counter or an outdoor table

SHOP

Limoné
Don't despair if you can't make it to Sorrento. This small factory in Naples offers tours and tastings of its lemon products, including *limoncello*, still prepared using a secret family recipe.

📍Piazza San Gaetano 72
🌐limoncellodinapoli.it

Where Coffee Is King
Espresso fuels Naples. It's cheap, eye-opening and delicious. Avoid elaborate caffeinated confections; instead rub shoulders with the locals at Centrale del Caffè *(www.centraledelcaffe.it)* and throw back thick shots of single-estate espresso at the counter. Across the city, Naples institution Il Vero Bar del Professore *(p63)* raises the bar with its super-strong brews.

Backstreet Cuisine

The lanes of Naples are lined with unrivalled street grub. Pop into a fried-food *friggitoria* like Vomero *(p135)* or Fiorenzano *(p71)* for a *cuoppo di pesce* or *terra* (fish or veg cone) and moreish morsels of *sciurilli* (courgette blossoms), aubergine, potato *crocchè* and cheesy arancini. Or eat your way down Tribunali and Toledo *(p60)*, the best streets for portable fried *pizza fritta* and folded *pizza a portafoglio*.

$\rightarrow$

A street food counter displaying what's on offer

TASTING NAPLES

From fresh shellfish to delicious street food to tantalizing desserts, Naples's plate is piled with a plethora of edible delights. The birthplace of Italy's most ubiquitous dish revels in finding new ways to toss a pizza. Discover them all – and prepare to add a notch on your belt.

Pizza, Pizza, Pizza

The birthplace of Italy's most famous foodstuff, Naples is suffused with the enticing scent of freshly baked pizza. Here, the ubiquitous dish is cooked quickly at searing temperatures, creating crisp crusts and a pillowy middle – perfection. Try the storied Da Michele *(p78)* – which sells only margheritas and marinaras – for a real Neapolitan experience. Look out for the "Vera Pizza" sign to find the most authentic pizzerias.

$\leftarrow$

Delicious-looking pizzas, an omnipresent Neapolitan meal

Did You Know?

Mozzarella DOP is a buffalo's milk cheese native to the Campania region.

Hook to Plate

You can expect amazing seafood the length of the Amalfi Coast, flanked as it is by fish-filled seas. Hook up with Salboat Sorrento *(www.salboatsorrento.com)* to try your hand at local fishing techniques, including night-time squid fishing, then cook your catch onboard following traditional recipes. Back on land, head to Il Miracolo dei Pesci *(p169)* in Posillipo, for plates of local favourite *scialatielli ai frutti di mare*, bursting with prawns, clams and sea truffles.

← Fresh-caught squid ready to cook on the grill

TOP 5 NEAPOLITAN PASTRIES

Sfogliatella
Moreish, crisp pastry shells filled with sweetened ricotta, semolina and candied citrus peel.

Rum Baba
Small yeast cakes drenched in rum and filld with sweet cream.

Zeppola
Deep-fried dough balls, sometimes laden with pastry cream or custard.

Torta Caprese
Walnut or almond flour chocolate cake.

Delizie al Limone
Limoncello-flavoured delicacy filled with lemon curd.

THE ANCIENT TABLE

Although the lower classes lacked meat and lead infused their wine, archaeological evidence shows the people of Herculaneum *(p164)* and Pompeii *(p158)* ate well. The fertile volcanic soil produced a variety of vegetables, grains, fruits, nuts and lentils, and fish and garum (fish sauce) were plentiful. Spices, ghee and sugar came from India, and olive oil, wine and bread were locally produced staples. Both cities had bakeries, and communal ovens for those who couldn't afford their own. Most people, however, ate at *thermopolia*, fast-food eateries scattered across both cities.

A local chef demonstrating ↑ how to prepare fish

Hands-On Cookery Classes

Go behind the scenes with local cooks to learn about authentic Neapolitan cuisine and how to create it. Follow Culinary Backstreets *(www.culinarybackstreets.com)* on a walking tour, sampling local fare – from salted cod to traditional Neapolitan pastries like *sfogliatella* – before trying your hand at whipping up a Neapolitan *caponata* salad. Outside the city, Casa Mele in Positano *(www.casamele.com)* runs hands-on classes in time for lunch.

Find Family-Friendly Foodstuffs

Neapolitan restaurants, especially pizzerias, are incredibly family-friendly, and taking a family to places like Di Matteo (p100) or an outpost of Sorbillo (p100) is easy. In the city's piazzas, lots of outdoor seating means less worry about navigating bags and prams, so there's no need to sacrifice an *aperitivo* stop – juice for the kids, of course. Plenty of options, low prices and a friendly welcome make dining out a no-fuss affair.

←

Antica Pizzeria Gino Sorbillo, perfect for a family meal

FAMILY ADVENTURES

Travelling with the family is made easy in laid-back Naples, where children are welcomed almost everywhere. Whether spending the day in child-friendly museums, plowing through plates piled with pizza or running wild on family-friendly beaches, there's plenty to please the whole family.

Roam Free

Let the whole family let off steam with a hike through the smouldering Phlegraean Fields. The family-friendly trails are easy even for little hikers. All along the Amalfi Coast, scenic trails link villages such as Maiori, Minori, Cetara (p179) and Marina di Puolo (p182) to sandy strands and gentle waves – ideal for a beachy bucket-and-spade day.

↑ Hiking the Sentiero degli Dei (Path of the Gods) along the Amalfi Coast

Stay Dry

Rain is rare in Naples, but if you do get caught out, the underground tunnels of Napoli Sotterranea *(p26)* make for a great, dry excursion. For an arty fix, try the Museo Archeologico Nazionale *(p96)*. Ask the kids to see how many animals they can find in ancient frescoes or to put crayon to paper and re-create the classical artworks on display.

←

Imposing gods greeting visitors to Naples's expansive Museo Archeologico Nazionale

💬 INSIDER TIP
Traffic Safety

Be sure everyone knows the rules and keep little ones close at crosswalks. Pedestrians are rarely given the right of way, so always be extra cautious, even at pedestrian crossings.

Indulge in the Holiday Spirit

Visits during the holidays are especially enticing, when the city is decked out with its famous *presepi* (nativity scenes). Check out Via San Gregorio Armeno, known by locals as "Christmas Alley", which explodes with colour as the wares of tiny shops spill into the street. Come back in the spring, when the weather is still cool and shops and bakeries such as Pasticceria Poppella *(p123)* fill with special pastries and chocolates. What kid could say no?

EAT

Fantasia Gelati
This whimsical gelateria is a family-friendly spot.
🏠 Via Toledo 381
🅦 fantasia gelati.it

€€€

Casa Infante
A huge hit with kids of all ages, this favourite has top-notch gelato.
🏠 Via Toledo 258
🅦 casainfante.it

€€€

Shops and displays on Via San → Gregorio Armeno and *(inset)* a traditional Neapolitan *presepe*

Ischia's Thermal Spas

Idyllic Ischia *(p190)* is stippled with beautiful beaches, but its real draw are its abundant hot springs and rejuvenating volcanic mud pools. Stick to a spa bearing the word *terme* – a good sign it uses its own natural underground resources. One of the largest is the Poseidon spa *(p191)*. Sprawled across 5 km (3 miles) of coast, it has three seawater pools for the children to play in while you sink into naturally heated alkaline hot springs. For true pampering, try the mud baths and spa treatment of super-chic Regina Isabella *(www.reginaisabella.com)*, over-looking the blue, blue sea.

→

The soothing thermal pools of the Poseidon spa and *(inset)* the luxury Regina Isabella hotel, adding to the allure of Ischia

ON THE COAST

On the Amalfi Coast, you're never far from the sea. Whether you want to enjoy a glamorous stay amid luxury yachts, relax in bubbling volcanic springs, paddle the craggy coastline or just lie back and worship the sun, the famous Amalfi Coast has you covered.

Glitz and Glamour

Part sun-kissed escape, part urban retreat, Capri *(p186)* has glamour to spare. A bouji resort island, it has attracted high flyers since the Romans. Hire a scooter to zip past spectacular panoramas of turquoise seas and theatrical views on your way into Capri Town. Splurge in the stores of Via Camerelle, where those with deep pockets go to fill their wardrobes. On the mainland, drift through pastel Positano *(p176)* to Buca di Bacco *(www.buca-di-bacco.be)* to sip a spritz and rub shoulders with the stars of the big and small screens.

←

Window-shopping along boutique-filled, bougainvillaea-lined Via Camerelle on Capri

TOP 5 BEACHES ON AMALFI COAST

Marina Grande
The nerve centre of the entire coastline, near Positano *(p176)*.

Gavitella
Surrounded by cliffs and natural beauty, in Praiano *(p177)*.

Lannio
A more intimate and hidden beach, near Cetara *(p179)*.

Spiaggia Arienzo
A sunny spot 300 steps down a cliff, just south of Positano *(p176)*.

Vietri sul Mare
Gorgeous sandy strands and calm water *(p177)*.

Bobbing on the turquoise waters leading to the sea caves of Capri ↑

Explore the Untamed Coast

The best way to explore any coastline is by sea. Climb aboard a Motoscafisti Capri boat *(www.motoscafisticapri.com)* to explore the craggy outcrops that fringe Capri. Stop to marvel at the mystical Grotta Azzurra *(p198)*, home to an AD 30 *nymphaeum* (shrine to water nymphs), then head out to the dramatic I Faraglioni rock formations. Alternatively, pick up a paddle with Kayak Napoli *(www.kayaknapoli.com)* to visit Posillipo's *(p172)* varied coastline.

Operatic Nuances

Staging opera since 1737, the Teatro di San Carlo *(p63)* is the world's oldest active opera house. The original burned down in 1816, but its 19th-century reconstruction is a confection of velvet and gold leaf. Take the guided tour through the building's nooks and crannies. Don't miss the theatre's state-of-the-art museum and archive, Memus, or the chance to attend one of the world-class concerts.

$\rightarrow$

Teatro di San Carlo, all red velvet, gold leaf and exquisite acoustics

MESMERIZING MUSIC

Naples has been a vibrant part of Italy's musical culture for centuries, with the world's oldest active opera house, a conservatory and streets that have a built-in soundtrack of arias, accordians and *canzone napoletana.*

THE NEAPOLITAN MANDOLIN

Distinct from others in Italy, the Neapolitan mandolin has been produced in the area since the 1700s. The instrument is tear-shaped with a bowl back and a uniquely triangulated sounding board. Most commonly associated with folk music, such as *canzone napoletana*, it is a mandatory part of the conservatory's curriculum and students regularly give classical performances on it.

Classical Moments

Hang around Piazza Bellini and you're almost guaranteed to hear harmonious melodies flowing from the conservatory, as Naples's latest talents practise never-performed and centuries-old compositions. Book through the Associazione Scarlatti *(www.associazionescarlatti. it)* to see these prodigies perform live in various theatres, palazzos and atmospheric churches across the city.

$\rightarrow$

A woodwind performance by students from the Naples Conservatory of Music

Jazz It Up

Naples serves up a twist with one of Italy's best jazz scenes. Find a little bit of New Orleans at the Bourbon Street Jazz Club *(www.bourbonstreet jazzclub.com)*. Hear world-class musicians riff through the night or get up on stage for a jam session, open to fans. Over on Capri, the scent of wood-fired pizza mingles with the hiss of craft beer bottles opening and the sound of jazz during Pizza Jazz *(www.pizzajazzbirra capri.com)*, while Ischia's annual Piano and Jazz Festival *(www. pianoejazz.it)* pumps out several fabulous days of jazz.

← Performers at a jazz event in Naples

TOP
5

NEAPOLITAN SONGS

'O Sole Mio
One of the most popular *canzone napoletana* is an ode to "my sunshine".

Funiculì, Funiculà
The opening of the funicular on Vesuvius *(p166)* is commemorated by this 1880 song.

'A Vucchella
This charming tune compares a woman's mouth to a rose petal.

Marechiare
An 1885 song by Salvatore di Giacomo praises the beauty of Posillipo *(p170)*.

Santa Lucia
Naples-born Enrico Caruso sang this air about a boatman's invitation to enjoy a boat ride in the Bay of Naples.

Canzone Napoletana

Traditional *canzone napoletana*, or the Neapolitan song – ballads of love, longing and sadness – drift by on the breeze in Naples. The genre was made popular by Naples-born Enrico Caruso, whose swoonworthy vocals are now the focus of a permanent exhibition at Teatro Trianon *(www.teatrotrianon.org)*. Head to Napulitanata *(www.napulitanata.com)*, a venue dedicated to the tradition, to be serenaded by the next generation of songsters.

↑ Enrico Caruso, the grandmaster of the *canzone napoletana*

A YEAR IN
NAPLES AND THE
AMALFI COAST

JANUARY

△ **Epiphany** *(6 Jan)*. The Befana gifts candies to children to celebrate the Three Kings' visit to Jesus.

Capri, Hollywood – International Film Festival *(early Jan)*. The festival before the Academy Awards.

O Cippo 'e Sant'Antuono *(17 Jan)*. Locals burn old belongings in bonfires to start the new year afresh.

FEBRUARY

Saint Biago Day *(3 Feb)*. Huge fireworks around Naples honour Saint Biago, the saint of the throat.

△ **Carnival** *(mid-Feb)*. Children dress in costumes to recognize the beginning of Lent.

Sant'Antonino in Sorrento *(14 Feb)*. Processions in Sorrento celebrate the town's patron saint.

MAY

Festa di San Gennaro *(Sat before 1st Sun in May)*. The first of three holidays dedicated to Naples' patron saint draws the faithful to the Duomo.

△ **Maggio dei Monumenti** *(throughout)*. Buildings usually closed to the public are open to visit.

Wine and the City *(mid-May)*. Free wine tastings in Naples showcase Campania's viticulture.

JUNE

Regatta of the Maritime Republics, Amalfi *(1st Sun every four years)*. Regional rowing teams compete.

△ **Pizza Village in Naples** *(Jun & Sep)*. Nearly a million people come to eat the iconic dish.

Ravello Festival *(Jun–Sep)*. A summer music festival.

Napoli Teatro Festival *(throughout)*. The city becomes a series of unexpected pop-up theatres.

SEPTEMBER

Festa di Piedigrotta *(8 Sep)*. This ancient cave hosts a feast marking the start of the rainy season.

Settembrata di Anacaprese *(1st week)*. Capri's second town hosts gastronomic contests.

△ **Festa di San Gennaro** *(19 Sep)*. The second of the patron saint's three festivals celebrates the liquification of his congealed blood.

OCTOBER

△ **Classical Music at San Carlo** *(throughout)*. The world-famous theatre kicks into high gear with its classical music season beginning in October.

Sagra Della Noce *(mid-Oct)*. Via Sabatao Borzillo hosts a festival dedicated to the walnut.

Naples International Film Festival *(late Oct)*. 2020 is the 12th edition of this multi-day event featuring dozens of screenings.

MARCH

△ **San Giuseppe** *(19 Mar)*. The Italian equivalent of Father's Day marks the switch from winter to spring attire, ushered in with deep-fried *zeppole*.

Settimana Santa *(last week of March)*. Processions and church services in the region prepare the faithful for Easter Sunday.

Festa della Primavera *(late Mar–early May)*. An international festival, Naples hosts events such as a food fair in Bagnoli, at the former NATO base.

APRIL

Easter *(early Apr)*. Good Friday processions, like the one on Procida, lead up to Easter Monday, when families picnic and relax out of the city.

△ **Piano City Naples** *(early Apr)*. Free piano concerts ring through Naples' most iconic cultural centers, public spaces and even homes.

Gran Premio della Lotteria di Agnano *(late Apr)*. Horses races thunder through the Agnano Hippodrome in Naples.

JULY

Festa di Madonna del Carmine *(16 Jul)*. A 13th century basilica is lit in a dazzling display of religious devotion to the Virgin Mary.

△ **Sant'Anna Ischia** *(26 Jul)*. Floats from each of the island's six towns are judged, followed by fireworks.

Amalfi Coast Music and Arts Festival *(throughout)*. Musicians and artists gather for events and concerts inspired by Italy's beauty.

AUGUST

La Notte di San Lorenzo *(10 & 11 Aug)*. Night-time events take place coinciding with a meteor shower.

△ **Ferragosto** *(15 Aug)*. Fireworks light up the coast of Positano to celebrate the feast of the Assumption.

Ischia Jazz Festival *(late Aug)*. The quiet island ignites with music across its coastal towns.

NOVEMBER

△ **Day of the Dead** *(1 Nov)*. Families lay flowers on tombs and vendors sell almond nougat.

Mushroom Festival at San Giuseppe Vesuviano *(early Nov)*. The humble *funghi* is the guest of honor at this quirky local festival.

La Festa dei Cornuti *(11 Nov)*. Cuckolds gather to celebrate their patron saint, San Martino.

DECEMBER

△ **Christmas markets** *(throughout)*. Traditional *presepi* (nativity scenes) fill Christmas markets around Via San Gregorio Armeno in Naples.

Festa di San Gennaro *(16 Dec)*. The third of the saint's feasts commemorates his protection during the 1631 eruption of Vesuvius.

New Year's Eve *(31 Dec)*. Fireworks light up the city, with rejoicing at the Piazza del Plebiscito.

A BRIEF
HISTORY

Said to have been born of a Siren, Naples has a history marked by the rise and fall of powerful rulers, going from a Greek colony to a Roman powerhouse to a jewel of the Baroque era. Having survived political turbulence, volcanoes, plagues, earthquakes and wars, Naples is now a city on the rise.

Greco-Roman Naples

Greek myth has it that Naples was founded where the body of the Siren Parthenope was washed ashore. By the 8th-9th century BC, Greek settlers had founded Parthenope on Pizzofalcone hill. Prosperity and population growth led to the founding of Neapolis, or "new city", nearby. The growing power of the city-state of Rome had become clear during its wars with the Samnite tribes of southcentral Italy; as a result, after losing a war with Rome in 328 BC, Neapolis agreed to become its ally. The region flourished until AD 79, when a catastrophic eruption of Vesuvius destroyed several towns around Naples.

1 A 16th-century map depicting Naples.

2 Artwork illustrating a view of Naples from the hill of Pizzofalcone.

3 A 6th-century mosaic in the Duomo in Naples.

4 A painting showing local revolutionary hero Masaniello.

Timeline of events

8th–9th century BC
The Greeks found Parthenope, one of their earliest settlements in Italy.

328 BC
Rome conquers Naples, but respects it as a centre of Greek culture and learning.

AD 305
Bishop Gennaro is decapitated by Emperor Diocletian in Pozzuoli; he is venerated as the patron saint of Naples.

6th century BC
The Greek settlers establish Neapolis further inland; Parthenope comes to be called Palaepolis or "old city".

536
Naples falls under Byzantine rule.

From the Byzantine Empire to the French

Naples remained a Roman city until 536, when Byzantine general Belisarius entered the city via its aqueduct and took control of it. It remained nominally under Byzantine rule until it became part of the Norman Kingdom of Sicily in the 12th century. By the 13th century the French House of Anjou had taken over and begun ambitious development schemes: land was reclaimed and castles, churches and monasteries were built.

The Spanish Viceroyalty

Joan II, the last Angevin queen, named Alfonso V of Aragon her successor in 1421, and by 1503 Naples had become a colony of Spain. The city began to expand and, with the building of Via Toledo, the focus of development shifted: Quartieri Spagnoli was established to house Spanish troops and palaces were built along the Riviera and Toledo. The city was now Italy's largest, facing overcrowding, poverty and disease as a result of its size. Growing resentment against the Spanish came to a head in 1647, when local rebel Masaniello led a violent uprising against them. By 1707, Naples had fallen under Austrian dominion.

REVOLUTION!

Naples has always been a hotspot for rebellion. The gladiator Spartacus made a stand against the Romans on the slopes of Vesuvius in BC 73. In 1647, local fisherman Masaniello led a mob against a new fruit tax levied by the Spanish rulers, while in 1943, Italian resistance fighters famously battled Third Reich soldiers during the popular Four Days of Naples uprising.

1486

Neapolitan barons rebel against Ferdinand I, son of Alfonso V of Aragon, but the revolt fails.

1503

Spain sends a viceroy to take control of Naples.

1656

A deadly epidemic of plague wipes out nearly half of Naples's population of 300,000.

1266

Charles I of Anjou enters Naples and makes it the capital of the new Angevin kingdom.

1562

Kissing in public is banned to prevent the spread of disease in the overcrowded city.

Bourbon Naples

In 1734 the Kingdom of Naples changed hands once more with the arrival of Charles of Bourbon, who set out to make Naples a metropolis. He suspended church building in favour of large-scale public works and industries, built a magnificent palace at Caserta and tried to introduce legislative and administrative reforms. Naples's art, antiquities and music attracted Grand Tour travellers; even its *lazzaroni* – street thieves and beggars – were seen as picturesque by visitors. The royal schemes lacked coherency, however, and were stopped as news of the French Revolution reached the city. Bourbon rule ended in September 1860 when republican General Giuseppe Garibaldi arrived in Naples after conquering Sicily; after a plebiscite in October, the city became part of the new Kingdom of Italy.

Naples after Unification

In 1884, a massive cholera epidemic brought old city planning problems to a head in crowded, densely populated Naples. The Urban Renewal Plan of 1885 was an attempt to tackle these issues, with authorities clearing out slums to develop new

↑ Illustration depicting Garibaldi entering Naples in September 1860

Timeline of events

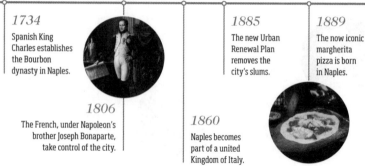

1734
Spanish King Charles establishes the Bourbon dynasty in Naples.

1806
The French, under Napoleon's brother Joseph Bonaparte, take control of the city.

1860
Naples becomes part of a united Kingdom of Italy.

1885
The new Urban Renewal Plan removes the city's slums.

1889
The now iconic margherita pizza is born in Naples.

3

districts in the centre and towards the hills. However, the plan failed to solve many of the problems and the work took much longer than expected, triggering a wave of corruption. The Fascist regime that followed contented itself with a new series of grand public works and the creation of more built-up areas.

Naples Today

After World War II Naples had to cope with the appalling damage inflicted by Allied bombs, and the 1950s and 60s saw extensive, indiscriminate construction backed by politicians for short-term gain. Factory closures in the 1980s aggravated the acute unemployment problem. The area also struggled with organized crime. Today, however, major changes are underway. The EU has pledged to invest €868 million in regional infrastructure and the restoration of Naples's historic core, a UNESCO World Heritage Site. This commitment to regeneration has led to an increase in tourism, one of the biggest contributors to the area's economy, which is now Italy's fourth largest. Always distinguished by its irrepressible vitality and creativity, Naples is today celebrating its rich past while looking ahead to an increasingly bright future.

1 A portrait of King Charles of Bourbon.

2 A vendor selling vegetables in a Naples slum, 1947.

3 An aerial view of modern Naples.

Did You Know?

In 1884, cholera killed 8,000 Italians, of which 6,000 were in Naples alone.

1943

Italy surrenders to the Allies at the end of World War II.

1960

Sophia Loren stars in the Hollywood romantic comedy *It Started in Naples*.

2018

My Brilliant Friend, one of Elena Ferrante's Neapolitan Novels, is made into a globally popular TV series.

1944

The most recent eruption of Vesuvius is photographed by US military pilots.

2020–22

The EU pledges to invest €868 million in infrastructure and restoration projects.

EXPERIENCE

Alley in the Quartieri Spagnoli area

The glass-roofed shopping area of Galleria Umberto I

TOLEDO AND CASTEL NUOVO

Millennia of history, bearing the imprints of successive civilizations, are concentrated in this quarter, from the ancient Greek ruins on the hill of Pizzofalcone to 19th-century buildings such as the magnificently restored Galleria Umberto I. Originally the site of an old Roman port, the harbour area became home to the imposing Castel Nuovo of the Angevins in the 13th century. The Aragonese dominion that followed brought with it the moulding of Naples into a city. The Spanish viceroy of the city established Via Toledo – the beating heart of this district – in the 16th century, and grand palaces, stately churches and numerous shops were built along its length, acting as a focal point for Neapolitan socializing. Flanking the avenue to the east, the gridded Quartieri Spagnoli was built to house the troops that were brought to the city by their Spanish masters to repress potential Neapolitan revolts. A century later, the viceroys began the construction of Palazzo Reale at the terminus of Via Toledo. Its magnificence was meant to reflect that this was one of the most important European courts of the time, and it remained the city's geographic and symbolic center of power for centuries. Although the 19th century saw a far-reaching reorganization of Naples into a metropolis, this historic area remains both the heart of the old capital and the commercial and administrative centre of modern Naples.

TOLEDO AND CASTEL NUOVO

Must Sees

1. Palazzo Reale
2. Castel Nuovo

Experience More

3. Galleria Umberto I
4. Piazza del Plebiscito
5. Gran Caffè Gambrinus
6. Via Toledo
7. Basilica di San Francesco di Paola
8. Piazza Municipio
9. Santa Maria Incoronata
10. Santa Brigida
11. Teatro San Carlo
12. Quartieri Spagnoli
13. Palazzo delle Poste e Telegrafi
14. Piazza Giovanni Bovio
15. Via Chiaia
16. Santa Maria degli Angeli
17. Pizzofalcone
18. Santa Maria Egiziaca a Pizzofalcone
19. Palazzo Serra di Cassano
20. Nunziatella

Eat

1. Pintauro's
2. Antica Pizza Fritta Zia Esterina Sorbillo
3. Trattoria Nanella

Drink

4. Cammarota Spritz
5. Il Vero Bar del Professore
6. Spuzzulè

Stay

7. Art Hotel Galleria Umberto
8. Barbarella Suite
9. Caruso Place

Shop

10. Gay Odin
11. Acampora Profumi
12. Casa Ascione

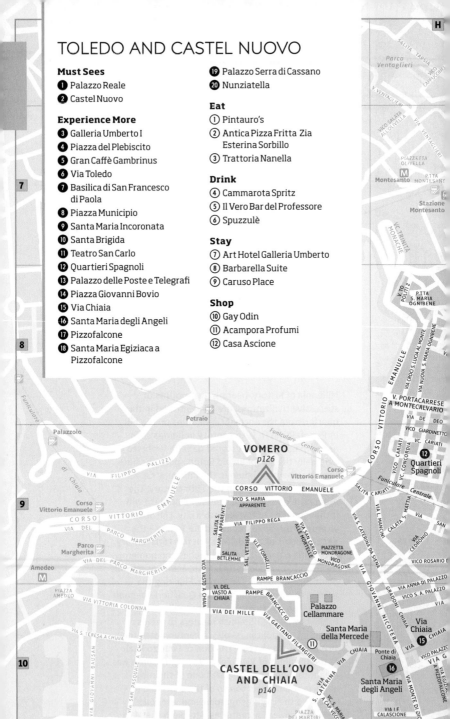

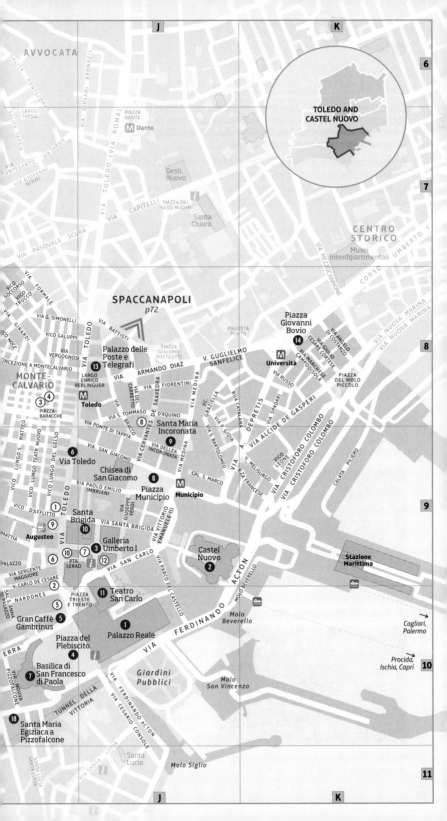

❶ ⚒

PALAZZO REALE

📍J10 🏛Piazza del Plebiscito 🚇Municipio 🚋4 🚌Centrale: Augusteo
🚌C25, E6, N1, N3, R2 🕐Appartamento Reale: 9am-8pm Thu-Tue (last adm: 7pm); biblioteca: 8:30am-7pm Mon-Fri, 8:30am-1:30pm Sat
🌐polomusealecampania.beniculturali.it

A masterpiece of Baroque and Neo-Classical architecture, the Palazzo Reale features decoration and ornamentation on every surface. The grand throne room alone makes it clear this was one of the most important courts in the Mediterranean in the 17th century.

The construction of the palace, designed by late-Renaissance architect Domenico Fontana, began in 1600 and was only finished in the mid-1800s. The Ala delle Feste wing now houses the Biblioteca Nazionale, home to the collection of papyrus scrolls from Herculaneum. The 30 rooms in the first-floor Museo dell' Appartamento Reale are arranged around a central courtyard. In the west wing are the Teatrino di Corte and the State Rooms; in the south are the private chambers. The east wing houses the Cappella Palatina, with a splendid 17th-century main altar, and the Sala di Ercole. The sumptuous objets d'art and furnishings are of the highest quality. The garden, laid out in 1841 on the site of the former stableyard, is filled with exotic plants, while in the palace stables the original mangers can still be seen.

↑ The façade, altered in the 18th century by Luigi Vanvitelli to hold statues of Neapolitan kings

↑ The Teatrino di Corte, beautifully decorated with papier-mâché sculptures

↑ The State Rooms, which feature important 16th- to 19th-century art

PAPER VIEW

As lavish as it all seems, the palace's Teatrino di Corte (court theatre) features some very low-cost decorations. Created in 1768 for the wedding of Maria Carolina of Austria and Ferdinand IV of Naples, the statues of Apollo and the Muses, by Italian sculptor Angelo Viva, are fashioned out of papier-mâché. Although used as a cheap alternative to marble, the sculptures proved resilient, even surviving the World War II bombings that damaged the theatre.

↑ The monumental staircase leading
from the central courtyard up to
the royal apartments

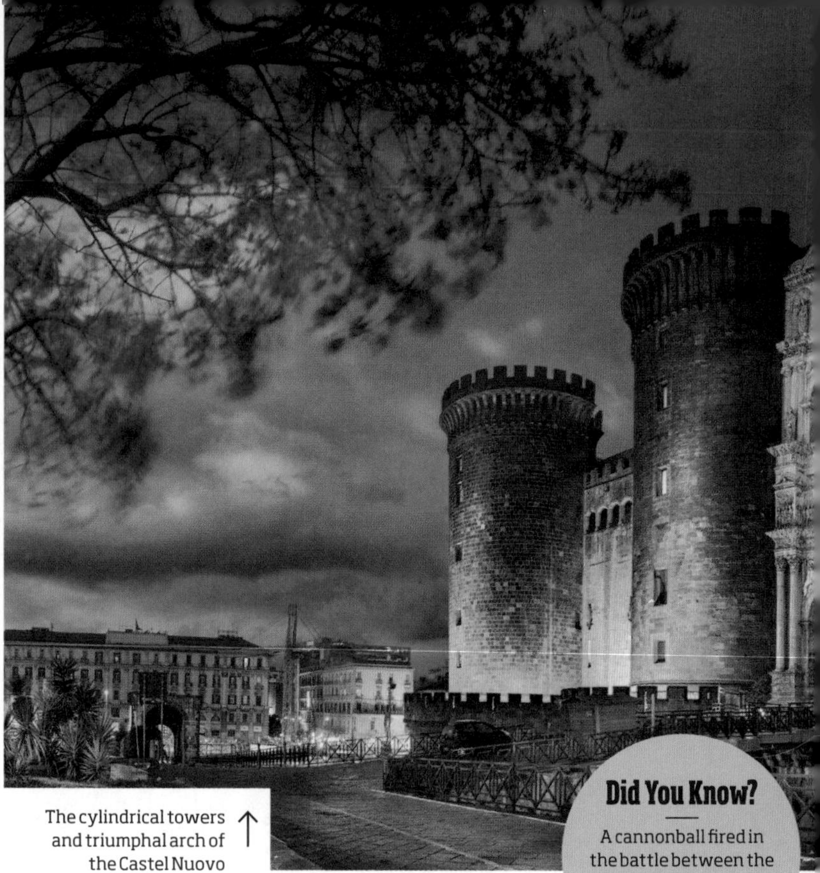

The cylindrical towers and triumphal arch of the Castel Nuovo

Did You Know?

A cannonball fired in the battle between the French and Genoese, in 1495, is still wedged in the bronze doors.

2

CASTEL NUOVO

J9 Piazza Municipio 081 795 77 22 Municipio Centrale: Augusteo C25, N1, N3, R2, 201, 202, 256 8:30am-7pm Mon-Sat

The imposing towers of Castel Nuovo housed royalty for centuries, as they reigned over Naples. Today, the medieval castle is no less intimidating, still standing watch over the harbour. Inside, its rooms allow visitors to peel back the layers of history that helped define the city.

The castle, more commonly known as the Maschio Angioino, was called *nuovo* (new) to distinguish it from two earlier ones, dell'Ovo *(p144)* and Capuano *(p105)*, which were too small to accommodate the entire Angevin court. Charles I of Anjou began construction in 1279, but the Cappella Palatina is the only part remaining of the original building. Alfonso V of Aragon (who later became Alfonso I, King of Naples and Sicily) began to rebuild it completely in 1443, the year that marked his triumphant entry into Naples. To celebrate this event, he later ordered the construction of the superb Arco di Trionfo, one of the most significant expressions of early Renaissance culture in southern Italy. Castel Nuovo, with its five cylindrical towers, is designed on a trapezoidal plan facing onto a central courtyard. From here you can gain access to the most famous chamber in the castle, the Sala dei Baroni (Barons' Hall), which is now used by the town council. Since 1990 a small but fine art collection, the Museo Civico, has occupied part of the west wing. The castle's upper walls and terraces offer visitors spectacular panoramic views of the city.

Cappella Palatina

▶ After the Middle Ages, Palatine Chapels such as this were increasingly used to link sacred and royal authority and consolidate royal status. This chapel, the only surviving part of the original castle, has a Renaissance doorway, and a rose window typical of the Catalan style. Its walls were once famously decorated with frescoes by Giotto, although only small fragments remain today.

Museo Civico

◀ The Civic Museum houses objets d'art, paintings and sculptures dating from the 14th to the 19th century, but by far the largest section consists of 19th-century Neapolitan paintings. Some of these – such as Vincenzo Caprile's *Vecchia Napoli* (Old Naples), depicting the famous Zizze fountain in its original state - offer views of a city that no longer exists.

Sala dei Baroni

The Barons' Hall owes its name to the grim events that took place there in 1486. Facing an uprising of his barons, Ferdinand I invited them to Castel Nuovo under the pretence of celebrating his niece's wedding, but instead arrested and executed them in this room. This grand hall, built by Spanish craftsman Guglielmo Sagrera in 1446, has a magnificent Catalan-inspired vault with ribs intersecting in the shape of a star.

Arco di Trionfo

▶ The monumental Arco di Trionfo (Triumphal Arch) was built in 1443 in honour of Alfonso V of Aragon. The bas-relief depicting the Triumph of Alfonso lies above the lower section, while the upper arch has figures representing, from left to right: Temperance, Justice, Fortitude and Magnanimity. On the tympanum, supporting two large symbolic statues of rivers, stands a figure of the archangel Michael.

↑ The splendid Spanish Gothic vaulted ceiling of the Sala dei Baroni

EXPERIENCE MORE

❸

Galleria Umberto I

📍 J9 🅰 Via San Carlo, Via Verdi, Via Santa Brigida, Via Toledo Ⓜ Municipio 🚆 Centrale: Augusteo 🚌 C25, E6, N1, N3, R2

This public shopping gallery was built as part of the Urban Renewal Plan, drawn up after a cholera epidemic struck the city in 1884 (*p48*). It features an impressive iron-and-glass roof and patterned marble pavement. The arcade soon became a meeting place for local composers and musicians. From the galleria,

Did You Know?

All 12 zodiac signs are depicted in the elaborate mosaic floors of the Galleria Umberto I.

visitors can enter the Salone Margherita, which was a well-known *café chantant*, and considered the heart of cabaret in Naples. It now hosts theatre shows and tango evenings.

---

❹

Piazza del Plebiscito

📍 H10 Ⓜ Municipio 🚆 Centrale: Augusteo 🚌 C25, E6, N1, N3, R2

Joachim Murat, Napoleon's brother-in-law, ruled the city of Naples from 1808 to 1815. Dissatisfied with the chaotic jumble of buildings opposite the Palazzo Reale, he decided to rebuild the whole area. Originally named Largo di Palazzo, the square was meant to play a major role in city life and was used for festivities, ceremonies and military parades. The first buildings to go up were the palace built for the Prince of Salerno, and the palazzo that is now the home of the Prefecture. The square's

two statues of Ferdinand I and Charles III are the work of Antonio Calì and Antonio Canova. Murat did not see the final results of his scheme, only managing to glimpse Leopoldo Laperuta's design for the Doric colonnade and the initial construction work, before the French were driven out of Naples. Today the piazza's name refers to the referendum that made the city part of the Kingdom of Italy (*p48*).

---

❺

Gran Caffè Gambrinus

📍 H10 🅰 Piazza Trieste e Trento Ⓜ Municipio 🚆 Centrale: Augusteo 🚌 C25, E6, N1, N3, R2 🕐 7am–1am daily (to 2am Fri, to 3am Sat) 🌐 grancaffegambrinus.com

This café dates from 1860, and its walls were decorated by leading Neapolitan painters of the time. It soon became the haunt of politicians, artists

←

Shoppers wandering beneath the soaring glass roof of the Galleria Umberto I

and writers, including Guy de Maupassant and Oscar Wilde, as well as the local composers Roberto Murolo and Giovanni Bovio. French philosopher Jean-Paul Sartre famously reflected on Naples and its contradictions here, writing at the café, "Does Naples exist?" When the literary hotspot also became popular with opponents of the Fascist regime, the Prefecture closed it down, initiating a long period of decline and neglect. Happily, its lavish belle époque decor has been restored, and this landmark is once again a local favourite. Neapolitans drop in for cakes, ice cream and tiny espressos, although visitors should note it is more pricey than most cafés around town.

---

6 🖼️ 🏛️

Via Toledo

📍 H9 Ⓜ️ Dante, Toledo 🚉 Centrale: Augusteo 🚌 E1, R4, 201

Commissioned by the Spanish viceroy Don Pedro de Toledo in 1536, this street features many famous buildings with rich histories. Inside Palazzo Cirella (No 228) artists planned an insurrection against the Bourbon king in 1848, while the composer Gioachino Rossini lived at No 205.

The road was popularized by Europeans on the Grand Tour; French writer Stendhal called it "the most crowded and gayest street in the universe". In 1870, to honour Italy's new capital, the road became Via Roma – an unpopular decision among locals. It was reversed in 1980.

Shopping in Via Toledo caters to all budgets. Locals stop at Gay Odin (p67) for chocolates and at Pintauro's for the *sfogliatelle* pastry.

7

Basilica di San Francesco di Paola

📍 H10 🏛️ Piazza del Plebiscito 📞 081 764 51 33 Ⓜ️ Municipio 🚉 Centrale: Augusteo 🚌 C25, E6, N1, N3, R2 🕐 8:30am–noon & 4–7:30pm Mon–Sat, 8:30am–1pm & 4–7pm Sun

In 1815 Ferdinand of Bourbon was reinstated to the throne of Naples and set about completing the restoration of the city begun by Napoleon's brother-in-law. Ferdinand commissioned this central royal basilica, which was dedicated to San Francesco di Paola. Inspired by Rome's Pantheon, the church has a circular plan with radiating chapels and a large cupola, complete with rosettes.

The church's sculptures and paintings are mostly Neo-Classical, except for the high altar, which was re-built in 1835 with multi-coloured marble and lapis lazuli taken from a 17th-century altar in the church of Santi Apostoli (*p120*). The interior is cool and formal. According to architectural historian Renato De Fusco: "Despite the large size of the interior… and garlanding decoration, the overall impression is not that of Neo-Classical rigour, but rather a lack of harmony between man and the setting, a funereal coldness compared to the exterior". The sobering effect is soon dispelled by emerging into the bustling Piazza del Plebiscito.

The classical façade of the basilica ↓

❽

Piazza Municipio

☑ J9 🏛 Piazza Municipio
Ⓜ Municipio 🚇 Centrale:
Augusteo 🚌 C25, N1, N3,
N8, R2, R4, 201, 202

Piazza Municipio – one of the largest squares in Naples – bustles with traffic and leads visitors to the Castel Nuovo (p58). Excavations for the city's metro system have left much of the area inaccessible for the past decade or so.

The piazza is dominated by the church of San Giacomo. Part of the 19th-century Palazzo San Giacomo (now the town hall), this church is sometimes called Nostra Signora del Sacro Cuore (Our Lady of the Sacred Heart). In 1540 Don Pedro Alvarez de Toledo, the viceroy responsible for the city centre's present-day appearance, built the church and adjoining hospital, which was for the Spanish community. The church, however, was for the local aristocracy and though rebuilt in 1741 it still belongs to the Real Hermandad de Nobles Hespanoles de Santiago, a confraternity founded more

3
———
The number of Roman ships found while excavating the old dock under Piazza Municipio.

than four centuries ago. San Giacomo contains tombs of Spanish nobles, including that of Don Pedro and his wife Maria. They were never buried here however; Don Pedro died in Florence and is buried in the cathedral there.

The square was once part of the original Roman port, and excavations have unearthed a number of intriguing archaeological finds. The new metro station (which is yet to be completed) is set to display many of these in its halls.

Also in the piazza is the Mercadante, Teatro Stabile. Built in 1778 to a design by Francesco Securo, this theatre was originally known as del Fondo because money for its construction came from a fund created by the sale of confiscated Jesuit property.

The 17th-century Fountain of Neptune has been moved, temporarily, to the corner of this piazza from Piazza Bovio (p64). It was the work of three artists: the statue of Neptune was sculpted by Michelangelo Naccherino, the balusters and lions were by Cosimo Fanzago, and the monsters at the base were by Pietro Bernini.

---

❾

Santa Maria Incoronata

☑ J9 🏛 Via Medina 60
📞 081 552 04 57 Ⓜ Toledo,
Municipio 🚇 Centrale:
Augusteo 🚌 N1, N3, N8,
R2, R4, 202 🕐 9am-6pm
Mon-Sat

This deconsecrated church was originally built to celebrate the coronation of Joan I

of Anjou in 1352. An identical, connected building was added in 1460, which doubled the church's size.

It is immediately obvious that Santa Maria Incoronata is at a lower level than Via Medina. This quirk dates to the 16th century, when Charles V built new moats for Castel Nuovo. Earth had been dug out to make room for the ditches, and when it was dumped nearby it partially buried this small Late-Gothic church.

↑ The gilded interior of the Teatro San Carlo, with six tiers of plush private boxes

⑩
Santa Brigida

☑ J9 🏠 Via Santa Brigida 72 ☎ 081 552 37 93 Ⓜ Toledo, Municipio 🚋 Centrale: Augusteo 🚌 C25, E6, N1, N3, R1, R2 🕐 7am–12:30pm & 5-7:30pm daily

The curious aspect of this 17th-century church is its dome, which had to be kept below 9 m (30 ft) high to avoid obstructing artillery fire from Castel Nuovo. However, the vivid fresco of a sky by Luca Giordano (1634–1705) on the cupola creates a feeling of immense space. Giordano, nicknamed Luca Fapresto (Luca the Swift) because he worked so rapidly, painted the dome in exchange for his tomb, which can be found in the left transept.

⑪
Teatro San Carlo

☑ J10 🏠 Via San Carlo 98d Ⓜ Municipio 🚋 Centrale: Augusteo 🚌 C25, E6, N1, N3, R2 🕸 teatrosancarlo.it

This is the oldest active opera house in the world. Designed by Giovanni Antonio Medrano

←

The ornate Fountain of Neptune, which currently stands in the Piazza Municipio

for the Bourbon King Charles, it was built in a few months and opened on 4 November 1737, 40 years before La Scala in Milan. It soon became one of the most important opera houses in Europe, known for its magnificent architecture and excellent productions. For many years, a performance at the San Carlo was considered the high point in the career of a singer or composer. One singer who did not enjoy the experience was Enrico Caruso; after being loudly booed by the audience, he vowed never to perform in Naples again, and to return to the city only for its famous pasta dishes.

In 1816 a fire severely damaged the interior, which was immediately rebuilt by Italian architect Antonio Niccolini, along with the addition of the foyer and balcony to the building. The focal point of the magnificent auditorium, with its six tiers of 184 boxes, is the royal box, topped by the crown of the Kingdom of the Two Sicilies.

Many great musical figures, including Gioachino Rossini and Gaetano Donizetti, were at one time artistic directors of the theatre. The world premieres of Donizetti's *Lucia di Lammermoor* and Rossini's *Mosè* were performed here.

Opera fans who miss out on performance tickets should head for the Museo e Archivio Storico del Teatro di San Carlo or **Memus**, located in the Palazzo Reale (*p56*). The museum is dedicated to the history of the opera house.

Memus

⊛ 🏠 Piazza Trieste e Trento 🕐 9am–5pm Tue–Sat, 9am–2pm Sun 🕸 memus.org

DRINK

Cammarota Spritz
Visitors and locals alike mingle here, drawn by the dangerously affordable €1 Aperol spritz.

☑ H8 🏠 Vico Lungo Teatro Nuovo 31 ☎ 320 277 56 87 🕐 Sun

Il Vero Bar del Professore
Opened in 1996, this cosy spot offers a fresh take on Neapolitan coffee.

☑ H10 🏠 Piazza Trieste e Trento 🕸 ilverobardel professore.com

---

Spuzzulè
A local hangout offering late-night wine and tasty small dishes.

☑ H9 🏠 Via Sergente Maggiore 54 ☎ 393 432 11 39

↑ A colourful street in the Quartieri Spagnoli, its balconies festooned with drying laundry

⑫ Quartieri Spagnoli

⑨H9 Ⓜ Toledo 🚋Centrale: Augusteo 🚌E3, E6

From an artists' district in the 18th century to a hub of organized crime in the 1980s, the Spanish Quarter has always been lively. Today it is one of the city's most densely populated districts, and tourists should take particular care when visiting the area. It was built in the 16th century to house Spanish troops, and its origins live on in the name, but today it is difficult to appreciate the original grid layout, as narrow alleys are draped with laundry, shielding the streets from daylight.

Despite the state of neglect, there is still some fine architecture, such as the church of Montecalvario (founded in 1560), which gives its name to one of the area's districts, and Santa Maria della Concezione, a Baroque masterpiece by Domenico Antonio Vaccaro.

The great Italian poet Leopardi once lived at No 24 Via Santa Maria Ognibene, and the local playwright Eduardo De Filippo used the area as a setting for his plays.

⑬ Palazzo delle Poste e Telegrafi

⑨J8 🏛Piazza Matteotti 2 Ⓜ Toledo 🚌C25, E1, N3, N8, R4, 201 🕐8am-6:30pm Mon-Fri, 8am-12:30pm Sat

The post office building was designed in 1935 by Giuseppe Vaccaro as part of an Urban Renewal Plan that resulted in the demolition of the San Giuseppe quarter. The flamboyant style of the civic architecture from this period (also found in the police headquarters, the tax office and the provincial administration building) is typical of buildings erected during the Fascist era (p49). The post office combines these emphatic features with other innovative elements of the European Modern Movement; its curvilinear façade and broad staircase make this one of the most interesting examples of 20th-century Neapolitan architecture.

⑭ Piazza Giovanni Bovio

⑨K8 Ⓜ Università 🚌E1, N1, N3, N8, R2, 202

Visitors will inevitably stumble upon this busy central square, which Neapolitans call Piazza della Borsa after the former Stock Exchange (Borsa) that dominates it. Built in 1895 when taste was eclectic, the old exchange is reminiscent of 16th-century buildings in the Veneto. It is now the home of the Chamber of Commerce. Incorporated into the left side of this building is the small church of Sant'Aspreno al Porto, originally medieval but completely rebuilt in the 1600s.

The square marks the beginning of Corso Umberto I, also known as the Rettifilo. This grand avenue was built after slum clearance around the harbour, to connect the city centre and the central railway station, giving a new look to early 20th-century Naples (p49). The frequently altered 17th-century Fountain of Neptune was moved several times before finding its

→

The Via Chiaia, a lively street renowned for its excellent shopping, at dusk

> **Although many tourists flock to Via Chiaia, Neapolitans still embrace it. Grab some gelato and relax with the locals in the leisurely atmosphere that fills this street day and night.**

home in Piazza Bovio in 1898, although it has since been moved – temporarily – to the corner of Piazza Municipio (*p62*) and Via Medina.

Via Chiaia

⊙ H10 Ⓜ Municipio 🚌 E6

This street was opened in the 16th century to connect what is now Piazza del Plebiscito (*p60*) with the coast – its name means "beach street" in Neapolitan dialect. Along with Via Toledo (*p61*), Via dei Mille and Via Calabritto, this is one of Naples's smartest shopping streets. While browsing, it is worth stopping to see the Ponte di Chiaia, a 17th-century gateway restored in the 1800s. Nearby is the 16th-century Palazzo Cellamare, known for the magnificent banquets and receptions once held there. Its portal was designed by architect Ferdinando Fuga. Although many tourists flock to Via Chiaia, Neapolitans still embrace it. Grab some gelato and relax with the locals in the leisurely atmosphere that fills this street day and night.

Santa Maria degli Angeli

⊙ H10 🏠 Piazza Santa Maria degli Angeli 📞 081 764 49 74 🚌 E6 🕐 7:30–11am & 5-7pm Mon-Sat, 8:30am-1:30pm Sun

Construction of this church began in the 17th century, on land donated to the devout Theatine religious order by Donna Costanza del Carretto Dira, the Princess of Melfi. The building was designed by the Theatine cleric Francesco Grimaldi, and it is clearly visible from any point overlooking the city. The three-nave interior is so well structured that Francesco Milizia described it in an 18th-century guide to Naples as "perhaps the most well-proportioned church in the city".

The frescoes on the vaults, which depict episodes from the life of the Virgin Mary, are the work of Italian painter Giovanni Battista Beinaschi.

17 Pizzofalcone

H11 **Mount Echia** **E6**

A nondescript hill rises over Naples as you approach the coast, behind Piazza Plebiscito (p60). Most visitors pay it little attention, but this was once the site of the early settlement Parthenope, and was also home to a group of splendid Roman villas. Today, the rosy-hued façades of the Nunziatella military academy mark Pizzofalcone, which overlooks the Castel dell'Ovo (p144). A few churches and residential buildings dot the hill, set alongside various military buildings that, over the centuries, took advantage of the strategic vantage point. Wandering the streets, it is easy to feel off the beaten track without going too far from bustling Via Toledo.

18 Santa Maria Egiziaca a Pizzofalcone

H10 **Via Egiziaca a Pizzofalcone 30** **081 764 51 99** **E6** **9-11am & 4:30-7:30pm Tue-Sun**

A portal on Via Egiziaca leads to this small Baroque church. Its construction began in 1661 at the request of the nuns who lived nearby in the Sant'Agostino convent. The design of the building was entrusted to Cosimo Fanzago (1593–1678), a Lombard architect and sculptor who was to become one of the most prestigious creators of the local Baroque style. The octagonal plan of the church was greatly admired by his contemporaries. The paintings in the main chapels are by Paolo De Matteis (1662–1728), while the sculptures are by Nicola Fumo (1647–1725). The high altar is in Rococo style.

The ornate church is named after St Mary the Egyptian, a 4th-century penitent who engaged in sex work; some believe that the choice of saint was intended as a lesson to the numerous prostitutes and their clientele in the nearby Quartieri Spagnoli (p64).

PARTHENOPE

In the 8th-9th century BC, Greek colonists from Rhodes founded the first urban settlement in Naples on the hill of Pizzofalcone: Parthenope, renamed Palaepolis "old city" 300 years later when Neapolis "new city" was founded to the east. The old city was later abandoned, and by the Middle Ages the area had reverted to farmland. The site of ancient Naples was revived in the 16th century, when it became a neighbourhood favoured by aristocrats and officials, attracted by the beauty of the area and its proximity to the Royal Palace. In the 18th century Via Monte di Dio was one of Naples's most important residential streets, and it still retains some of its original character.

19 Palazzo Serra di Cassano

H10 **Via Monte di Dio 14-15** **081 795 11 11** **E6** **11am-4pm daily, by appt only**

The original doorway to Prince Aloisio Serra di Cassano's palace is no longer the main

← Spectacular views over the Bay of Naples from the summit of Pizzofalcone

contrasts dramatically with the building's imposing, grey volcanic stone.

The *piano nobile* (upper floor) of the palazzo is now home to the Istituto Italiano per gli Studi Filosofici, an international cultural institution.

20 ⓂB
Nunziatella

🔲 H11 🏠 Via Generale Parisi 16 🚌 E6 🕑 9–10am for occasional Mass; by appt at other times 🌐 nunziatella.it

At the beginning of the 18th century, the Jesuits at the Nunziatella asked architect Ferdinando Sanfelice – who was working on the nearby Palazzo Serra di Cassano – to build the church and restore the convent, which dates from the 16th century. Entering the little church, visitors are struck by the harmonious balance between the architectural space and the decorative elements. The most important frescoes were painted by Neapolitan artist Francesco de Mura (1696–1782); in the apse is the *Adoration of the Magi*, on the ceiling is the *Assumption of the Virgin*, and on the inside of

entrance to this beautiful example of 18th-century Neapolitan civic architecture. To express his grief over the execution of his son Gennaro, one of the leaders of the 1799 revolution in Naples, the prince ordered the entrance (at No 67 Via Egiziaca) to be closed that same year. The doorway is now at Via Monte di Dio. The uniqueness of the palazzo, which was designed by one of the leading architects of the time, Ferdinando Sanfelice (1675–1748), lies in the majestic staircase with its double flight of steps. Set in the entrance hall, it is decorated with white marble that

the façade is *Rest during the Flight to Egypt*. The altar, by sculptor Giuseppe Sanmartino (1720–93), is one of the main examples of Neapolitan Baroque that still exists today.

The Nunziatella has been the city's military college since 1787. It was the site of revolutionary uprisings when the French took over Naples and later trained some of Italy's top military leaders. Still a school today, it also contains three different museums for visitors, with each one housing donations of items from alumni.

SHOP

Gay Odin
The finest chocolates and candles in Naples are found at this 19th-century institution. Their "Forest" line is a particular speciality - distinctive "branches" of delicious chocolate.

🔲 H9 🏠 Via Toledo 214 🌐 gay-odin.it

Acampora Profumi
Visitors can sample artisanal perfumes at this family-run laboratory. Made with old-school care, each bottle of perfume here is sealed and stamped with wax.

🔲 J8 🏠 Via Gaetano Filangieri 71 🌐 en.brunoacampora.com

Casa Ascione
Located in a fashionable corner of Naples, this museum and shop celebrates a tradition dating back to 1855 with its coral jewellery and engraved items.

🔲 H9 🏠 Galleria Umberto 1 🌐 ascione.it

↑ Interiors of the Palazzo Serra di Cassano, which dates from the 18th century

A SHORT WALK
TOLEDO AND CASTEL NUOVO

Distance 1 km (0.5 miles) **Time** 15 minutes
Nearest Metro Toledo

Naples is a city of contrasting moods: the quiet solemnity of Piazza del Plebiscito, a symbol of the city's rebirth, is very different from the animation – you might even call it confusion – of the surrounding streets. Visitors to this area can mingle with the crowd in Via Toledo, drop in at the Gran Caffè Gambrinus or Galleria Umberto I, pause in the shade of the historic Basilica di San Francesco di Paola, or visit the museums at Palazzo Reale and Castel Nuovo. In addition to the rich history and art treasures in this area, Via Toledo is also a good spot for shopping.

Galleria Umberto I (p60) *was built in the late 1800s by Boubée and has an iron-and-glass dome.*

START

VIA TOLEDO

PIAZZA TRIESTE E TRENTO

PIAZZA DEL PLEBISCITO

Via Toledo (p61), *named after a Spanish viceroy, borders the Quartieri Spagnoli.*

Teatro San Carlo (p63) *is richly decorated in gilded stucco and has excellent acoustics.*

San Ferdinando *hosts a performance of the Stabat Mater, every year on Good Friday, for the confraternity based here since 1837.*

Entrance to the **National Library**

Gran Caffè Gambrinus (p60) *was frequented by the writer Gabriele d'Annunzio.*

The Neo-Classical **Basilica di San Francesco di Paola** (p61)

Bustling **Piazza del Plebiscito** (p60) *is a popular public square.*

← Waiters outside the Gran Caffè Gambrinus, a historic city café

↑ The imposing Maritime Terminal building at Naples's busy Molo Beverello port

The Palazzo Reale stables

VIA VITTORIO EMANUELE III

VIA SAN CARLO

VIA PARCO DEL CASTELLO

VIA FERDINANDO ACTON

FINISH

This lovely courtyard is the venue for summer events and concerts.

Castel Nuovo's (p58) triumphal arch stands out between the Mezzo (middle) and Guardia (watch) towers.

The **Molo Beverello**, the port's passenger terminal

The **gardens** next to Palazzo Reale are overlooked by the historic Neapolitan rowing club, Circolo Canottieri Napoli.

Palazzo Reale (p56) was begun in 1600 for a visit by Philip III of Spain that ultimately did not take place.

Did You Know?

The National Library of Naples is the third-largest in Italy, following those of Rome and Florence.

0 metres	100	N
0 yards	100	↑

Filling up fresh
fruit stock at a market ↑
on Via Pignasecca

A LONG WALK
MONTESANTO

Distance 3 km (2 miles) **Walking Time** 60 minutes
Nearest Funicular Centrale: Augusteo

A visit to Naples would not be complete without a stroll through at least one of its fascinating open-air markets. This walk begins on the wide shopping street Via Toledo and winds its way past the imposing Fascist structures of Piazza Matteotti and through the lively Pignasecca in the Montesanto district. Though officially a *mercatino* (little market), the Pignasecca is a favourite among Neapolitans. In addition, several atmospheric churches here make for welcome havens from the jostling and haggling crowds.

Locator Map
For more detail see p54, p74, p90

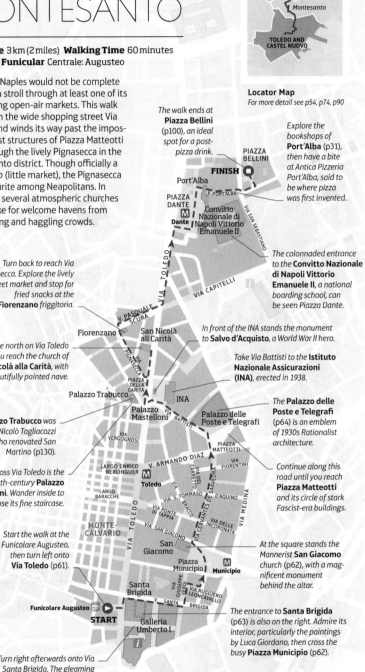

The walk ends at **Piazza Bellini** (p100), *an ideal spot for a post-pizza drink.*

Explore the bookshops of **Port'Alba** (p31), *then have a bite at Antica Pizzeria Port'Alba, said to be where pizza was first invented.*

The colonnaded entrance to the **Convitto Nazionale di Napoli Vittorio Emanuele II**, *a national boarding school, can be seen Piazza Dante.*

In front of the INA stands the monument to **Salvo d'Acquisto**, *a World War II hero.*

Take Via Battisti to the **Istituto Nazionale Assicurazioni (INA)**, *erected in 1938.*

The **Palazzo delle Poste e Telegrafi** (p64) *is an emblem of 1930s Rationalist architecture.*

Continue along this road until you reach **Piazza Matteotti** *and its circle of stark Fascist-era buildings.*

At the square stands the Mannerist **San Giacomo** *church (p62), with a magnificent monument behind the altar.*

The entrance to **Santa Brigida** (p63) *is also on the right. Admire its interior, particularly the paintings by Luca Giordano, then cross the busy* **Piazza Municipio** (p62).

Turn back to reach Via Pignasecca. Explore the lively street market and stop for fried snacks at the **Fiorenzano** *friggitoria.*

Continue north on Via Toledo until you reach the church of **San Nicolà alla Carità**, *with its beautifully painted nave.*

Palazzo Trabucco *was built by Nicolò Tagliacozzi Canale, who renovated San Martino (p130).*

Across Via Toledo is the striking 18th-century **Palazzo Mastelloni***. Wander inside to glimpse its fine staircase.*

Start the walk at the Funicolare Augusteo, then turn left onto **Via Toledo** (p61).

Turn right afterwards onto Via Santa Brigida. The gleaming **Galleria Umberto I** *arcade (p60) will be on your right.*

0 metres 250
0 yards 250

N ↑

71

Laundry draping over a narrow street in Spaccanapoli

SPACCANAPOLI

The arrow-straight street of Spaccanapoli, corresponding to the lower decumanus, was one of the three main thoroughfares in Greco-Roman Naples; seen from above, it appears to cut the city in half. It was in the district traversed by this road that Thomas Aquinas taught at the University of Naples, located in San Domenico Maggiore, which was built in the late 1200s. At the end of the 13th century, after the construction of Castel Nuovo, the administrative hub of the city began to shift away from the Spaccanapoli area and towards the seafront. However, commercial activity still developed in the Piazza Mercato zone, while in the old centre, a concentration of churches and convents, notably Santa Chiara, developed. When the city expanded around the newly built Via Toledo, during the era of the Spanish viceroyalty, the area which is now Piazza del Gesù Nuovo became the junction point between the old and modern cities. In the 19th century, urban renewal projects attempted to revamp the city following the cholera epidemic, cutting through slums in the area with Corso Umberto I. Some districts witnessed rejuvenation, however others, such as historic Forcella, have remained largely untouched. Today much of the area seems frozen in time, enchanting visitors who stroll through the bustling pedestrian streets which are crammed with lively eateries, independent shops and some of Naples's most fascinating sites.

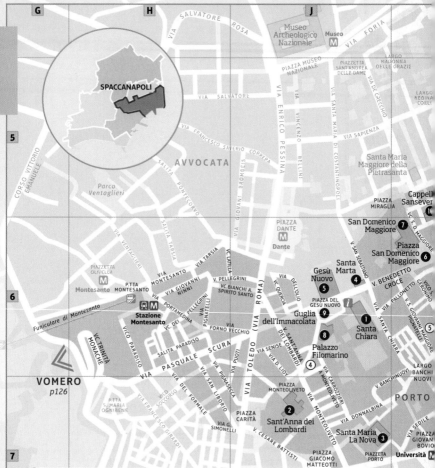

SPACCANAPOLI

Must See
1 Santa Chiara

Experience More
2 Sant'Anna dei Lombardi
3 Santa Maria La Nova
4 Santa Marta
5 Gesù Nuovo
6 Piazza San Domenico Maggiore
7 San Domenico Maggiore
8 Palazzo Filomarino
9 Guglia dell'Immacolata
10 Capella Sansevero
11 Sant'Angelo a Nilo
12 Palazzo Carafa Santangelo
13 Statue of the Nile
14 San Giorgio Maggiore
15 Museo Civico Filangieri
16 Archivio di Stato
17 Santi Marcellino e Festo
18 Gesù Vecchio

19 Corso Umberto I
20 Monte de Pietà
21 Capella Pappacoda
22 Santissima Annunziata
23 Santi Severino e Sossio
24 Santa Maria del Carmine

Eat
① L'Antica Pizzeria Da Michele
② Tandem Ragù

Drink
③ Archeobar
④ Red Wine

Stay
⑤ Decumani Hotel de Charme
⑥ Hotel Naples

Shop
⑦ Forcella Market
⑧ Porta Nolana Market

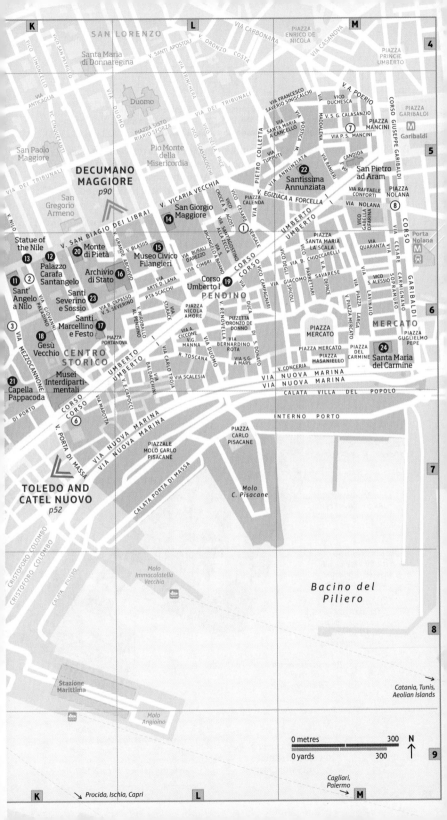

❶ 🔶

SANTA CHIARA

📍J6 🏛Church: Via B Croce; cloister & museum: Via S Chiara 49c Ⓜ Dante,
Università 🚋Montesanto 🚌E1, N1, R4, 201 🕐9:30am–5:30pm daily,
10am–2:30pm Sun & hols 🌐monasterodisantachiara.it

Behind its imposing façade, this monastic complex hides a resplendent cloister
surrounded by arcades and tiled walkways. A relatively sober interior forms
the last resting place of Angevin and Bourbon royalty, while Roman ruins
below reveal a past beyond anything the monks would have remembered.

In 1310 Robert of Anjou laid the first stone of the convent and church that the Angevin rulers later chose as the site for their tombs. Santa Chiara was where the kingdom's assemblies were held, as well as ceremonies, such as the one celebrating the miracle of San Gennaro's blood (p95). In the mid-1700s, the church's Gothic lines were obscured by the addition of elaborate Baroque ornamentation.

After the church was completely destroyed by fire in 1943, restoration work tried to recover as much as possible of the original; the present interior is simple and austere, typical of a Franciscan church. Near the apse are the fine sculpture groups of the royal Angevin tombs; a beautiful wooden 14th-century crucifix executed by an unknown artist is on the altar. The lovely cloisters are an oasis of calm.

The bell tower still has its original base, with Gothic inscriptions describing the foundation.

Poor Clares' Choir, built by Leonardo di Vito, is a great example of Neapolitan Gothic frescoed by Giotto; only fragments of the original remain.

The tombs of Charles of Calabria and his wife Mary of Valois were built by Tino da Camaino (c 1285–1337).

The rose window tracery consists of six marble circles.

The projecting porch is a structure in piperno stone set against the yellow tufa façade.

The main gateway is a 14th-century portal with a large jutting vault.

The marble pavement was designed by Ferdinando Fuga.

Clarissa cloister

The tomb of Philip of Bourbon (son of King Charles III of Spain) was designed by Ferdinando Fuga and is one of the few 18th-century works that survived the fire in 1943.

An illustration showing the elegant features of Santa Chiara ↑

EXPERIENCE Spaccanapoli

76

1310
▽ Robert of Anjou lays the first stone.

1340
Santa Chiara consecrated and declared a royal church.

1769
▽ The church is rebuilt in Baroque style.

1343
Giovanni and Pacio Bertini sculpt the Tomb of Robert of Anjou.

1742
△ The tiled cloister is built.

The simple arches of the 14th-century tiled cloister frame the garden redesigned by Domenico Antonio Vaccaro in 1739–42. The pillars are punctuated by seats decorated with majolica tiles painted by Donato and Giuseppe Massa.

The Museo dell'Opera houses objects, decorative ornaments and sculptures from Santa Chiara. In the section devoted to archaeology, you can see the ruins of a Roman bathhouse.

The Roman baths, once marking the city's western limit, are located between the first two rooms of the Museo dell'Opera and the outer courtyard.

→
The cloister of Santa Chiara, featuring colourful pillars and majolica tiles

EXPERIENCE MORE

❷ Sant'Anna dei Lombardi

Q J7 **A** Piazza Monteoliveto **C** 081 551 33 33 **M** Toledo **R** Montesanto **E** E1, N3, N8, R4, 139, 201 **O** 10am–1pm & 4–6pm Mon–Sat; 10am–noon Sun

Founded in 1411 as Santa Maria di Monteoliveto, this was the favourite church of the Aragonese kings, who summoned leading artists of the time to decorate it. Its name changed when it was assigned to the Confraternity of Lombards (to whom it still belongs), whose church had collapsed in the 1805 earthquake. The church's roof was damaged during World War II and has not been restored, but the interior contains some examples of Renaissance sculpture. The skilfully realistic sculptural tableau *Lamentation over the Dead Christ* was created by Guido Mazzoni (1450–1518) in 1492. It displays seven life-size terracotta figures leaning over the body of Christ in mourning. Their grief-stricken faces are said to be modelled on those of the Aragonese kings. In the Vasari Sacristy, the stunning ceiling frescoes were painted by Tuscan artist Giorgio Vasari (1511–74) in 1545, while the Tolosa Chapel was decorated by the della Robbia workshop in Florence. The church also contains the tomb of the architect Domenico Fontana.

At No 3 Via Monteoliveto is the 16th-century Palazzo Gravina, now occupied by the Faculty of Architecture.

❸

Santa Maria La Nova

Q J7 **A** Piazza Santa Maria La Nova 44 **M** Toledo, Università **R** Montesanto **E** C25, E1, N1, N3, R2 **O** 9:30am–3pm Mon–Fri, 9:30am–2pm Sat & Sun **W** santamarialanova.info

In order to make room for the grand Castel Nuovo (*p58*), a Franciscan church devoted to the Virgin Mary had to be torn down. In exchange, Charles I of Anjou had this new church built at his own expense. The richly decorated ceiling was painted by leading artists of the time (such as Imparato and Corenzio), creating a gallery of 16th- and 17th-century Neapolitan painting. In the fourth chapel on the right is Giovanni da Nola's (1488–1558) altarpiece of Sant'Eustachio. Other chapels contain works by Caracciolo and Santacroce. In the former monastery, now the seat of the provincial government, there are two cloisters; the smaller one (No 44) has Renaissance frescoes and marble tombs, while the other (No 43) contains a garden.

The complex is also home to the **Museo ARCA** (Arte Religiosa Contemporanea). Exhibits here include a tomb thought to be that of Vlad the Impaler.

Museo ARCA
⊛ **A** Piazza Santa Maria la Nova 44 **O** 9:30am–3pm Mon–Fri, 9:30am–2pm Sat & Sun **W** oltreilchiostro.org/museo-arca

❹ Santa Marta

Q J6 **A** Via San Sebastiano 42 **M** Dante, Cavour-Museo **R** Montesanto **E** E1

This small church was founded by Margherita di Durazzo in the 15th century and became the headquarters of one of the city's most important

← A tomb in Santa Maria La Nova, thought to be that of Vlad the Impaler

confraternities. The church stands opposite the bell tower of Santa Chiara (p76). The doorway still retains its original depressed arch structure. On the high altar is a painting by Andrea and Nicola Vaccaro (1670), depicting Santa Marta, to whom the church is dedicated. The *Codice di Santa Marta (Codex of St Martha)*, with its valuable miniatures, came from this church and is now kept in the Archivio di Stato, or state archive (p84). You can reach the underground cemetery from the room next to the sacristy. Santa Marta is usually closed to the public, but it does open its doors from time to time.

---

⑤

Gesù Nuovo

◩ J6 ◨ Piazza del Gesù Nuovo 2 Ⓜ Dante ▦ Montesanto ▭ E1 ◷ 8:30am-12:30pm & 4:30-7pm daily ▥ gesunuovo.it

The façade of this building, which is covered in diamond-point rustication, was once part of a 15th-century palazzo. This portion was retained by the Jesuits who bought the building and transformed it in 1584 into the large church seen today. The 17th-century doorway incorporates the original Renaissance entrance to the palazzo.

The Baroque interior is richly decorated with multi-coloured marbles and ornate works of art, including statues, vivid frescoes and a two-sided

The rich interior and (inset) diamond-patterned façade of Gesù Nuovo →

reliquary from 1617 that is decorated with 70 busts of martyred saints. In the chapel of St Ignatius of Loyola are two of Cosimo Fanzago's finest works: the sculptures of *David* and *Jeremiah*. The cupola, frescoed by Lanfranco, collapsed in the earthquake of 1688; only the corbels

showing the four Evangelists in flight remain. Above the main entrance is a huge fresco by Francesco Solimena titled *Expulsion of Heliodorus from the Temple* (1725). The statue of the Virgin, on a lapis lazuli globe, dates from the mid-1800s. One chapel on the right houses the remains of the physician San Giuseppe Moscati (1880–1927), who was canonized in 1987. On its walls are silver images of specific body parts, which were purchased by worshippers hoping to be healed.

GIUSEPPE MOSCATI'S MEDICAL MIRACLES

A devoutly religious man and an excellent doctor, Giuseppe Moscati helped fight cholera outbreaks in Naples and treated soldiers during World War I. Many attributed miraculous healings to him, in part due to his holistic and humanizing approach to medicine. After his death, a mother dreamed of Moscati in a white coat, and her son, who was dying of leukaemia, went into remission. The pope recognized this as a miracle, leading to Moscati's canonization - a first for modern doctors.

6

Piazza San Domenico Maggiore

K6 **M** Dante, Università
Montesanto **E1**

This piazza was the result of a rare Renaissance town-planning project in Naples. In the 1500s the area was still being used for kitchen gardens. Rebuilding by the Aragonese rulers transformed the zone into a setting appropriate for the church of San Domenico, which had been chosen to house the royal tombs. They also wanted to improve the area around the statue of the Nile, which was the aristocratic residential district. The top of the piazza is dominated by the apse of San Domenico, while imposing buildings line the other sides of the square. Opposite the church is the 17th-century Palazzo Sangro di Casacalenda; to the left is Palazzo Petrucci, with its 15th-century portal; to the right are Palazzo Corigliano, now home to the Oriental Studies department of the University

of Naples, and Palazzo Sangro di Sansevero. In the centre stands the Guglia di San Domenico, built to honour its namesake saint for bringing about the end of the plague of 1656. The spire was designed by Cosimo Fanzago and finished only in 1737 by Domenico Antonio Vaccaro.

7

San Domenico Maggiore

K6 **A** Vico San Domenico Maggiore 18
M Dante, Cavour-Museo
Montesanto **E1**
9:30am-noon, 5-7pm daily **W** museo san domenicomaggiore.it

In 1283 Charles I of Anjou ordered the construction of a new church and monastery for the Dominican order. The Gothic three-nave building was built onto the pre-existing church of Sant'Arcangelo a Morfisa, which was the original seat of Naples's University of Theology, founded by Thomas Aquinas. A relic of the saint's arm is said to be kept inside the monastery. Visitors can also see the painting of the crucifix that miraculously spoke to the saintly scholar.

Scandal struck in the church in the 1560s, when 18 friars were sentenced to death for sexual misconduct, creating ill-will between the order and then-young friar Giordano Bruno. The Dominican monk would go on to challenge the Church and be charged for heresy, ultimately burning at the stake in 1600.

Federico Travaglini rebuilt the interior in Neo-Gothic style in 1850–53, removing much of the original spirit of the building. In the second chapel are some 14th-century frescoes ascribed to Pietro Cavallini, a pupil of Giotto. The sacristy houses 42 coffins, some of which contain the embalmed corpses of the Aragonese kings, including Alfonso V and Ferdinand I.

↑ Elaborately carved tombs within the Cappella Sansevero

DRINK

Archeobar

This cosy cocktail bar, where patrons spill out onto the streets at night-time, is the perfect place to mingle with the locals.

📍 K6 🏠 Via Mezzocannone 101/Bis 📞 081 1917 88 62

Red Wine

Does what it says on the tin; a large selection of wines pair nicely with the cheese and charcuterie plates on offer at this relaxed wine bar just off Piazza del Gesù Nuovo.

📍 J6 🏠 Calata Trinità Maggiore 19 📞 081 1956 91 31

8
Palazzo Filomarino

📍 J6 🏠 Via Benedetto Croce 12 📞 081 551 71 59 Ⓜ Dante 🚋 Montesanto 🚌 E1 🕐 Italian Institue of Historical Studies: 9am-1pm & 4-7pm daily

This is the first of many noble buildings visitors will glimpse upon entering the Decumano Maggiore and Spaccanapoli areas. These mansions and palaces are often in a state of disrepair, yet have retained an air of splendour and still bear traces of the aristocrats who built and lived in them. The original Palazzo Filomarino dates back to the 14th century, but the building was substantially altered in the

←

Crowds seated in the Piazza San Domenico Maggiore, beneath the plague column

16th century. It underwent restoration in the next century after being damaged during Masaniello's uprising (p47). The 18th-century doorway is the work of the architect Sanfelice. The philosopher Benedetto Croce, a leading figure in Italian culture and politics in the early 20th century, lived in this palazzo in the latter part of his life. The Italian Institute of Historical Studies, founded by Croce, takes up the whole of the first floor with its 40,000-volume library. Croce's apartment and personal library, however, are closed to the public.

9
Guglia dell' Immacolata

📍 J6 🏠 Piazza del Gesù Nuovo Ⓜ Dante 🚋 Montesanto 🚌 E1

The Jesuits commissioned this gigantic marble spire – the newest of the three Spires of Naples – in honour of the Virgin Mary, and as a tangible sign of their power. The monument, designed by Giuseppe Genoino, was begun in 1747. The complex stone ornamentation, which depicts Jesuit saints and stories of Mary, was sculpted by Francesco Pagano and Matteo Bottigliero and is a key work of 18th-century Neapolitan sculpture. The Madonna's statue is the centre of festivities on the Feast of Immaculate Conception.

10
Cappella Sansevero

📍 K5 🏠 Via Francesco de Sanctis 19 (off Via San Severo) Ⓜ Dante, Cavour-Museo 🚋 Montesanto 🚌 E1 🕐 9am-6:30pm Wed-Mon (last adm 6pm) 🌐 museo sansevero.it

The focal point of this chapel is its extraordinary Veiled Christ, the masterpiece of Neapolitan

sculptor Giuseppe Sanmartino (1720–93). Created from a single block of marble, the recumbent figure of Christ is draped with a translucent veil.

The lavish decoration of the chapel was planned by the Prince of Sansevero, Raimondo di Sangro (1710–71), in the 18th century. Each sculpture group features a member of his family as an allegorical figure. Antonio Corradini's Modesty, located to the left of the altar, is set on the tomb of the prince's mother. On the tomb of his father, who was said to be a dissolute man who later repented, is Francesco Queirolo's Disillusion.

The mysterious di Sangro himself headed the city's Masonic Lodge and was excommunicated from the Church; he was, however, later readmitted, probably due to his family's influence. The tales about the prince – lover of science and the occult – have engendered legends depicting him as a demon or a sorcerer. Chapel visitors incorrectly believed that he turned a veil on the Veiled Christ into marble through mystical chemical processes. In fact, it was simply a testament to Sanmartino's skill.

← Visitors standing outside the intricately carved walls of Sant'Angelo a Nilo church

From the church you can visit the courtyard of Palazzo Brancaccio where the first public library in Naples was founded in 1690.

12

Palazzo Carafa Santangelo

⊙K6 **⌂Via San Biagio dei Librai 121** **Ⓜ Dante, Cavour-Museo, Università** **🚃E1, E2** **🕐8:30am–1:15pm & 3:30–4:45pm Mon–Sat (courtyard only)**

This important example of Neapolitan Renaissance architecture is known as Palazzo della Capa di Cavallo because of the terracotta copy of a horse's head (now in the courtyard). This was a gift from Lorenzo de' Medici to his friend Diomede Carafa in 1471 to embellish his new palace. The original sculpture, a Roman bronze, has been in the Museo Archeologico (p96) since 1809.

The marble portal, similar to that of Palazzo Petrucci in Piazza San Domenico (p80), and the façade are examples of the new Renaissance style. In late 15th-century Naples this look merged with the Late Gothic style, as can be seen in the arches and pilasters and the inlay in the wooden doors with the Carafa family coats of arms. Opposite the palace is the animated

→ The statue of the Nile god, topped by a bearded head

11

Sant'Angelo a Nilo

⊙K6 **⌂Piazzetta Nilo** **📞081 211 08 60** **Ⓜ Dante, Cavour-Museo, Università** **🚇Montesanto** **🚃E1** **🕐9am–1pm & 4:30–7pm Mon–Sat, 9am to 1pm Sun & public hols**

Built in the early 15th century by Cardinal Brancaccio next to his family palace, this church was remodelled by Arcangelo Guglielminelli four centuries later. It houses the earliest Renaissance work in Naples: the cardinal's funerary monument, sculpted in Pisa by Donatello and Michelozzo in 1426–7 and sent to Naples by ship. On the front of the sarcophagus, in the bas-relief representing the *Assumption of the Virgin*, Donatello created one of the first examples of his revolutionary "stiacciato" technique – the relief receding gradually from the foreground to give the illusion of depth.

Baroque façade of the church of San Nicola a Nilo, which is also the site of a second-hand dealer's stall.

13

Statue of the Nile

⊙K6 **⌂Largo Corpo di Napoli (off Via Nilo)** **Ⓜ Dante, Cavour-Museo, Università** **🚇Montesanto** **🚃E1, E2**

Walking along busy Via Nilo visitors may catch sight of this imposing marble statue. Alexandrian merchants who

↑ An array of exhibits on display at the Museo Civico Filangieri

once worked in the area of the Greco-Roman city had the statue sculpted in honour of the Egyptian god Nile. The statue disappeared after the merchants left Naples, and, when found in the 1400s, it was missing its head. At that time the recumbent putti next to Nile – symbols of the many tributaries of the river god – were interpreted as babies at their mother's breast, so the sculpture was called "the Body of Naples", the mother-city suckling her children. The statue has kept this name despite the addition of a bearded head in the 17th century – since removed and restored again.

---

⑭

San Giorgio Maggiore

📍L5 🏛 Via Duomo 237a
📞081 28 79 32 🚌C57, E1, E2, N1, N3, R2 🕐8am–noon & 5–7pm daily, 8am to 1pm Sun & public hols

San Giorgio Maggiore, originally an early Christian basilica, is one of the city's oldest churches. It was completely rebuilt in the mid-1600s to a design by Cosimo Fanzago. The only surviving part of the original church is the semicircular apse at the entrance of the 17th-century church, which was originally built facing a different direction. The right-hand nave of the rebuilt church was demolished in the late 19th century to make room for the Via Duomo extension. Before visiting the church, pause for a moment at Palazzo Marigliano (at No 39 Via Duomo). Though run-down, it is one of the most important examples of 16th-century Neapolitan civic architecture.

---

⑮

Museo Civico Filangieri

📍L6 🏛 Via Duomo 288
📞081 20 31 75 🚌C57, E1, E2, N1, N3, R2 🕐10am–4pm Tue–Sat, 10am to 2pm Sun

The building now occupied by this civic museum was built in the Florentine Renaissance style during the 15th century as the Como family residence. It became a monastery in the late 1500s, was demolished during work on Via Duomo (1879), and then rebuilt 20 m (66 ft) from its original site.

In 1882 Prince Gaetano Filangieri established his fine art collection here and donated it to the city in 1888. Much of the collection was scattered during World War II but was reassembled. Today it consists of objects including weapons, furniture, paintings, medallions and porcelain.

The spiral staircase leads from the ground floor to the Sala Agata (named after the founder's mother), which leads to the prince's library via a suspended passageway.

THE ART OF NAPLES IN WORLD WAR II

During the infamous Four Days of Naples in September 1943, retreating German troops burned huge sections of the city and its artworks, including much of the Filangieri Museum's collection. This final rush of looting and destruction only ended as Allied forces arrived. The Filangieri Museum, however, was reborn thanks to donations from private art collectors. After years of closures and renovations, the museum finally reopened in 2012, and today it is a thriving cultural institute in the historic heart of Naples.

16
Archivio di Stato

L6 **Piazzetta del Grande Archivio 5** **C57, E1, E2, N1, N3, R2** **8am-6:30pm Mon-Fri, 8am-1:30pm Sat** **archiviodi statonapoli.it**

In 1835, Ferdinand II decided to use the former Benedictine monastery of Santi Severino e Sossio to house administrative documents that had accumulated since the Angevin period. The old monastery, built in the 9th century and enlarged in 1494, was remodelled to allow for this new function. The State Archive contains over a million files, registers, documents and parchments, and is one of the most important of its kind in Europe.

The huge complex has four cloisters and many rooms containing numerous works of art. One cloister is known as the Chiostro del Platano, named after an ancient plane tree (felled in 1959 because it was dying) that, according to tradition, had been planted by St Benedict himself. The mid-16th-century frescoes depicting the life of the saint are the work of Antonio Solario, known as Lo Zingaro or "gypsy".

By the entrance to the former monastery is the 17th-century Fontana della Selleria, a public fountain with Baroque detailing.

A NUMBER FOR EVERY OCCASION

At noon every Saturday, life in Naples stands still for a few minutes in anticipation of the lottery draw, which takes place in the hall of the lottery office at No 17 Via del Grande Archivio. Devised in Genoa in the 16th century, the lottery was legalized in the 1700s and grew rapidly in popularity in the 1800s. As Matilde Serao wrote in the late 19th century: "Even Neapolitans who can't read know La Smorfia by heart". La Smorfia is a guide to the significance of numbers and is the lottery "bible". First published in the 19th century, the book is regularly updated to offer interpretations of events and dreams.

17
Santi Marcellino e Festo

K6 **Largo San Marcellino 10** **081 253 73 95** **Università** **E1, N1, N3, R2, 202** **9am-7pm Mon-Fri**

The two adjacent monasteries of Santi Marcellino e Pietro and of Santi Festo e Desiderio date from the 8th century. In the mid-15th century they were combined to create a single large complex. The site's church, built the following century, is adorned with 18th-century marble inlay. Luigi Vanvitelli, architect of the Royal Palace of Caserta (p194) worked on its renovation in 1770. The building is now used as a congress centre. The spacious cloister has piperno stone arches and a garden in the centre; from the south-facing side there is a panoramic view of the Bay of Naples. By royal decree, the complex became the property of the University of Naples in 1907, and it is still used as a centre of study today. The building next to the church is open to the public, and is occupied by the **Museum of**

← A colonnaded courtyard, where the Archivio di Stato is now housed

library was given to the Royal Mineralogy Museum, the most important such museum in Italy. Its Vesuvian collection is especially noteworthy. Other sections house the Zoology Museum and the Anthropology Museum, founded in 1811.

Back in Via Paladino, look out for the beautiful Baroque interior of the **College Church** (at No 38), begun in 1564, which contains works by Solimena and Fanzago.

Museums
⌖ 📞 081 253 75 87 🕐 9am-1:30pm Mon-Fri (also 2:30-4:45pm Mon & Thu)

Church
⌖ 📞 081 552 66 39
🕐 7:30am-noon, 4:30-6:30pm daily

---

⑲
Corso Umberto I
📍 L6 Ⓜ Università, Garibaldi 🚌 E1, N1, N3, R2, 202

This wide street, known to Neapolitans as the Rettifilo, connects the central railway station (Stazione Centrale) with the city centre. It was built in the late 19th century after the cholera epidemic. The idea of decongesting cities was popular at this time – as seen in the Urban Renewal Plan. However, critics maintained that the street's renovated areas merely covered up shabby neighbourhoods behind it, while destroying many architectural treasures. Its namesake, King Umberto I, was similarly criticized by leftists and anarchists who ultimately assassinated the monarch, but his legacy lives on through the avenue.

---

⑳
Monte di Pietà
📍 K6 🏛 Palazzo Carafa, Via San Biagio dei Librai 114 Ⓜ Dante, Cavour-Museo, Università 🚌 E1, E2 🕐 9am-7pm Sat, 9am-2pm Sun

This majestic building was built in the late 1500s for a charitable institute set up to grant loans to those in debt to moneylenders. Its Cappella della Pietà at the end of the courtyard has a Renaissance façade with sculptures at the entrance by Pietro Bernini and on the tympanum by Michelangelo Naccherino. The church interior was frescoed by Belisario Corenzio and Caracciola in the early 1600s. It includes many works by Naples's Baroque artists.

Palaeontology. Inside, the museum has a fine painted majolica floor and more than 50,000 artifacts on display.

Museum of Palaeontology
⌖ 📞 081 253 75 16 🕐 9am-1:30pm & 2:30-4:45pm Mon-Thu, 9am to 1:30pm Fri

---

⑱
Gesù Vecchio
📍 K6 🏛 Via Giovanni Paladino 39 Ⓜ Università 🚌 E1, N1, N3, R2, 202
🕐 9am-6:45pm Mon-Fri

The home of the University of Naples since 1777, this late 16th-century building was the city's first Jesuit college. In the 19th century, the Urban Renewal Plan *(p48)*, expanded the university with the addition of a factory building looking out over Corso Umberto I. One part of the original college that still remains is the area that has been occupied by the university library since 1808, and is home to one million volumes.

Other parts of the building have been turned into a number of **museums**. In 1801 the hall that was once the Jesuits'

↑ Sculptures by Michelangelo Naccherino adorning the tympanum of Monte di Pietà

↑ The elaborately carved Gothic doorway of the splendid Cappella Pappacoda

SHOP

Forcella Market

Sift through mountains of goods at this lively catch-all flea market, and don't be afraid to haggle if your Italian is up to scratch.

🔲 M5 🏛 Via Pasquale Stanislao Mancini ⏱ Morning daily

Porta Nolana Market

This outdoor market specializes in fresh local seafood (although a range of food is also available). A trip here is a great way to explore Forcella's local culture.

🔲 M5 🏛 Porta Nolana, Piazza Nolana ⏱ Morning daily

㉑

Cappella Pappacoda

🔲 K6 🏛 Largo San Giovanni Maggiore Ⓜ Università 🚌 E1, R2 🔒 To the public

In the early 15th century Artusio Pappacoda, Grand Seneschal and councillor in the Angevin court, founded this small church. The original late Gothic doorway is the work of Antonio Baboccio (1351–1435), a sculptor, architect and goldsmith who also crafted the main portal of the city's cathedral (p94). The campanile is particularly interesting because of the dramatic colour contrast created by the different materials; most of the building is a faded yellow, while the façade's portal is intricately carved from white marble. The church is now deconsecrated and is used as the Great Hall of the nearby Istituto Universitario Orientale (Oriental Institute).

㉒

Santissima Annunziata

🔲 M5 🏛 Via dell'Annunziata 34 Ⓜ Piazza Garibaldi 🚌 E2, N1, N3, R2, 202 ⏱ 8am–noon & 5–7:30pm Mon–Sat, 8am–1:30pm Sun 🌐 annunziatamaggiore.it

The Santa Casa dell'Annunziata was a charitable institution that existed from the early 1300s to help abandoned children. The church was destroyed by fire in 1757 and rebuilt by Luigi and Carlo Vanvitelli, who designed the cupola and one-nave interior. Among the parts fortunately untouched by the fire is the sacristy, which features frescoes by Corenzio (1605) along with 16th-century inlaid wooden cupboards. To the left of the church, an impressive marble doorway leads to the former foundling hospital (now a pediatric hospital). A wheel system that dates to the 17th century has been renovated, so visitors can see how desperate mothers could leave their children in the safety of the church by placing them in a basket and turning the wheel to the church's interior. By the late 19th century, the wheel was no longer in use, but the church maintained its role as an orphanage until the 1950s.

㉓

Santi Severino e Sossio

🔲 K6 🏛 Via Bartolomeo Capasso 22 Ⓜ Università 🚌 E1, N1, N3, R2, 202 ⏱ Church: 9:15am–noon daily; cloister: 9am–7pm daily

Founded in the 9th century together with the adjoining monastery – which became the Royal Archives in 1835 (p84) – this church was rebuilt from the late 1400s on. Inside both church and monastery

FORCELLA

While much of Naples has been renovated in recent years, Forcella can still feel caught in the past. It's one of the poorest parts of the city - with grand buildings and former municipal landmarks that have crumbled over the years as the wider landscape transformed - but Forcella still attracts locals for its cheap markets and lively pizzerias. Its reputation is perhaps undeservedly harsh, but tourists are not a common sight here.

are some excellent works of art from the 16th–18th centuries. Among these are canvases by the Sienese painter Marco Pino, while the sculptures include the tomb of Andrea Bonifacio, a masterpiece by the Spanish sculptor Bartolomeo Ordoñez.

24

Santa Maria del Carmine

M6 Piazza del Carmine 2 Garibaldi E2 Hours vary, check website santuariocarminemaggiore.it

In Mercato, the former civic centre of Naples, this church stands in remembrance to the people of this district, which is now undergoing significant redevelopment. Among the famous residents was Swedish memoirist Dr Axel Munthe, who slept in the church when he came to Naples to help during the 1884 cholera outbreak.

Despite its surroundings, the church has maintained much of its grace. Neapolitans are devoted to its many works of art, particularly the *Madonna Bruna*, a 14th-century painting kept behind the altar. This famous effigy is celebrated annually at the feast of the Madonna del Carmine. Except for the cross dome in the presbytery, little remains of the original Angevin construction. Instead the church displays typical 18th-century architectural forms both inside and out. The interior was decorated by the architect Tagliacozzi Canale; the ceiling, destroyed in World War II, has been rebuilt in keeping with the original. Left of the nave is the tomb of Corradino, Duke of Swabia, who was beheaded in 1268 in Piazza Mercato opposite the church. The medieval crucifix placed in a tabernacle under the triumphal arch is also the object of devout worship. The 75-m (246-ft) campanile, completed by the architect Fra Nuvolo in 1631, is the tallest in Naples.

The lavish interior and *(inset)* bright exterior of Santa Maria del Carmine ↓

A SHORT WALK
SPACCANAPOLI

Distance 1 km (0.5 miles) **Time** 15 minutes
Nearest Metro Dante

The long street commonly known as Spaccanapoli is divided into seven sections bearing different names. Because of its rich array of churches, squares and historic buildings the street has been called an "open-air museum", like nearby Via dei Tribunali. It is also one of the liveliest and most atmospheric places in Naples, with shops, crafts and cafés. Piazza San Domenico Maggiore, near the university, is always crowded with young people. During your stroll, be sure to stop to enjoy the excellent pastries at the Scaturchio pasticceria.

Piazza San Domenico Maggiore (p80) *is a significant Neapolitan square with a spire at its centre.*

Cappella Sansevero (p81)

San Domenico Maggiore (p80) *was built by Charles I of Anjou in 1283.*

Santa Marta (p78) *is a small church dating from the 15th century.*

Gesù Nuovo (p79), *a historic church, was once part of Palazzo Sanseverino.*

VIA S. SEBASTIANO

VIA BENEDETTO CROCE

START PIAZZA DEL GESÙ NUOVO

VIA S. CHIARA

CALATA TRINITA MAGG.

Scaturchio pasticceria

Sant'Angelo a Nilo (p82) *houses the tomb of Cardinal Brancaccio, sculpted by Donatello and Michelozzo.*

Palazzo Filomarino *is where philosopher Benedetto Croce died in 1952.*

Santa Chiara (p76), *a church commissioned by Robert of Anjou*

Guglia dell' Immacolata (p81) *is an 18th-century spire that is named after the statue of the Virgin at its pinnacle.*

→
The ornate Guglia dell'Immacolata spire, illuminated at night

Locator Map
For more detail see p74

↑ Musicians and produce stalls fighting for space on the lively street of Spaccanapoli

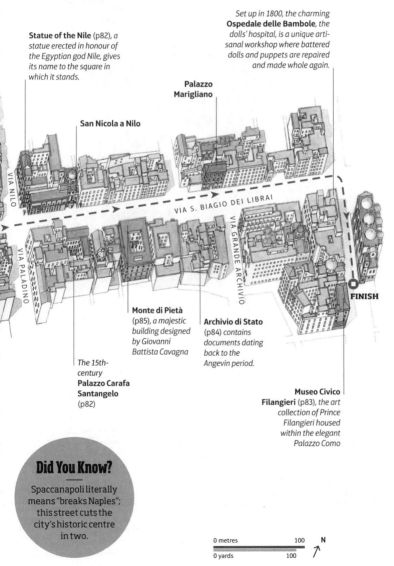

Set up in 1800, the charming **Ospedale delle Bambole**, *the dolls' hospital, is a unique artisanal workshop where battered dolls and puppets are repaired and made whole again.*

Statue of the Nile (p82), *a statue erected in honour of the Egyptian god Nile, gives its name to the square in which it stands.*

Palazzo Marigliano

San Nicola a Nilo

VIA NILO

VIA S. BIAGIO DEI LIBRAI

VIA GRANDE ARCHIVIO

VIA PALADINO

FINISH

Monte di Pietà (p85), *a majestic building designed by Giovanni Battista Cavagna*

Archivio di Stato (p84) *contains documents dating back to the Angevin period.*

The 15th-century **Palazzo Carafa Santangelo** (p82)

Museo Civico Filangieri (p83), *the art collection of Prince Filangieri housed within the elegant Palazzo Como*

Did You Know?

Spaccanapoli literally means "breaks Naples"; this street cuts the city's historic centre in two.

| 0 metres | 100 |
| 0 yards | 100 |

N

DECUMANO MAGGIORE

Now called Via dei Tribunali, the Decumano Maggiore was the main east-west avenue in the heart of the Greek city of Neapolis. Remnants of the old Greek walls, still visible at Piazza Bellini, emphasize the area's ancient roots. It was here that the Norman kings decided to create their stronghold when they conquered the city. In the 12th century, King William I started building Castel Capuano, which remained a royal residence through the subsequent Angevin and Aragonese eras, even after the construction of Castel Nuovo. The following centuries saw a great deal of development taking place in this quarter, and many of the structures from that period still stand, including the city's magnificent Duomo. In 1585, the royal barracks was built at the northern edge of this district; two centuries later, it was rebuilt as a magnificent royal museum housing the Farnese treasures. Around the time that the barracks was constructed, a market sprang up at the western end of the Decumano Maggiore, outside the old city walls, which was transformed into the splendid pedestrian hub of Piazza Dante in the 18th century. The area also became famous for workshops making *presepi*, the nativity scenes that rose to an art form in Naples and can still be seen today. This historic quarter gained a more contemporary institution in 2005: the acclaimed art museum MADRE.

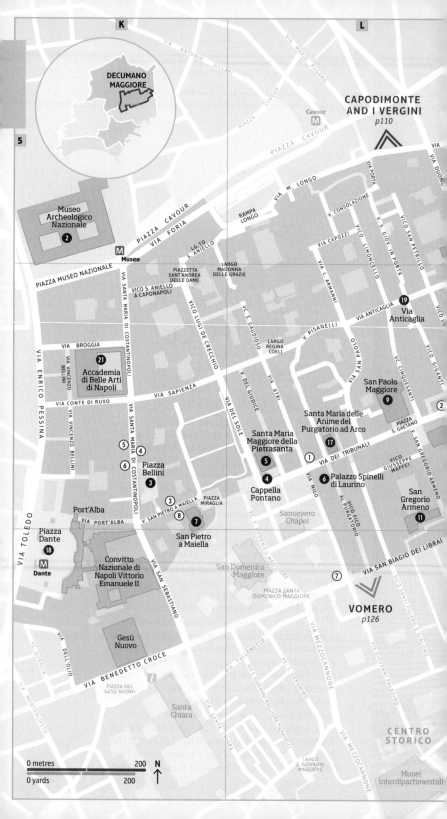

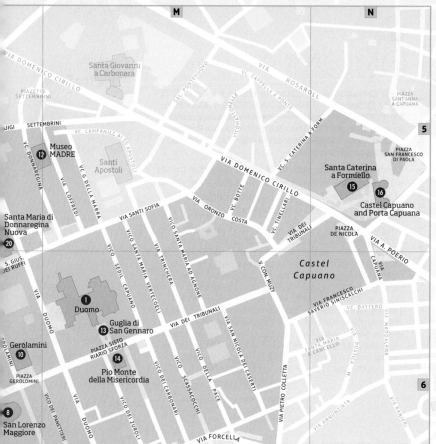

DECUMANO MAGGIORE

Must Sees

① Duomo

② Museo Archeologico Nazionale

Experience More

③ Piazza Bellini

④ Capella Pontano

⑤ Santa Maria Maggiore della Pietrasanta

⑥ Palazzo Spinelli di Laurino

⑦ San Pietro a Maiella

⑧ San Lorenzo Maggiore

⑨ San Paolo Maggiore

⑩ Gerolamini

⑪ San Gregorio Armeno

⑫ Museo MADRE

⑬ Guglia di San Gennaro

⑭ Pio Monte della Misericordia

⑮ Santa Caterina a Formiello

⑯ Castel Capuano and Porta Capuana

⑰ Santa Maria delle Anime del Purgatorio ad Arco

⑱ Piazza Dante

⑲ Via Anticaglia

⑳ Santa Maria di Donnaregina Nuova

㉑ Accademia di Belle Arti di Napoli

Eat

① Antica Pizzeria Gino Sorbillo

② Pizzeria di Matteo

Drink

③ Perditempo

④ Spazio Nea

Stay

⑤ Costantinopoli104

⑥ Piazza Bellini

Shop

⑦ Museum Shop

⑧ Libreria Antiquaria Colonnese

❶ ⊗

DUOMO

📍 M6 🏛 Via Duomo 147 Ⓜ Cavour-Museo, Garibaldi 🚌 C57, E1, E2 🕐 Cathedral: 8:30am-1:30pm & 2:30-7:30pm Mon-Sat, 8:30am-1:30pm & 4:30-7:30pm Sun & hols; museum: 9am-4:30pm Mon-Fri, 9am-5:30pm Sat; Santa Restituta: 8:30am-noon & 4:30-6:30pm Mon-Sat, 8:30am-1pm Sun 🌐 museosangennaro.it/en

Sandy white on the outside, Naples's cathedral bursts with colour and decorations on the inside. A patchwork of styles and renovations, it houses countless treasures on its walls and in its chapels.

This great cathedral was built for Charles I of Anjou in the late 1200s–early 1300s. It incorporated older Christian buildings and has been altered substantially over the centuries. The left-hand nave leads to the early Medieval basilica of Santa Restituta, radically changed in the 17th century, and the San Giovanni in Fonte baptistry. The Cappella Minutolo has retained its original Gothic structure and decoration; the mosaic pavement and 13th-century frescoes are by artist Montano d'Arezzo. The Crypt of the Succorpo was built under the apse in 1497 to house the relics of San Gennaro, kept until then in the Montevergine sanctuary. In the early 1600s the Reale Cappella del Tesoro di San Gennaro was built in thanksgiving to the saint; the attached museum displays a rich collection of jewellery and art.

The Baptistry is the oldest in the Western world. It was built around AD 550 and has splendid mosaics.

Santa Restituta contains the beautiful mosaic Madonna and saints Gennaro and Restituta, executed by the painter Lello da Orvieto.

The underground archaeological area reveals layers of buildings from three periods: Greek, Roman and early Middle Ages.

The middle portal bears two 14th-century lions and the sculptor Tino da Camaino's Virgin and Child in the lunette.

The font features a basin made of Egyptian basalt. The right-hand nave also has Greek sculptures and a 14th-century episcopal throne.

↑ The façade of the cathedral, an array of architectural styles

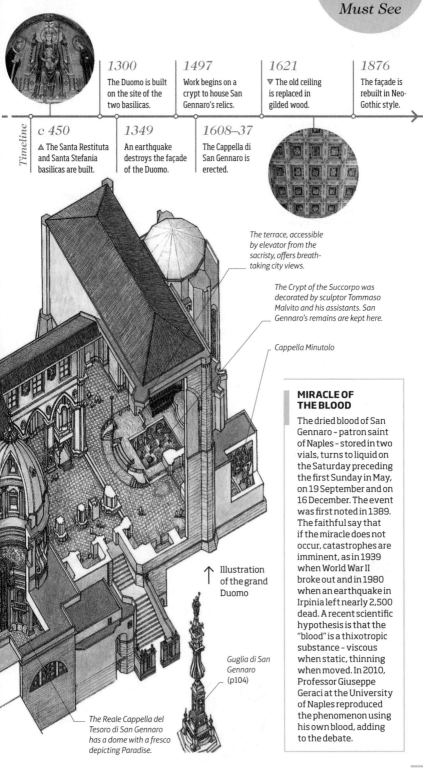

Timeline

c 450
△ The Santa Restituta and Santa Stefania basilicas are built.

1300
The Duomo is built on the site of the two basilicas.

1349
An earthquake destroys the façade of the Duomo.

1497
Work begins on a crypt to house San Gennaro's relics.

1608–37
The Cappella di San Gennaro is erected.

1621
▽ The old ceiling is replaced in gilded wood.

1876
The façade is rebuilt in Neo-Gothic style.

The terrace, accessible by elevator from the sacristy, offers breath-taking city views.

The Crypt of the Succorpo was decorated by sculptor Tommaso Malvito and his assistants. San Gennaro's remains are kept here.

Cappella Minutolo

↑ Illustration of the grand Duomo

Guglia di San Gennaro (p104)

The Reale Cappella del Tesoro di San Gennaro has a dome with a fresco depicting Paradise.

MIRACLE OF THE BLOOD

The dried blood of San Gennaro – patron saint of Naples – stored in two vials, turns to liquid on the Saturday preceding the first Sunday in May, on 19 September and on 16 December. The event was first noted in 1389. The faithful say that if the miracle does not occur, catastrophes are imminent, as in 1939 when World War II broke out and in 1980 when an earthquake in Irpinia left nearly 2,500 dead. A recent scientific hypothesis is that the "blood" is a thixotropic substance – viscous when static, thinning when moved. In 2010, Professor Giuseppe Geraci at the University of Naples reproduced the phenomenon using his own blood, adding to the debate.

2 🔧 🎨 🏛

MUSEO ARCHEOLOGICO NAZIONALE

📍K5 🚇Piazza Museo 19 Ⓜ️Cavour-Museo 🚌CS, C51, C52, E1, R1 and others 🕘9am-7:30pm Wed-Mon 🚫1 Jan, 25 Dec 🌐museoarcheologiconapoli.it/en

One of the most important archaeological museums in the world, the Museo Archeologico Nazionale makes history come to life as artifacts created over millennia are given a voice in an unbeatable collection of humankind's history.

The museum is housed in a grand building that started life in 1585 as the home of the royal cavalry and barracks, and was rebuilt in the early 17th century as the seat of the University of Naples. In 1777, when King Ferdinand IV transferred the university to Gesù Vecchio (p85), the building was again adapted to house the Real Museo Borbonico and library. The frequent reconstructions are reflected in the palace's architecture, which combines both Baroque and Neo-Classical elements.

The Making of the Museum

The Real Museo Borbonico initially held the Farnese Collection of paintings – works of art from the royal houses of Rome and Parma that Charles of Bourbon had inherited from his mother Elizabeth Farnese. The collection also contained books, ancient artifacts and archaeological finds from sites across Campania and southern Italy. In 1925 the books were moved to the Palazzo Reale (p56), and in 1957 the Farnese Collection paintings were returned to Museo di Capodimonte (p114). The remaining material consisted of finds from the Greek, Roman and Renaissance periods, particularly artifacts from the nearby Vesuvian cities of Pompeii, Herculaneum and Stabiae. This collection is what became the Archaeological Museum. In 1860 the collection was nationalized, and the restoration and reorganization of exhibits still continue.

SALONE DELLA MERIDIANA

When the building was being fitted out as a museum, the architects had the idea of adding an observatory. A large sundial (meridiana) was created for the hall, which had initially been destined to be the Bourbon library. The observatory, however, was scrapped, and, as originally planned, the Salone della Meridiana was opened to the public in 1804 as a library, with a ceiling fresco that is among the most impressive in Europe. Today the space is used to display artworks.

1616
The building becomes the seat of the University of Naples.

1738
▽ Excavations of Vesuvian towns begin; Charles III collects finds.

1860
The collection of the museum becomes public property.

Timeline

1585
△ The structure that will house the museum is built as the home of the royal cavalry.

1957
The museum is renamed after the picture collection moves.

1980
△ An earthquake causes serious damage to several of the museum's exhibits.

The Salone della Meridiana, with a ceiling frescoe painted by Pietro Bardellino in 1781

Exploring the Museo Archeologico

The impressive Farnese Collection and sculpture from Herculaneum, Pompeii, Stabiae and other destroyed Vesuvian cities can be seen on the ground floor, the mezzanine level and the first floor. Beautiful Pompeiian mosaics on the mezzanine and domestic items, weapons and frescoes on the first floor show daily life in the ancient cities. The mezzanine also hosts the coin collection, while the first floor also has the Gabinetto Segretto and the Salone della Meridiana. The lower ground floor has a collection of Pompeiian epigraphs and the Egyptian Collection, Italy's second-largest with over 2,500 objects. The arrangement aims to display the exhibits in context.

→
Fresco from a Stabiae villa depicting a maiden gathering flowers in spring

→
Visitors admiring Classical sculptures in the impressive collection

GABINETTO SEGRETO

Ancient Romans had a fairly robust appreciation of the erotic, which came as a shock to the 19th-century archaeologists excavating the cities of Pompeii and Herculaneum. Museum authorities, finding the explicit artifacts inappropriate, locked them away in a "secret cabinet" and bricked up its door in 1849. The room, which includes a collection of phalluses, finally reopened to the general public in 2000.

Mosaics

▶ The majority of the mosaics on display come from Pompeii, Herculaneum, Stabiae and Boscoreale, and date from the 2nd century BC to AD 79. The realistic images, such as the female portraits from Pompeii, are particularly fascinating. Another masterpiece is the *Battle of Alexander (right)* found at Pompeii's House of the Faun (p163).

The Egyptian Collection

Artifacts from the Ancient Kingdom (2700-2200 BC) to the Roman age are exhibited here. As well as human and animal mummies, this section includes canopic vases, containers for the internal organs of the deceased with lids in the shape of animal heads.

Sculpture

The fine collection of Greco-Roman sculpture consists mostly of works found around Vesuvius and the Phlegraean Fields, as well as the treasures from the Farnese Collection. Among the many sculptures - most of which are the only existing copies of lost Greek originals - are the statues of Harmodios and Aristogeiton, or the "Tyrannicides", young Athenians who killed the 6th century BC tyrant, Hipparchos.

Frescoes

◀ Most of the frescoes here are from Herculaneum and Pompeii. The frieze from the Pompeii house of Julia Felix, with a still life of apples and grapes *(left)* and scenes from the forum, gives a fascinating glimpse of daily life in a 1st-century AD city.

Incised Gems

This precious collection, begun by Cosimo de' Medici, holds Greek, Roman and Renaissance gems. The highlight is the veined sardonyx Farnese Cup, a large and beautiful cameo carved in Egypt around the 2nd and 1st centuries BC.

Temple of Isis

The artifacts from Pompeii's Temple of Isis re-create the sanctuary as it appeared to the first archaeologists in 1764. The marble head of the goddess Isis dates from the 1st century AD.

The Model of Pompeii

Based on archaeologist Giuseppe Fiorelli's idea, this scale model was built between 1861 and 1879. The exact reproduction of every detail found in the ruins make this an extremely important historical document and, in some cases, the only useful source that remains.

Villa dei Papiri

This villa in Herculaneum (p164), still partly buried today, contained a rich array of exceptional artworks; this ancient private collection has been preserved intact at the museum. Among the pieces on display are life-sized statues and small sculptures in marble and bronze, such as the *Dancing Faun* from the atrium of the villa. Most of the pieces were inspired by Greek figurative art. Also found here was a vast library of around 1,800 papyrus scrolls, now in the Palazzo Reale (p56).

EXPERIENCE MORE

❸ Piazza Bellini

◉K6 Ⓜ️Dante, Cavour-Museo 🚋Montesanto 🚌E1, N3, R4, 201

Dating back to the 1600s, Piazza Bellini is one of the liveliest hubs in the city, and attracts an artsy, intellectual crowd all year round. A mix of old and new, the square is a popular spot for Neapolitans to relax and spend time with friends. It buzzes morning and night with revellers sipping drinks at one of the numerous cafés, or cracking open local beers that have been purchased from inexpensive bars. A statue of the 19th-century opera composer Vincenzo Bellini, for whom the square is named, holds court in the centre of the square, while underfoot, remains of part of the walls of the ancient Greek city of Neapolis are on display, unearthed during excavations in 1954. Music drifts across from the nearby conservatory, humming through the discussions and debates among local students who linger here between classes.

❹ Cappella Pontano

◉L6 🏠Piazzetta Pietrasanta 16 Ⓜ️Dante, Cavour-Museo 🚋Montesanto 🚌E1, R4, 201 🕘9am–1pm daily

Giovanni Pontano, renowned humanist and secretary to King Ferdinand of Aragon, commissioned this small chapel in 1492. Based on a design for a pagan temple, it has harmonious proportions that make it one of the most significant works produced in Renaissance Naples. It has a frescoed triptych by Francesco Cicino da Caiazzo and a 15th-century pavement of coloured tiles. The numerous Latin epigraphs were written by Giovanni Pontano himself.

❺ Santa Maria Maggiore della Pietrasanta

◉L6 🏠Piazzetta Pietrasanta 📞081 797 12 31 Ⓜ️Dante, Cavour-Museo 🚌E1, R4, 201 🕘9am–6:30pm Sun

A wall of Neapolis and a Roman villa lie directly

underneath the church, as does a 3-km- (2-mile-) long Roman aqueduct that was used as a bomb shelter during World War II. A church was first erected in this location in AD 566 by Bishop Pomponio, but the majestic, centrally planned church that is seen today was built in the 17th century by Cosimo Fanzago. The campanile belonged to the original basilica; it was built after the main building in the 10th century and is the sole remaining example of early medieval architecture in Naples.

←

The domed roof of Santa Maria Maggiore della Pietrasanta

↑ The ornate ceiling of San Pietro a Maiella, standing *(inset)* at the end of a close-packed street

day. The courtyard, designed by Ferdinando Sanfelice, is open to the public.

6

Palazzo Spinelli di Laurino

◑ L6 ◐ Via dei Tribunali 362 ☎ 081 29 95 79 Ⓜ Dante, Cavour-Museo 🚇 Montesanto 🚌 E1 ◔ Courtyard: 8am-7pm Mon-Sat

The former grandeur of this 16th-century palazzo, which once belonged to the dukes of Laurino, can be seen in its oval courtyard and double-flight staircase. Many visitors here claim to see the ghost of a young woman. According to legend, she was named Bianca and worked as a maid for the duke. One day, Bianca displeased her mistress, who had the girl walled up in a room. The story goes that Bianca's spirit never left and haunts the building to this

7

San Pietro a Maiella

◑ K6 ◐ Piazza Miraglia 393 Ⓜ Dante, Cavour-Museo 🚇 Montesanto 🚌 E1, R4, 201 ◔ 7:30am-1:30pm Mon-Sat, 7:30am-1pm Sun 🌐 sanpietroamajella.it

The founder of this church, the nobleman Pipino da Barletta, dedicated it to Pietro Angelerio, also known as Pietro da Morrone, a hermit friar from Maiella who became Pope Celestine V in 1294. The church's original Gothic architecture, modified by numerous additions over the centuries, was restored between 1888 and 1927. The restoration uncovered some wonderful 14th-century frescoes in two of the chapels and also revealed splendid gilded wooden ceilings in the nave and transept with paintings by Mattia Preti, regarded as among the most supreme examples of 17th-century Neapolitan painting. Since 1826 the monastery annexed to the church has housed one of Italy's music conservatoires.

THE HERMIT POPE

Serving as pope for just five months in 1924, Pietro Angelerio had started his religious career by founding the Celestines of the Benedictine order. He was a cave-dwelling recluse and an ascetic, but when a new pope was needed, leaders chose him – despite his opposition. The cardinals accompanied him to Naples, where he was dubbed Pope Celestine V, but, lacking any authority or skills, he resigned. The only other pope to resign since was Pope Benedict XIV, who stepped down 719 years later in 2013.

↑ The arched cloisters of San Lorenzo Maggiore, which lead to the ruins beneath the church

8 ⊘ ⋈

San Lorenzo Maggiore

♀L6 ♠Via dei Tribunali 316 Ⓜ Dante, Cavour-Museo 🚋Montesanto 🚌E1 ⏰7:30am-12:30pm & 5-7:30pm daily 🌐laneapolis sotterrata.it

The heart of Greco-Roman Naples once beat where the church of San Lorenzo Maggiore stands. The cloister affords access to the excavation site, which has revealed important remains including a vast *macellum* (market). Thanks to recent discoveries, visitors can now follow ancient streets, identifying the bakery, the laundry shop and the treasury. A model of the market is displayed to help situate the ruins.

The construction of San Lorenzo itself began in 1265 for Charles I of Anjou, on the site of a 6th-century church. The façade was totally rebuilt by Sanfelice in 1742, but the 14th-century portal and original wooden doors are intact. The interior has an apse with nine chapels placed around the ambulatory. Here is the tomb of Catherine of Austria, a fine sculpture by Tino da Camaino (c 1323) and frescoes by a local pupil of Giotto. It was in this church that Boccaccio first saw the girl he celebrated in his writings as Fiammetta.

To the right of San Lorenzo is the monastery, where you can visit the chapterhouse; the cloister; and the refectory, which was the assembly hall of the royal Parliament from 1442. It also houses the Museo dell'Opera, which has local artifacts dating from the 3rd century BC to the 19th century.

9

San Paolo Maggiore

♀L6 ♠Piazza San Gaetano ☎081 45 40 48 Ⓜ Dante, Cavour-Museo 🚋Montesanto 🚌C57, E1, E2 ⏰Church: 9am-6pm Mon-Sat, 10am-6pm Sun; crypt: 8-10am & 5-7pm daily

In Greco-Roman Naples, the present-day Piazza San Gaetano was the site of the Greek *Agora* and later, of the Roman Forum. The Romans built a Temple of the Dioscuri here, which was converted into a Christian basilica in the 8th century. This ancient church was then remodelled from 1583 to 1603; the new church also incorporated the pronaos of the pagan temple, but only two Corinthian columns of the latter survived the 1688 earthquake.

In the richly decorated interior there are frescoes by Massimo Stanzione on the vault over the central nave. Sadly, they were damaged by water and bombardments during World War II. The Cappella Firrao, on the left side of the apse, has many 17th-century tombs, frescoes and sculptures. The marvellous paintings in the sacristy are by Francesco Solimena (1689–90). A stairway leads down to the crypt, which is the final resting place of San Gaetano, one of Naples's patron saints.

←

A marble sculpture by Domenico Antonio Vaccaro in San Paolo Maggiore

---

BENEATH THE CITY

Underneath Naples there is a fascinating world to be explored. Since its early days, the city has been built out of material quarried from the ground. Over time, caves and tunnels were left in this way, and became catacombs, aqueducts, passages, and shelter areas during World War II. The caves grew to their current size during Spanish rule (*p47*), when it was forbidden to import raw building materials. You can descend into the bowels of Naples and wander (*p26*)– there is an entrance at San Paolo Maggiore.

Gerolamini

◎L6 **⌂**Piazza Gerolamini
☎081 29 23 16 **Ⓜ**Dante,
Cavour-Museo **🚇**Monte-
santo **🚌**C57, E1, E2
◷8:30am–7pm Mon–Fri,
8:30am–2pm Sat & Sun

This monastery was founded
in the late 16th century by the
Oratorio di San Filippo Neri
congregation, also called "dei
Gerolamini" because they
came from San Girolamo alla
Carità in Rome. The church
was built in Tuscan Renaissance style; the interior was
rebuilt in the early 1600s; and
the façade was modified by
Ferdinando Fuga in 1780.

Alongside the church there
are two cloisters. The first,
designed by Giovanni Dosio,
shares features with the
cloister he created at the
Certosa di San Martino (p130).
There are fine paintings in
the Quadreria (art gallery),
including Ribera's *Saint Andrew*,
which depicts the apostle with
his cross behind him. Also on
display are works by Caracciolo
and Luca Giordano.

⑪ San Gregorio Armeno

◎L6 **⌂**Via San Gregorio
Armeno 44 **☎**081 552 01
86 **Ⓜ**Dante, Cavour-
Museo **🚇**Montesanto
🚌E1 **◷**9:30am–noon daily
(to 12:30pm Sun)

Carlo Celano described the
sumptuous Baroque interior
of this church as a "room of
Paradise on Earth". It was
designed in the mid-18th
century by Niccolò Tagliacozzi
Canale, and notable works
include the late 16th-century
wooden ceiling and frescoes
by Luca Giordano.

The monastery is located
on Via San Gregorio Armeno,
a street known as "Christmas
Alley", where artisans sell items
for the *presepe* (nativity scene).
It was founded in the 8th
century by a group of nuns
who had fled persecution in
Byzantium, and was rebuilt
in the 1500s and enlarged
the following century. The
campanile was erected in
1716 on a footbridge that
connected two parts of
the complex.

DRINK

Perditempo

Located just off Piazza
Bellini, this atmospheric
venue can get a little
smoky and loud when
patrons take over the
street in front. Those in
search of an authentic
evening out won't
be disappointed!

◎K6 **⌂**Via San Pietro
a Maiella 8
☎081 44 49 58

Spazio Nea

The café-bar of this
local gallery is a great
place to start your
night, before moving
on to the nearby Piazza
Bellini, which is riddled
with intriguing bars
and nightlife venues.

◎K6 **⌂**Via Santa Maria
di Costantinopoli 53
◷9am–2am daily
🌐spazionea.it

↑ Bustling artisanal shops on
Via San Gregorio Armeno,
or "Christmas Alley"

↑ Museo MADRE's entrance, by French artist Daniel Buren

STAY

Costantinopoli 104

With elegant rooms set inside a former villa, this well-located spot also has a charming shady garden and a pool, perfect for relaxing.

📍K6 🏠 Via Santa Maria di Costantinopoli 104
🌐costaninopoli104.it

€€€

Piazza Bellini

It's worth upgrading to a room with a view at this budget-friendly hotel. Interiors are fresh and comfortable, and the location – right in the historic centre of Naples – is arguably the best in town.

📍K6 🏠 Via Santa Maria di Costantinopoli 101
🌐hotelpiazzabellini.com

€€€

---

12 🎨 🖥 🛍

Museo MADRE

📍M5 🏠 Via Settembrini 79 🚇 Cavour-Museo
🚌C57, E2, N4, 182, 203
🕐 10am-7:30pm Mon, Wed-Sat; 10am-8pm Sun
🌐madrenapoli.it

Opened in 2005, the Museo d'Arte Contemporanea Donna Regina Napoli (MADRE) houses a remarkable collection of works by artists such as Mimmo Paladino, Jeff Koons, Anish Kapoor, Jannis Kounellis, Damien Hirst and Giulio Paolini, among others. The first floor has a library and a children's area, while the third floor is used for temporary exhibitions. The museum often hosts special events such as cinema screenings, concerts and theatrical performances.

The back of the museum is also the entrance to the 8th-century church of Santa Maria di Donnaregina Vecchia, rebuilt in 1293 at the request of Marie of Hungary, wife of Charles II of Anjou. The church contains the marble tomb of the queen, sculpted by Tino da Camaino in 1325–6.

13

Guglia di San Gennaro

📍M6 🏠 Piazza Riario Sforza 🚇 Dante, Cavour-Museo 🚌C57, E1, E2

This marble spire is dedicated to San Gennaro, patron saint of Naples, for having protected the city during the 1631 eruption of Vesuvius. The *guglia*, the oldest of Naples's three spires, was designed by Cosimo Fanzago in 1636, and has a bronze statue at the top that was sculpted by Tommaso Montani. Behind the spire you can glimpse the stairway of the side entrance to the Duomo *(p94)*.

---

14 🎨

Pio Monte della Misericordia

📍M6 🏠 Via dei Tribunali 253 🚇 Cavour-Museo, Garibaldi 🚌C57, E1, E2
🕐 9am-6pm Mon-Sat, 9am-2:30pm Sun 🌐piomonte dellamisericordia.it

Pio Monte is one of the most important charitable

> Inside the Pio Monte della Misericordia, the eye is immediately drawn to the extraordinary altarpiece: *The Seven Acts of Mercy*, a masterpiece by Caravaggio.

institutions in Naples. It was founded in 1601 to aid the poor and ill and to free the Christian slaves in the Ottoman Empire. The entire complex was designed by Francesco Antonio Picchiatti in the 17th century. Inside the church, the eye is immediately drawn to the extraordinary altarpiece: *The Seven Acts of Mercy*, a masterpiece by Caravaggio (1571–1610), which depicts the seven good deeds Catholics should perform for others. The art gallery on the first floor of the building houses the fine Pio Monte collection.

---

⑮

Santa Caterina a Formiello

📍 N5 🏠 Piazza Enrico De Nicola 65 ☎ 081 44 42 97
Ⓜ Garibaldi 🚌 C57, E2, 203
🕐 8:30am–12:30pm & 4:30–8pm daily, 9am–1:30pm public hols

The dome of Santa Caterina a Formiello dominates the surrounding area. The 16th-century church was called *formiello* because it was built next to *formali*, the ancient city aqueducts. Inside there is Baroque decoration; painters Luigi Garzi and Guglielmo Borremans executed the frescoes (1695–1709). The marble tombs of the Spinelli family are in the apse area.

---

⑯

Castel Capuano and Porta Capuana

📍 N5 🏠 Piazza Enrico De Nicola and Via Concezio Muzy Ⓜ Garibaldi 🚌 C57, E2

Functioning as a court of law since 1540, this palace

and fortress was built by the Normans in 1165 to defend the nearby city gateway. Castel Capuano is one of only four castles in Naples, and it remained a royal residence for the Angevin and Aragonese rulers even after the construction of Castel Nuovo (*p58*), before Don Pedro de Toledo turned the fortress into law courts. On the first floor is the huge frescoed Court of Appeal, which leads to the splendid Renaissance Cappella della Sommaria. The chapel was decorated by the Spanish painter Pietro Roviale, also known as Pedro de Rubiales (1511–82).

A short distance away from the courts stands the imposing gateway of Porta Capuana, where the ancient road to Capua entered the city. Although much older in origin, its present appearance is the result of late-15th-century reconstruction by the Italian architect and sculptor Giuliano da Maiano. The gateway's two towers, which are named Honour and Virtue, enclose the marble arch, repeating the pattern established in the Arco di Trionfo in Castel Nuovo.

---

⑰ 🎨 🅼

Santa Maria delle Anime del Purgatorio ad Arco

📍 L6 🏠 Via dei Tribunali 39
Ⓜ Dante, Cavour-Museo
🚇 Montesanto 🚌 E1
🕐 10am–6pm Mon–Fri, 10am–5pm Sat 🌐 purgatorioadarco.it

Evidence of the importance attached to worship of the dead in 17th-century Naples is shown by the many skulls, bones and other funerary motifs on this church's façade and in the interior. The church still belongs to the confraternity of the same name, founded in 1604 to collect alms to pay for masses for the souls of the dead. Inside, it has a single nave and lavish Baroque decoration. In the apse area there is a relief with a winged skull by Cosimo Fanzago, who also designed the church.

A steep staircase leads to the underground church, a large, sombre space that is used to worship the souls of the dead. In the centre of the floor, surrounded by black chains, is an anonymous tomb. Along a corridor there is a crypt of bones, which include those of the virgin-bride Lucia, who died of consumption shortly before her wedding day in the 1700s.

↑ The arched Porta Capuano gateway, framed by two circular stone towers

18 🚇 🏛

Piazza Dante

📍K7 Ⓜ Dante 🚋 Montesanto 🚌 C63, N3, N8, R4, 201

Until the 1700s this square lay outside the city walls and was used as a marketplace, hence the name Largo del Mercatello (Market Square).

In the second half of the 18th century it took on its present form and was renamed Foro Carolino by Charles III, King Charles of Bourbon and ruler of Naples from 1735 to 1759, who commissioned the new layout. The semicircular façade with its colossal columns was designed by architect-of-the-day Luigi Vanvitelli as a setting for the king's statue, which was intended for the central niche but was never sculpted. The 26 figures on the cornice are allegories of the sovereign's qualities.

Following the unification of Italy, a statue of Dante was placed in the middle of the square, and the site renamed again. The square is now lined with book shops all the way up to Via Port'Alba and Port'Alba, the gateway built in 1625 to connect the city with

outlying districts. It's a very popular place for locals to stroll, growing especially lively in summer.

19

Via Anticaglia

📍L6 Ⓜ Cavour-Museo 🚌 C57, E1, E2

The third, northernmost *decumanus* (east–west major road) in Greco-Roman Naples today has four official sections (Via Sapienza, Via Pisanelli, Via Anticaglia and Via Santi Apostoli), as does the lower *decumanus*, Spaccanapoli

(p76). The name "Anticaglia", meaning ruins, derives from the remains of the brick walls of a Roman building in this stretch of the street. These walls connected the ancient theatre, seen on the left as you go towards Via Santa Maria di Costantinopoli, and the bathhouse on the opposite side of the street. The theatre, where Emperor Nero is known to have acted, had a seating capacity of about 8,000.

NERO ON STAGE

He was known for killing his mother and possibly setting Rome ablaze during his short reign that began in AD 54, so it's no surprise that Emperor Nero was something of a drama lover. A patron of the arts, he would come to Naples and perform songs - including many that he had composed himself - to great crowds in the theatre. He never performed in Rome, preferring Naples, where he once sang right through an earthquake, thanking both the audience and the gods for the applause.

Nearby was the *odeion*, or ancient roofed theatre, which was used for concerts and poetry readings.

On the corner of Via Duomo and the third *decumanus*, there is a fine marble-and-piperno double stairway; from here you can visit the atrium of the church of San Giuseppe dei Ruffi, which was added in the early 18th century. Once past the Roman ruins, a right-hand turn at Via Armanni takes you to the Ospedale degli Incurabili. Inside is the unusual *Farmacia* (pharmacy), which features about 400 brightly coloured majolica vases on shelves of inlaid wood – a positive art gallery of Neapolitan ceramics. Public access is limited, however, with visits allowed only during the month of May for the "Maggio dei Monumenti", a month-long cultural festival *(p44)*.

People relaxing in the open space of Piazza Dante ↓

20 ⊕
Santa Maria di Donnaregina Nuova

📍 L5 🏛 Largo Donnaregina 7 Ⓜ Cavour-Museo 🚌 C57, E1, E2 🕐 9:30am-4:30pm Mon, Wed-Sat; 9:30am-2pm Sun 🌐 museo diocesanonapoli.com

The single-nave interior of this Baroque church, built in the early 1600s for the Poor Clares, an order of nuns, is decorated in multicoloured marble. Frescoes by Italian painter Francesco Solimena can be admired in the nuns' choir. The second floor houses the Diocesan Museum of Naples, which has two hallways of paintings, including *St Paul's Landing in Pozzuoli* by Baroque painter Giovanni Lanfranco. Other artists displayed along these corridors include Vaccaro, De Matteis and several Neapolitan artists from the 16th to the 19th centuries. Between the two hallways, a lookout point provides views of the church.

21 ⊕
Accademia di Belle Arti di Napoli

📍 K6 🏛 Via Vincenzo Bellini 36 Ⓜ Cavour-Museo 🚌 E1, N3, N8, R4, 201 🕐 10am-2pm Tue-Thu & Sat, 2-6pm Fri 🌐 abana.it

Italian architect Errico Alvino (who was particularly known for his work in Naples) transformed the 18th-century convent of San Giovanni delle Monache into the Academy of Fine Arts in the 1840s. The Neo-Renaissance style throughout the building reflects the prevailing fashion of that time, and a broad staircase with plaster casts of ancient sculptures leads to the first floor. The academy contains an important collection of modern painting, especially works by 19th-century Neapolitan and southern Italian artists.

SHOP

Museum Shop
Kitsch decor and quirky home goods inspired by local art and culture line the shelves of this shop and bar in the city centre. The selection of ceramics is particularly good.

📍 L7 🏛 Largo Corpo di Napoli 3 📞 389 119 41 69

Libreria Antiquaria Colonnese
Located off Piazza Bellini, this atmospheric book and stationery shop is a stand-out on a street packed with stalls selling photographs, postcards and second-hand books.

📍 K6 🏛 Via San Pietro a Majella 32-33 📞 081 459 858

A SHORT WALK
VIA DEI TRIBUNALI

Distance 1.5 km (1 mile) **Time** 25 minutes
Nearest Metro Dante

Via dei Tribunali was named after Castel Capuano, visible in the distance at the end of this long avenue, when it became the home of the civil courts (*tribunali*) in the 1500s. One of the streets crossing the Decumano Maggiore is Via San Gregorio Armeno, which is surely among the loveliest streets in Naples.

Art and handicrafts flourish here, and you can slow your pace to a crawl to watch as locals work. The craftsmen still carve shepherds and other figures for the *presepi*, traditional Neapolitan nativity scenes, just as they did four centuries ago – to the delight of visitors and Neapolitans alike.

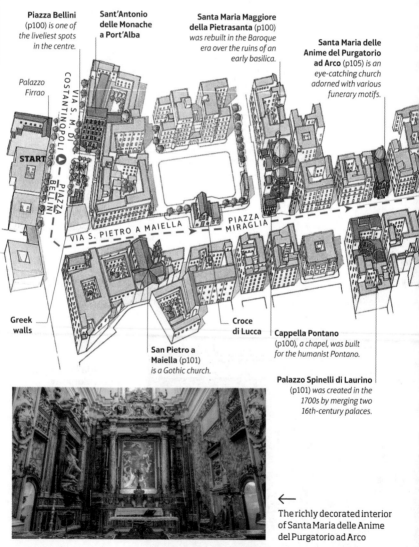

Piazza Bellini
(p100) *is one of the liveliest spots in the centre.*

Sant'Antonio delle Monache a Port'Alba

Santa Maria Maggiore della Pietrasanta (p100) *was rebuilt in the Baroque era over the ruins of an early basilica.*

Santa Maria delle Anime del Purgatorio ad Arco (p105) *is an eye-catching church adorned with various funerary motifs.*

Palazzo Firrao

VIA S. M. DI COSTANTINOPOLI

PIAZZA BELLINI

START

VIA S. PIETRO A MAIELLA

PIAZZA MIRAGLIA

Greek walls

Croce di Lucca

San Pietro a Maiella (p101) *is a Gothic church.*

Cappella Pontano
(p100), *a chapel, was built for the humanist Pontano.*

Palazzo Spinelli di Laurino
(p101) *was created in the 1700s by merging two 16th-century palaces.*

← The richly decorated interior of Santa Maria delle Anime del Purgatorio ad Arco

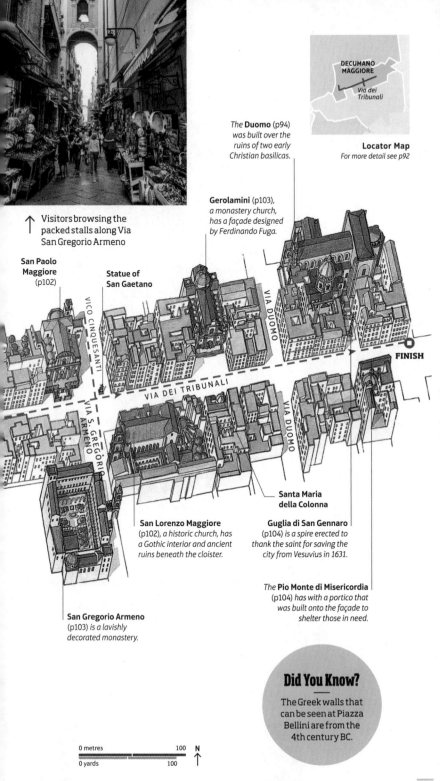

Visitors browsing the packed stalls along Via San Gregorio Armeno

The **Duomo** (p94) was built over the ruins of two early Christian basilicas.

Gerolamini (p103), a monastery church, has a façade designed by Ferdinando Fuga.

San Paolo Maggiore (p102)

Statue of San Gaetano

VICO CINQUESANTI

VIA DUOMO

FINISH

VIA DEI TRIBUNALI

VIA S. GREGORIO ARMENO

VIA DUOMO

Santa Maria della Colonna

San Lorenzo Maggiore (p102), a historic church, has a Gothic interior and ancient ruins beneath the cloister.

Guglia di San Gennaro (p104) is a spire erected to thank the saint for saving the city from Vesuvius in 1631.

San Gregorio Armeno (p103) is a lavishly decorated monastery.

The **Pio Monte di Misericordia** (p104) has with a portico that was built onto the façade to shelter those in need.

Locator Map
For more detail see p92

DECUMANO MAGGIORE

Via dei Tribunali

Did You Know?

The Greek walls that can be seen at Piazza Bellini are from the 4th century BC.

0 metres 100

0 yards 100

N

The stunning ballroom of Capodimonte palace

CAPODIMONTE AND I VERGINI

Towering over this neighbourhood is the hill of Capodimonte, and hewn into its stone are San Gennaro's 2nd-century catacombs. These tunnels, designed for Christian rituals and burial, bring to light the early history of this area. High above, and centuries later, the Kings of Two Sicilies used the hill as a hunting area, eventually building a splendid summer residence on it. This palace would go on to house one of Europe's most important museums: the Museo di Capodimonte. Meanwhile, from the 17th century onwards, suburban development had continued apace in this area, despite the attempts of the Spanish viceroys to block construction outside the city walls. During the devastating plague of 1656, caves in the area became makeshift graveyards where the Italian *pezzentelle* tradition, or the Cult of the Dead, developed. In 1751 the city began an ambitious project to ameliorate poverty and homelessness, building the palatial Albergo dei Poveri to assist the growing number of struggling citizens. A century later, further growth took place in the northern suburbs as roads were widened to accommodate the increasing population. The old Sanità, Fontanelle and Vergini districts developed into lively areas where, even today, tenements alternate with historic churches and buildings and little English can be heard.

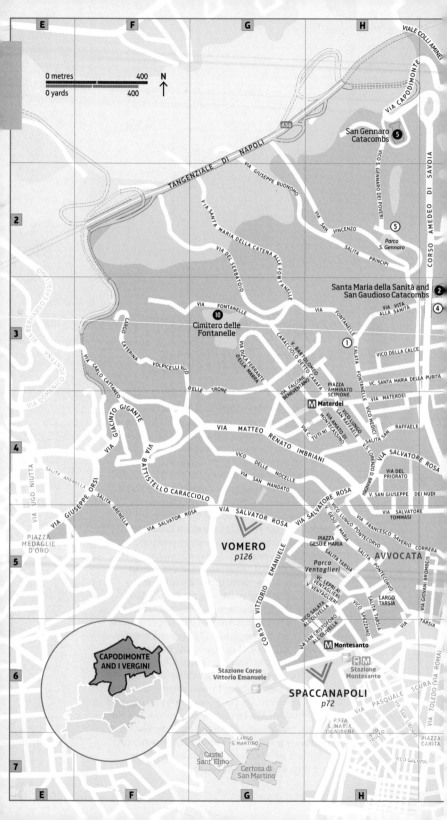

CAPODIMONTE AND I VERGINI

0 metres	400
0 yards	400

N ↑

San Gennaro Catacombs 5

Parco S. Gennaro 5

Santa Maria della Sanità and San Gaudioso Catacombs 2, 4

Cimitero delle Fontanelle 10

VIALE COLLI AMINEI

VIA CAPODIMONTE

CORSO AMEDEO DI SAVOIA

TANGENZIALE DI NAPOLI

A56

VIA GIUSEPPE BUONOMO

VIA SANTA MARIA DELLA CATENA ALLE FONTANELLE

VIA DEL SERBATOIO

VIA SAN VINCENZO

SALITA PRINCIPI

VICO S. GENNARO DEI POVERI

VIA FONTANELLE

CALATA FONTANELLE

VIA VITA ALLA SANITÀ

VICO DELLA CALCE

VIA FONTANELLE

LARGO CATERINA

VIA CARLO CATTANEO

VOLPICELLI VICO

DELLE TRONE

VIA DUCA FERRANTE DELLA MARRA

CARACCIOLO DETTO CARAFA

V. BARTOLOMEO

VC. SANTA MARIA DELLA PURITÀ

VIA MATERDEI

PIAZZA AMMIRATO SCIPIONE

VIA FALCONE BENCIVENGA

M Materdei

VICO LUNGO SAN RAFFAELE

VIA AMATO DI MONTE CASSINO

RAFFAELE

VIA MEDICI

SALITA SAN

VIA GIACINTO GIGANTE

VIA BATTISTELLO CARACCIOLO

VIA MATTEO RENATO IMBRIANI

VICO DELLE NOCELLE

VIA SAN MANDATO

VIA C. TUTINI

VIA LORENZO D. BININO

VIA SALVATORE ROSA

VIA DEL PRIORATO

V. SAN GIUSEPPE DEI NUDI

VIA SALVATORE TOMMASI

SALITA ARENELLA

VIA UGO NIUTTA

VIA GIUSEPPE ORSI

SALITA ARENELLA

VIA SALVATOR ROSA

VIA SALVATOR ROSA

VIA SALVATORE ROSA

VIA FRANCESCO SAVERIO CORRERA

VIA GIOVANNI BROMBES

PIAZZA MEDAGLIE D'ORO

VOMERO *p126*

VICO LUNGO PONTECORVO

GESÙ E MARIA

PIAZZA GESÙ E MARIA

SALITA TARSIA

SALITA PONTECORVO

AVVOCATA

LARGO TARSIA

CORSO VITTORIO EMANUELE

Parco Ventaglieri

VC. LEPRI AI VENTAGLIERI

V. VENTAGLIERI

VICO SALATO ALL'OLIVELLA

VIA SAN CRISTOFORO ALL'OLIVELLA

VICO SPEZZANO

SALITA TARSIA

VIA TARSIA

M Montesanto

Stazione Corso Vittorio Emanuele

RM **Stazione Montesanto**

SPACCANAPOLI *p72*

VIA PASQUALE SCURA

VIA SAN LIBORIO

VIA TOLEDO (VIA ROMA)

P.TTA S. MARIA OGNIBENE

VICO TRUCIO

PIAZZA CARITÀ

VICO GALUPPI

LARGO S. MARTINO

Castel Sant'Elmo

Certosa di San Martino

CAPODIMONTE AND I VERGINI

Must See

1. Museo e Real Bosco di Capodimonte

Experience More

2. Santa Maria della Sanità and San Gaudioso Catacombs
3. Palazzo dello Spagnolo
4. Palazzo Sanfelice
5. San Gennaro Catacombs
6. San Giovanni a Carbonara
7. Santi Apostoli
8. Santa Maria degli Angeli alle Croci
9. Porta San Gennaro
10. Cimitero delle Fontanelle
11. Albergo dei Poveri
12. Osservatorio Astronomico
13. Torre del Palasciano
14. Orto Botanico

Eat

1. Cantina del Gallo
2. A'Cucina'e Mammà Napoli
3. Pasticceria Poppella

Drink

4. Caffe' del Principe
5. Bar Aversano
6. Caffè Carlo III

① 🖌️ 🏛️ 🖥️ 🛍️

MUSEO E REAL BOSCO DI CAPODIMONTE

📍 J1 🏠 Via Miano 2 🚌 C63, R4, 168, 178 🕐 Museum: 8:30am-7:30pm Thu-Tue (last adm: 6:30pm); park: 7am-1 hr before sunset 🌐 museocapodimonte. beniculturali.it

Contained within an airy hilltop palace surrounded by a woodland oasis, this museum offers a welcome respite from bustling city life, alongside a collection of stunning art and architecture.

From the beginning, Capodimonte was intended to be both a royal palace and a museum because Charles of Bourbon wanted to create a home for the works of art from the royal houses of Rome and Parma that he had inherited from his mother, Elizabeth Farnese. Construction began in 1738 under architect Antonio Medrano, but the palace was only completed a century later, despite the fact that a large part of the Farnese Collection had been on display there since 1759. The collection was dispersed after the French occupation in 1799, but, following the Bourbon restoration in 1815, it was enlarged considerably. With the Unification of Italy in 1860,

Capodimonte became the property of the House of Savoy and was the residence of the Dukes of Aosta until 1947. The museum opened its doors to the public again in 1957.

The Farnese Collection, which is the core of the Art Gallery, features the major Italian and European schools of painting from the 15th to the 17th centuries. When the Real Museo Borbonico – now the Museo Archeologico Nazionale *(p96)* – was created in Palazzo degli Studi in the early 1800s, the paintings were transferred from Capodimonte, but they were returned in 1957, along with other works purchased since the 19th century by the Bourbon rulers and the Italian government.

← The three-storey palace housing the Museo di Capodimonte, set in extensive parkland

1 This grand dining room in the Royal Apartments is typical of the palace of Capodimonte.

2 Mount Vesuvius can be seen in the distance from the Capodimonte park.

3 An armour-clad knight on horseback is part of the decorative arts collection displayed at the Capodimonte museum.

THE ROYAL FOREST OF CAPODIMONTE

Charles of Bourbon was initially drawn to Capodimonte by its good hunting oppor-tunites. As this was his favourite pastime, he decided to build a hunting lodge here. The first section of this vast royal forest – spread across 1.2 sq km (0.5 sq miles) – was laid out by Baroque architect Ferdinando Sanfelice in 1742. It is centred around five main avenues, radi-ating out from the Porta di Mezzo gate and lined with oaks. The buildings that were once used for various court activ-ities can still be found in the woods.

Collection of ceramics
and broznes at the
Museo di Capodimonte

Exploring the Museo di Capodimonte

The ground floor is home to the Collection of Drawings and
Prints, containing, among other works, cartoons by Raphael
and Michelangelo. The ticket office, auditorium and the
museum bookshop are also on this floor. The first floor is
devoted to the Farnese Collection, the Royal Apartments,
porcelain and armour. The second floor has 13th- to 18th-
century Neapolitan paintings and sculpture, while the third
floor has 19th-century art. The two upper floors also have a
fine collection of 20th-century and contemporary works.

Did You Know?

The Farnese collection
was one of the first
compilations of art
from the Greco-
Roman world.

Inside the grand Bourbon
Palace of Capodimonte, the
embodiment of elegance

ROYAL PORCELAIN FACTORY

Charles of Bourbon established the Real Fabbrica in 1739, and a new pavilion for the Royal Factory was opened in the park of Capodimonte in 1743. The factory flourished until 1759, when the king returned to his native Spain and took it and the staff with him. The factory was reopened in 1771 by Ferdinand, and the production of top-quality pieces began again.

Paintings from the 13th to the 16th Centuries

▷ As the Farnese Collection did not focus on Medieval works, paintings from this period are later purchases or come from churches in the Naples region. Important 14th-century works include Simone Martini's Gothic masterpiece *San Ludovico di Tolosa*. The 15th century is represented by Giovanni Bellini's masterpiece, *Transfiguration* (c 1480-85), considered one of the gems of the Farnese Collection since the 1600s. Other works from his studio include *Madonna and Child in a Landscape*, painted around 1490 *(right)*. The focal point of the 16th-century paintings are the splendid works by Titian and Raphael. Other major works are Correggio's masterpiece *Mystic Marriage of St Catherine* and *Antea* by Parmigianino, a portrait of a young woman in an elegant dress and a marten stole.

Paintings from the 17th to the 20th Centuries

Among the 17th-century works in the museum, Bartolomeo Schedoni's *Charity* (1611) is one of the most famous, admired for its expressive intensity. The astounding *Flagellation of Christ* by Caravaggio was painted in stages from 1607 to 1610, and hung in San Domenico Maggiore until its move to Capodimonte. It is regarded as the lynchpin of 17th-century Neapolitan art. No less astounding is *Judith Slaying Holofernes* by the Baroque painter Artemisia Gentileschi *(p28)*. Capodimonte also has a large body of 19th-century Neapolitan paintings, including works by Anton Pitloo, the Dutch painter who settled in Naples, and Giacinto Gigante. Don't miss the latter's famous painting of the Cappella del Tesoro in the Duomo.

Decorative Arts

◁ The major section in the fine decorative arts collection is the armoury. Many of the objects here come from the Naples Royal Arms Factory, founded in 1734 by Charles III. There are also over 4,000 ceramic pieces here, including the De Ciccio majolica collection and samples of the superb porcelain manufactured in Naples. A fine example of this craftsmanship is Queen Maria Amalia's Porcelain Parlour *(left)*.

Drawings and Prints

▷ Among the museum's huge inheritance there are about 2,900 drawings and watercolours and about 24,000 prints and engravings. One of the most famous works is a cartoon (a preparatory drawing made with charcoal or chalk) made by Michelangelo around 1546. It was drawn for part of the fresco of *The Crucifixion of St Peter* in the Cappella Paolina in the Vatican. Another important cartoon is Raphael's *Moses before the Burning Bush*, a preparatory drawing for a detail of a fresco in the Stanza di Eliodoro in the Vatican.

EXPERIENCE MORE

2

Santa Maria della Sanità and San Gaudioso Catacombs

📍 J3 🏛 Piazza Sanità 14
🚌 C51, C52, R4 🕐 10am–1pm daily 🌐 catacombedinapoli.it

The heart of the working-class Sanità quarter is the basilica of Santa Maria. Designed by Fra Nuvolo, the church was built on a Greek cross plan in 1603–13, with 24 columns supporting one central dome and 12 lateral domes (a reference to Christ and the Apostles). The central tiled dome is overlooked by the 19th-century Ponte della Sanità, linking the city centre to Capodimonte.

Inside, the main altar was raised to allow worshippers to see the space that serves as a kind of atrium for the underground cemetery. The entrance to the catacombs, which is through the 5th-century crypt, can be clearly seen.

Tradition has it that, in 452, the African bishop Settimio Celio Gaudioso died in exile in Naples, and was buried in the Sanità valley. The catacombs grew up around his tomb, which had begun to stir up devotion among other Christians, and were named after him. Today these are the second-largest catacombs in Naples. The many corridors still bear traces of frescoes and mosaics (4th–6th centuries AD). Later, the Dominicans added their own burial methods and macabre artistic sense to the crypt. They would drain the blood from the deceased, propping up the corpses on seats that are still in evidence. After removing the head and burying the body elsewhere, they would embed the skull into the tufa stone.

The morbid but fascinating tours of the catacombs are an hour long. Tour tickets can be purchased online, but email ahead in order to book an English-speaking guide.

Did You Know?

The Palazzo dello Spagnolo's stairs are shallow so that horses could walk down to the stables unaided.

3

Palazzo dello Spagnolo

📍 K3 (9 C1) 🏛 Via Vergini 19
Ⓜ Cavour-Museo 🚌 C51, C52, E1, 182, 184, 201, 203 🕐 Courtyard only

This palace, built in 1738 for the Marquis Nicola Moscati, is said to have been designed by the famous Neapolitan architect Ferdinando Sanfelice (1675–1748). The architect's name does not appear in any of the notary deeds; however, since Sanfelice built his own palazzo just a few streets away, it seems likely that he consulted and advised on this building too. Indeed, once through the majestic doorway of the Palazzo dello Spagnolo, visitors will notice a feature taken from the Palazzo Sanfelice: the double-flight external staircase, which effectively separates the main courtyard from the smaller one.

Nicola Moscati ran into massive debt during the construction of this palazzo and was forced to sell the building to the Marquis of Livardi. In 1813, Spanish nobleman Tommaso Atienza bought the property, which has since been called the "Palace of the Spaniard".

←

The elaborate main altar of Santa Maria della Sanità, raised above the congregation

→ Visitors exploring the atmospheric caverns of the San Gennaro Catacombs

4

Palazzo Sanfelice

📍 J3 🏛 Via Sanità 2-6 Ⓜ Cavour-Museo 🚌 C51, C52 🕐 Courtyard only

The architect Ferdinando Sanfelice built this large palazzo for his own family from 1723 to 1728. Despite now being in a dilapidated state, the building was once thought to be one of Naples's' finest palazzos. It was here that Sanfelice first created the unusual external staircase that was later adopted, with some variations, in the Palazzo dello Spagnolo. This type of strikingly original staircase became Sanfelice's trademark. His contemporaries likened the design to a large bird with outspread wings, and it became known as a stair *ad ali di falco* – a "falcon's wing" staircase.

The best way to grasp the beauty of the design is to walk up the steps. On the far side of the second courtyard (at Via Sanità No 2), which has unfortunately lost its original decoration, there is yet another elliptical staircase.

The crumbling splendour of Palazzo Sanfelice has attracted film-makers over the years. The comedy *Questi Fantasmi* (1950) by Neapolitan writer Eduardo de Filippo and the 2011 remake of the Oscar-nominated classic *Four Days in Naples* (1962) were both shot here.

———

5

San Gennaro Catacombs

📍 H1 🏛 Via Tondo di Capodimonte 13 🚌 C63, C67, N4, N8, R4, 178 🕐 10am-5pm Mon-Sat, 10am-2pm Sun 🌐 catacombedinapoli.it

The original nucleus of this large subterranean cemetery may have been the tomb of a pagan aristocrat donated in the 2nd century to the Christian community. The catacombs grew in importance in the 3rd century after acquiring the tomb of Sant'Agrippino, but it was as the burial site of the saint, bishop and martyr Gennaro, brought here in the 5th century, that they became famous. The cemetery also housed the tombs of the bishops of Naples up to the 11th century. The vast size and two-level layout of this holy site distinguish it from other catacombs of the same era, making it the most important complex in southern Italy. Hewn into the rock, with vaulted ceilings, it feels like an underground city, and dramatic LED lighting highlights the tombs, a carved bishop's chair and an altar that adorn the caverns. Remains of 2nd- to 10th-century mosaics and frescoes (including the oldest known portrayal of San Gennaro, dating from the 5th century) decorate the walls. Don't miss the Bishops' Crypt on the upper floor and the Sant'Agrippino Oratory and baptistry on the lower level. The basilica of San Gennaro extra Moenia was erected over the catacombs in the 5th century but greatly modified in the 11th century and in 1932.

CULT OF THE DEAD

After plagues killed thousands over the centuries, many Neapolitans were given quick, anonymous burials in local caves. Devout Catholics took to caring for these bones in the late 19th century. Many began to name the unknown skulls, talking to them and leaving tokens in return for favours. The Church had ended this practice by 1969, but tokens still find their way to the skulls in the catacombs and in Fontanelle Cemetery *(p121)*.

⑥
San Giovanni a Carbonara

**⑨ L4 ⓐ Via Carbonara 5
ⓒ 081 29 58 73 Ⓜ Cavour-Museo 🚌 C57, E1, E2, 203
ⓒ 8am-noon & 4:30-8pm daily**

The imaginative double-flight staircase that was designed by Ferdinando Sanfelice in the early 1700s leads to the 14th-century Chapel of Santa Monica, which stands in the middle of the district of San Lorenzo. Left of the chapel is the doorway to San Giovanni a Carbonara. Founded in 1343 by Augustinian monks, this church was restored and enlarged at the end of the century by King Ladislas to make it a worthy burial site for the Angevin rulers.

When the king died in 1414, his tomb, the work of anonymous Tuscan and Lombard sculptors was erected at the request of his sister, Joan II, who succeeded him to the throne. The grandiose funerary monument, with seated statues of Ladislas and Joan, dominates the single-nave interior. Through a small

doorway beneath it is the circular Cappella Caracciolo del Sole, built in 1427 and paved with coloured Tuscan tiles. Behind the altar is the tomb of Giovanni Caracciolo, Joan's lover and Grand Seneschal at the court; he died in 1432. To the left of the presbytery is the Cappella Caracciolo di Vico, built in 1517 by sculptor Giovan Tommaso Malvito, following a design by the architect Bramante. Another work by Malvito is the richly decorated tomb of the Miroballo family opposite the entrance of the church.

⑦
Santi Apostoli

**⑨ L4 ⓐ Largo SS Apostoli
Ⓜ Cavour-Museo 🚌 C57, E2, 203 ⓒ 9am-noon & 5-8pm daily**

To reach the church of Santi Apostoli you have to go along a short stretch of Via Pisanelli, which turns into Via Anticaglia (*p106*). The church was founded in the 5th century and restructured at the start of the 17th century by Francesco Grimaldi (1610) and, after 1627, by

Giovanni Conforto. The church is best known for a superb fresco cycle by Giovanni Lanfranco (1638–46) which influenced artistic development in Naples. The artist also frescoed the cupola of the Cappella del Tesoro di San Gennaro in the Duomo (*p94*).

⑧
Santa Maria degli Angeli alle Croci

**⑨ L2 ⓐ Via Veterinaria 2
ⓒ 081 44 07 56 Ⓜ Cavour-Museo 🚌 12 ⓒ 8-11am & 5-7:15pm Mon-Sat, 8-11am Sun**

The name of this church refers to the Stations of the Cross, once marked by wooden crosses (*croci*) alongside the ascent to the church. Santa Maria was founded at the end of the 16th century by Franciscans and rebuilt in 1638 by sculptor Cosimo Fanzago. The façade is simply decorated with white and grey marble. This was a daring shift from the usually lavish architecture of Neapolitan Baroque. The interior houses a magnificent marble pulpit

sculpted by Fanzago. The eagle supporting it symbolizes St John the Evangelist. The extraordinary bas-relief of the dead Christ on the altar was sculpted by Carlo Fanzago, Cosimo's son.

9
Porta San Gennaro

📍 K4 🏛 Piazza Cavour
Ⓜ Cavour-Museo 🚌 C51, C52, E1, 182, 184, 201, 203

This gateway was named after San Gennaro, the city's patron saint, because it marked the start of the street leading to the catacombs where he was buried *(p119)*. After the plague of 1656, Baroque artist Mattia Preti painted a fresco on each city gate as an *ex voto* from those who survived. Porta San Gennaro is the only one that still has traces of the artist's work. On the inner façade is a bust of San Gaetano with a dedication and the date – 1658.

→

Visitors wandering amid carefully stacked skulls in the Cimitero delle Fontanelle

---

←
Sculptures inside San Giovanni a Carbonara

10
Cimitero delle Fontanelle

📍 G3 🏛 Via Fontanelle 80
📞 338 965 22 88 🚌 C51, C52
🕐 9:30am–4:30pm daily

Inside the cathedral-like caverns on the rocky hill of Materdei, visitors enter the Fontanelle Cemetery, named after the numerous freshwater springs that once flowed here.

Thousands who died during the plague of 1656 were interred anonymously in the caves. After the plague had ended, the ossuary continued to be used as the final resting place of the very poor and those unable to pay for a dignified church burial. The last to be interred here were the victims of the 1836 cholera epidemic.

Skulls and bones are arranged almost artistically for visitors to wander past. Some people may find this upsetting, as did the tourist played by Ingrid Bergman in *Viaggio in Italia* (1954), which made the cemetery famous. The Cult of the Dead *(p119)* sparked controversy over "adoptions" of skulls to bring good luck, though today visitors are discouraged from touching the bones.

DRINK

Caffe' del Principe
One of many local cafés, this simple place has outside seats where you can relax before hiking up to hilly Capodimonte.

📍 J3 🏛 Via Sanità 17
📞 081 564 26 28

Bar Aversano
If you're in need of a break in this somewhat non-touristy part of town, then this café near the San Gennaro Catacombs is a great option.

📍 H2 🏛 Via San Gennaro dei Poveri 25/f
📞 081 741 99 69

Caffè Carlo III
A classic café with a varied selection of drink choices, this place is a convenient pit stop when wandering near the Botanical Gardens. They have a good assortment of pastries on offer.

📍 M2 🏛 Piazza Carlo III
📞 081 299 348

⑪
Albergo dei Poveri

📍M2 🏛Piazza Carlo III
📞081 795 11 11 🚇N4, 12,
201, 202, 540

The enormous building visible today is only one-fifth of the large-scale complex that King Charles wanted to build to provide a refuge for the kingdom's poor. Construction of the "Hotel of the Poor" began in 1751 according to a design by Ferdinando Fuga, and work continued until 1829. In reality, the building was more like a prison, hated by the poor, including orphans, who were compelled to live and work there without hope of leaving. In 1981 a wing of the building collapsed following earthquake damage. After many years of neglect, restoration is underway, though no concrete plans for its future have been set.

Did You Know?

Covering an area of 10 ha (25 acres), the Albergo dei Poveri is one of Europe's largest public buildings.

⑫
Osservatorio Astronomico

📍K2 🏛Salita Moiariello 16
🚇C63, C66 🌐oacn.inaf.it

Set in a large park on Miradois hill, 150 m (490 ft) above sea level, the observatory has a splendid vantage point, with fine panoramic views of the city and the bay. Founded in 1819 by Ferdinand IV, this was the first scientific facility of its kind in Europe. The Bourbons had always been keenly interested in astronomic studies, and it was King Charles who established the first university chair of astronomy in Naples in 1735. The observatory was originally planned for the Museo Archeologico, and in fact construction had begun there in 1791 (p96), but the project was discarded. A few years later, the elegant Neo-Classical building that now houses the observatory was built by the Gasse architect brothers. Today part of the observatory is occupied by the **Museo degli Strumenti Astronomici** with a fine collection of telescopes, clocks and old scientific instruments.

Museo degli Strumenti Astronomici

⊛⊛ 🕐10am–4pm Mon–Sat
🌐beniculturali.inaf.it/musei/napoli

⑬
Torre del Palasciano

📍K1 🏛Salita Moiariello 65
🚇C63, C66 🚫To the public

Located just behind the observatory, and inspired by the Palazzo della Signoria in Florence, this dwelling was commissioned and owned by the physician and surgeon Ferdinando Palasciano (1815–91). He became famous for providing medical care in Messina to the wounded of both sides during the popular revolts of 1848. For this serious act of insubordination, Palasciano was sentenced to be executed. The intervention of King Ferdinand II of Bourbon spared his life, and Palasciano's sentence was commuted to one year in prison. His case

attracted a great deal of international attention, providing the starting point for the Geneva Convention of 1864, which in turn led to the creation of the Red Cross.

Construction was directed by the architect Antonio Cipolla (1822–74), and the building was completed in 1868. The grounds once included a temple, two gardens and an orchard for fruit trees. Today the area, which is sited on the hill of Capodimonte, provides a pleasant walk with great views of the city.

↑ Lush ferns within a greenhouse at the impressive Orto Botanico

🄮
Orto Botanico

📍 L2 🏛 Via Foria 223 Ⓜ Cavour-Museo 🚌 12, 182, 184, 201, 203 🕑 9am–1:30pm Mon-Fri (also Sun in May) 🌐 ortobotanico. unina.it

Established in 1807 by Joseph Bonaparte, the "Royal Plant Garden" is now one of Italy's leading botanical gardens, renowned for the high quality of its collections as well as for its sheer size. It has a rich stock of tree and shrub specimens from all latitudes and examples of many plant species, as well as several greenhouses with varying climatic conditions. The temperate house is an early 19th-century Neo-Classical building. The collections of citrus trees, desert plants and tree ferns are particularly interesting. A walk along the paths of this green oasis makes for a very pleasant break from the city. Ring the bell at the gate, and the custodian will let you in.

EAT

Cantina del Gallo
A local favourite for pizza, this is a great spot to unwind after a trip to the nearby Fontanelle Cemetery. If you're keen to experiment, try the *pizzicotti*.

📍 H3 🏛 Via Alessandro Telesino 21 🌐 cantina delgallo.com

€ € €

A' Cucina 'e Mammà Napoli
Warm and welcoming, this tiny, family-run restaurant serves up delicious pizza and pasta, with seafood options aplenty.

📍 L3 🏛 Via Foria 99 📞 081 1808 78 07

€ € €

Pasticceria Poppella
A top bakery in Naples, this place sells cakes, chocolates and an impressive assortment of seasonal treats, especially at Easter.

📍 J3 🏛 Via Arena della Sanità 29 📞 081 45 53 09

€ € €

↑ The vast façade of the Albergo dei Poveri, which is over 350 m (1,150 ft) long

A SHORT WALK

NORTH OF THE ANCIENT WALLS

Distance 1.5 km (1 mile) **Time** 25 minutes
Nearest Metro Materdei

The area north of the city walls has been used for burials and worship of the dead since it was first inhabited. A visit to the catacombs, first built in the early Christian era, is an unforgettable experience. Less appealingly, the area outside the walls was also used to dump rubbish. The district known today as Via San Giovanni a Carbonara was once called the Fosso Carbonario (literally, "coal ditch"), and this is how the street and the beautiful 14th-century church acquired their current names.

Did You Know?

Legend says Santi Apostoli was built on a temple of Mercury - god of luck and a guide to the underworld.

The **Padri della Missione Church** was designed by architect Luigi Vanvitelli.

The **Basilica of San Severo** is built on the burial site of St Severus, who was Bishop of Naples from 364 to 410.

The church of **Santa Maria dai Vergini**, built in the 14th century, was badly damaged during World War II.

VIA S. SEVERO A CAPODIMONTE

VICO MARESCA

VIA SANTA MARIA ANTESAECULA

VIA DELLA SANITA

VIA ARENA DELLA SANITA

VIA S. NICANDRO

LARGO VERGINI

VIA MARIO PAGANO

PIAZZA DELLA SANITA

GRADINI NICANDRO

START

Santa Maria della Sanità (p118) *has a raised high altar so that the entrance to the San Gaudioso catacombs could be seen.*

Palazzo Sanfelice (p119) *has a notable staircase in its smaller courtyard.*

The highlight of the **Palazzo dello Spagnolo** (p118) *is the double-flight staircase, accessed through this monumental gateway.*

0 metres	50
0 yards	50

N

↑ San Giovanni a Carbonara, a church that houses many magnificent sculptures

Locator Map
For more detail see p112

San Carlo all'Arena *is so named because in the 1600s the street nearby was covered in sand (arena).*

San Giovanni a Carbonara (p120), *one of the most important churches in Naples, features a double-flight winding staircase designed by Ferdinando Sanfelice.*

FINISH

Santi Apostoli (p120), *a church originally founded in the 5th century, has a dome painted by Baroque artist Giovanni Battista Beinaschi in 1680.*

In the mid-15th century the city walls were extended and this gateway, **Porta San Gennaro** (p121), *was rebuilt in its present location.*

Santa Maria Succurre Miseris, *founded in the 14th century, was rebuilt in the 1700s by Neapolitan architect Ferdinando Sanfelice.*

→ Visitors photographing the elegant staircase at Palazzo Sanfelice

VOMERO

Vomero's name likely references a ploughshare in Italian, although the district's agricultural roots led to it being nicknamed the "hill of Broccoli". The area caught the eye of the Angevins who began the construction of what became the imposing Castel Sant'Elmo and the grand Certosa di San Martino in the Middle Ages, alongside the stepped street known as the Pedamentina. During the later plague epidemics, the clergy and nobles often fled to this lofty spot to escape the chaos in the city below. In 1885, the Naples city council approved a plan for a new district to be developed in the hills that would accommodate some 30,000 inhabitants. The new neighbourhood of Vomero soon grew famous for its scenic beauty and wealthy residents. Wide streets and more modern housing, influenced by urban redesigns popularized in Paris, contrasted sharply with the more densely populated old districts below. Despite uncontrolled property development since World War II, Vomero has remained a haven for the Neapolitan bourgeoisie. Crowning the neighbourhood today – as it did 700 years ago – is San Martino. One of the world's oldest funiculars, opened in 1889, still whisks people up and down the hill in a matter of minutes, making the district easily accessible.

VOMERO

Must See

❶ Certosa di San Martino

Experience More

❷ Villa Floridiana
❸ Castel Sant'Elmo
❹ Pedamentina
❺ Via Scarlatti
❻ Via Luigi Sanfelice

Eat

① Friggitoria Vomero
② Pizzeria Acunzo Patrizio Vomero
③ Trattoria Caprese

Shop

④ Dolce Idea Gennaro Bottone
⑤ Riot Concept Store

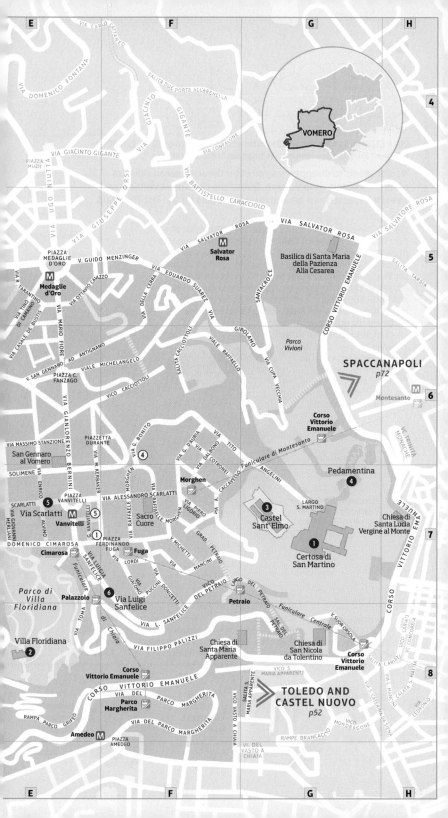

CERTOSA DI SAN MARTINO

📍G7 🏛Largo San Martino 5 🚇Montesanto: Via Morghen 🚌V1 🕐8:30am-6:30pm Thu-Tue 🌐polomusealecampania.beniculturali.it

Naples seems to disappear as you enter the sun-soaked cloisters of this monastery atop Vomero. One of the city's most visible structures, it has acted as a beacon for Neapolitans for the last 700 years.

In 1325 Charles, Duke of Calabria, began the construction of what is one of the richest monuments in Naples. From the 16th to the 18th centuries the greatest artists of the time worked at the *certosa*, or charterhouse, of San Martino. The original look of San Martino was gradually altered by Mannerist and Baroque rebuilding. The French deconsecrated the monastery in 1806, and since 1866 it has housed the fascinating San Martino museum, with displays of Neapolitan art and history that document the rich and varied forms of artistic expression that thrived in Naples between the 15th and the 19th centuries. The church, the Quarto del Priore (prior's residence), the cloister and the gardens are also noteworthy.

The Chiostro dei Procuratori cloister was built in the late 16th century by Giovanni Antonio Dosio.

Naval section

The prior's garden

The Quarto del Priore is richly decorated and has a splendid panoramic view over the Bay of Naples.

Timeline

1325
Construction begins under Charles of Anjou; the church is consecrated in 1368.

1578
Architects Dosio and Conforto decorate and enlarge the monastery.

1623
▽ Sculptor Cosimo Fanzago begins work on the Chiostro Grande.

1631-56
The complex is rebuilt and redecorated by Fanzago.

1799
The monastery is damaged during the Parthenopean revolution.

1807
▽ The last monks are compelled to leave the Certosa di San Martino.

1866
The Certosa becomes state property and a part of it is turned into a museum.

The Chiostro Grande cloister, encircled → by 64 slender marble columns

The church and its subsidiary rooms feature sumptuous Baroque decoration.

In 1580 Giovanni Antonio Dosio closed the aisles in the central nave and built six side chapels. The vaults of the original 14th-century nave are still visible.

Nativity section

Entrance

Historical section

The Chiostro Grande, the main cloister, was designed by Giovanni Antonio Dosio at the end of the 16th century, then remodelled by Cosimo Fanzago.

Museo dell'Opera

Monks' cemetery

↑ Illustration of the Certosa di San Martino, set in lush and fragrant gardens

Did You Know?

Until the 19th century women were not allowed into the complex as it was a monastery for men.

→

The central nave, rich with brightly coloured marble and gilded stucco trim

THE CHURCH AND ITS SUBSIDIARY ROOMS

In 1568, the prior Severo Turboli set up an elaborate plan for the complete restructuring of the Certosa (charterhouse) di San Martino. The original Angevin church was enlarged and modernized – its Gothic structure almost completely disappeared under the multitude of frescoes, stuccowork and marbles produced by leading artists of the time. The most radical changes to the building were carried out in the 17th century by architect and sculptor Cosimo Fanzago, who worked at San Martino from 1623 to 1656. He designed the interior of the church and its lavish decoration. Coloured marble adorns the nave and chapels, such as the Cappella di San Bruno. The rooms adjacent to the church are also richly ornamented. In the sacristy, the panels of the beautiful inlaid walnut wardrobes contain 56 intarsia scenes with striking perspective effects (16th century). *The Triumph of Judith* fresco on the vault of the brightly lit Cappella del Tesoro Nuovo was painted by Luca Giordano in 1704.

> **In the sacristy, the panels of the beautiful inlaid walnut wardrobes contain 56 intarsia scenes with striking perspective effects (16th century).**

HISTORICAL SECTION

These interesting rooms are dedicated to the history of the Kingdom of Naples. Paintings, furnishings, sculptures, medallions, arms and memorabilia recreate the key moments in the political, social and cultural history of Naples, from the Aragonese to the Bourbon dynasties.

←

Visitors admiring the artwork in the monastery's historical section

This valuable collection's importance is exemplified in two famous works that combine historical and artistic documentary significance: *The Revolt of Masaniello* (p47), painted in 1647, and *Piazza del Mercatello during the 1656 Plague*, both painted by Micco Spadaro. These dramatic compositions tell the story of two important events in the history of 17th-century Naples. They are also an accurate and useful representation of what the city looked like at that time.

THE QUARTO DEL PRIORE

The charterhouse's prior, who was the only individual allowed contact with the outside world, governed the workings of the monastery from his private apartments, otherwise known as the Quarto del Priore. This was a fabulous residence, rich with priceless works of art adorning the walls and opening onto lush gardens overlooking Naples and the sea.

Built in the 17th century and enlarged the following century, these luxurious quarters have undergone scrupulous restoration. Originally, this part of the complex was used to exhibit the rich art collection of the Carthusian monks.

Following the restoration, an attempt has been made to recreate the Quarto del Priore as it was when inhabited by the prior, with paintings, sculpture, fabric and furniture adorning the various rooms. The art collection and high-quality furnishings reflect the refinement and great artistic sensitivity of the Carthusian monks as well as their ability to keep abreast of the latest artistic and architectural developments. With its stunning decor, works of art and sculpture and spectacular panoramic views over the city, the Quarto del Priore is one of the highlights of a visit to the Certosa di San Martino.

↑ The Quarto del Priore, the opulent quarters of the monastery's prior

---

NINETEENTH-CENTURY NEAPOLITAN ART

This collection also displays pieces that are significant from both an artistic and historical standpoint. The collection contains purchases made by the Italian government but owes its strength primarily to donations of important private Neapolitan collections. All the schools of painting that flourished in this area during the 19th century are represented here. A favourite and recurring theme was the serene, beautiful landscape of Campania landscape, as depicted in Giacinto Gigante's *Panorama of Naples Viewed from the Conocchia*. Among the noteworthy sculptures are Vincenzo Gemito's *Il Malatiello* (The Sick Child) and *Testa della Popolana* (Head of a Peasant Woman).

↑ *Panorama of Naples Viewed from the Conocchia*, by Giacinto Gigante

NATIVITY SECTION

Only towards the end of the 19th century did the *presepe* or nativity scene start to be considered an artistic genre in its own right, worthy of a museum. This section of the museum has one of the most important public collections of its kind, with displays of entire nativity scenes as well as individual figures, such as Mary and Joseph, the Three Kings or the shepherds. Animals and accessories, such as the crib, are also displayed.

Among the most important nativity scenes is a creation by the Neapolitan playwright, Michele Cucinello. The manger scene is hidden amid 18 shepherds, 10 horses, 8 dogs, folk going about their business, a Moroccan musical ensemble and much more. Many of the statuettes were executed by famous Neapolitan artists. *Blind Beggar with Cataracts* (c 1780), in the Perrone Collection, is by the artist Giuseppe Sanmartino, who sculpted the *Veiled Christ* in the Cappella Sansevero *(p81)*.

↑ Stone steps leading to the façade of Villa Floridiana, fringed by greenery

EXPERIENCE MORE

②

Villa Floridiana

📍 E8 📭 Via Domenico Cimarosa 77, Via A Falcone 171 ☎ 081 578 8418 Ⓜ Vanvitelli 🚉 Centrale: Piazza Fuga; Chiaia: Via Cimarosa 🚌 V1, 128 🕐 Villa: 8:30am–4:30pm daily; park: 8:30am–1 hr before sunset daily

In 1817 Ferdinand I acquired an estate on the Vomero hill as a present for his second wife Lucia Migliaccio, the Duchess of Floridia, whom he had married shortly after the death of Maria Carolina of Austria. The estate, which was named La Floridiana in honour of the duchess, included a park with a magnificent view of the city, and there were two buildings on the property. The first, the Villa Floridiana, was rebuilt as a summer residence in the Neo-Classical style by Antonio Niccolini in 1817–19. The Italian government purchased the villa in 1919, and it now houses the **Museo Nazionale della Ceramica Duca di Martina**, a well-regarded museum of ceramics. There was also a "Pompeiian" coffee-house, later called Villa Lucia, which was also designed by Niccolini and later became private property.

Placido de Sangro, the Duke of Martina and member of an illustrious noble family, was a passionate collector of decorative art objects, especially porcelain and ceramics. When the duke died in 1891, his valuable collection of about 6,000 pieces was inherited by his grandson Placido, who donated them to the city of Naples in 1911.

Since 1927 the villa has been the home of the Museo Nazionale della Ceramica Duca di Martina, where curators aim to reproduce as closely as possible the arrangement and spirit of the collections in the De Sangro residence. The pleasant, unusual atmosphere of a home-cum-museum has remained unchanged, despite additions and later donations.

The many porcelain pieces come from the most significant Italian factories and from elsewhere across Europe. There is also a collection of Oriental art – consisting mostly of 18th- and 19th-century porcelain – which is one of the best in Italy.

Alongside its porcelain collections, the museum also contains some 15th-century ivory pieces, stunning majolica, Limoges enamel, tortoiseshell objects and drawings by 17th- and 18th-century Neapolitan artists, including Solimena, Giordano and De Matteis.

↑ A vase on display in the Museo Nazionale della Ceramica Duca di Martina

Museo Nazionale della Ceramica Duca di Martina
 Villa Floridiana 8:30am–4:30pm Wed–Mon polomusealecampania.beniculturali.it

---

3

Castel Sant'Elmo

G7 Via Tito Angelini 22 Vanvitelli Montesanto: Via Morghen; Centrale: Piazzetta Fuga; Chiaia: Via Cimarosa V1 8:30am–7:30pm Wed–Mon polomuseale campania.beniculturali.it

In the 1330s the Angevin rulers instigated a flurry of building on the Vomero hill west of Naples – the construction of the Certosa di San Martino (*p130*) and the enlargement and reconstruction of the nearby fortified residence of Belforte, which had been inhabited by Charles I of Anjou's family since 1275. In the 16th century Pedro Scriba, a leading military architect of the time, completely transformed the 14th-century castle, giving it its present six-pointed star configuration.

Because of its strategic position, under viceroy Pedro de Toledo Castel Sant'Elmo

The ramparts of Castel Sant'Elmo, renowned for their great views

became the focal point of the new defence system for Naples. For centuries it was used as a military prison, a purpose that it fulfilled into the 1970s. Among the prison's illustrious "guests" were the great Renaissance philosopher Tommaso Campanella, the 1799 revolutionaries and patriots involved in the 19th-century Risorgimento.

Today, the entrance to the castle bears Charles V's coat of arms and a fine epigraph. The complex, which also contains a large lecture hall, has been the venue for temporary exhibitions and cultural events since 1988. Visitors to the fortress can find the best views of the city at the castle's ramparts, where the walls offer a spectacular 360-degree view of Naples' rooftops and the picturesque bay spread out below.

Art lovers will also want to stop by the **Museo del Novecento a Napoli**, a contemporary art gallery in the castle's prison. Over 170 works from the 20th century are on display, with an emphasis on those created by local artists between 1919 and 1980. The museum was inaugurated in 2010, following a trend for more modern art venues at that time.

Museo del Novecento a Napoli

9:30am–5pm Wed–Mon polomuseale campania.beniculturali.it

EAT

Friggitoria Vomero
Fried aubergine, arancini and other essential Neapolitan street foods are on offer at this historic eatery located by the funicular.

E7 Via Domenico Cimarosa 44 081 578 31 30 Sun

€€€

Pizzeria Acunzo Patrizio Vomero
Hiking around the steep streets of Vomero merits a pizza, and this tucked-away, family-run spot serves up all the classics.

E7 Via Belisario Corenzio 4 081 049 18 68 Mon

€€€

Trattoria Caprese
This spacious, airy restaurant has plenty of well-known pasta dishes on the menu, along with a variety of other local favourites to try.

E7 Via Luca Giordano 25 081 558 75 84

€€€

↑ The Pedamentina
snaking its way up
to the top of Vomero

If you decide to do it the other way around and climb up the Pedimentina, you will be rewarded by some delightful cafés at the top where you can relax and take in the glorious scenes.

SHOP

Dolce Idea Gennaro Bottone

Chocolate and spreads from this local artisan's boutique make great gifts – while for yourself, there's ice cream on site.

📍 F6 🚇 Via Giuseppe Bonito 2 ☎ 081 556 05 63

Riot Concept Store

Pop into this trendy, catch-all shop to browse clothing and home-wares, and stay for a cocktail at their bar.

📍 E7 🚇 Via Michele Kerbaker 19 ☎ 081 1957 84 91

❹ Pedamentina

📍 G7 🚋 Montesanto: Via Morghen 🚌 V1

The snaking steps connecting Castel Sant'Elmo and the city sprawling below allow visitors today to descend towards the sparkling sea much as visitors would have done in the 14th century when these stepped streets were first built. The atmospheric Pedamentina stairway is one of the oldest in the city, having been built around the same time that construction began on the Certosa di San Martino (p130) at its base. The 414 shallow, zigzagging steps run 650 m (2,132 ft) down from San Martino to Corso Vittorio Emanuele and offer beautiful panoramic views that change at every stage – those of the Bay of Naples are particularly rewarding. If you decide to do it the other way around and climb up, you will be rewarded by some delightful cafés at the top of the stairs where you can relax and take in the glorious scenes.

❺ Via Scarlatti

📍 E7 🚇 Vanvitelli 🚋 Centrale: Piazza Fuga; Chiaia: Via Cimarosa 🚌 C31, V1, 128

Descending from Piazza Vanvitelli towards Via Cilea, this is Vomero's most elegant street. Lined with tall plane trees and closed to traffic, Via Scarlatti is the perfect place for a pleasant walk, which can be interspersed with plentiful shopping breaks. Lift your gaze above the line of shops to take in the striking contrast between the 19th-century buildings and the more modern constructions that were built when a wave of property development altered the area.

❻ Via Luigi Sanfelice

📍 F7 🚋 Centrale: Piazza Fuga; Chiaia: Via Cimarosa 🚇 Vanvitelli 🚌 E4

Any visitor asking for the "Santarella" will be pointed to Via Luigi Sanfelice. The key to this riddle lies in a curve in the road, where stands a villa with a curious nameplate: Qui Rido Io ("this is where I laugh"). This was the home of Neapolitan playwright and actor Eduardo Scarpetta (father of writer and actor Eduardo De Filippo), whose best-known work is *Na santarella*. The elegant houses of Via Luigi Sanfelice and Via Filippo Palizzi nearby are good examples of Neo-Renaissance or Art Nouveau styles.

FROM THE "FERROVIA DI DELIZIA" TO THE FUNICULAR RAILWAY

In 1875 the engineers Bruno and Ferraro designed a rail system to take passengers up the Vomero hill using two funiculars, connected so that the ascent of one caused the descent of the other. The "train of delights" allowed travellers to admire stupendous views of the bay while crossing the hill, in those days a rural area. The scheme gradually evolved into two independent funicular railways offering an efficient means of transport between Vomero and the city. The Chiaia funicular opened in 1889, and Montesanto in 1891. To improve connections, the Centrale funicular was built in 1928 and is the longest of the three. There is also a fourth line, the Mergellina funicular, connecting the seafront with Via Manzoni. The funiculars are fast and reliable, running about every ten minutes.

A SHORT WALK
VOMERO

Distance 1 km (0.5 miles) **Time** 15 minutes
Nearest Metro Vanvitelli

Take one of the funicular railway lines up the hill
to Vomero for fine views of the city centre and the
Bay of Naples. Art-lovers will find that Neapolitan
masters are well represented in the museums of
the Certosa di San Martino and Villa Floridiana
(the Duca di Martina). Meanwhile, a walk along the
atmospheric streets in the heart of the district
reveals an eclectic range of shops and goods,
including, in Via Scarlatti, the Caffè Scarlatti, which
sells excellent coffee and delectable cakes. In
Via Luigi Sanfelice, make a stop at the villa of
Neapolitan actor Eduardo Scarpetta.

Locator Map
For more detail see p126

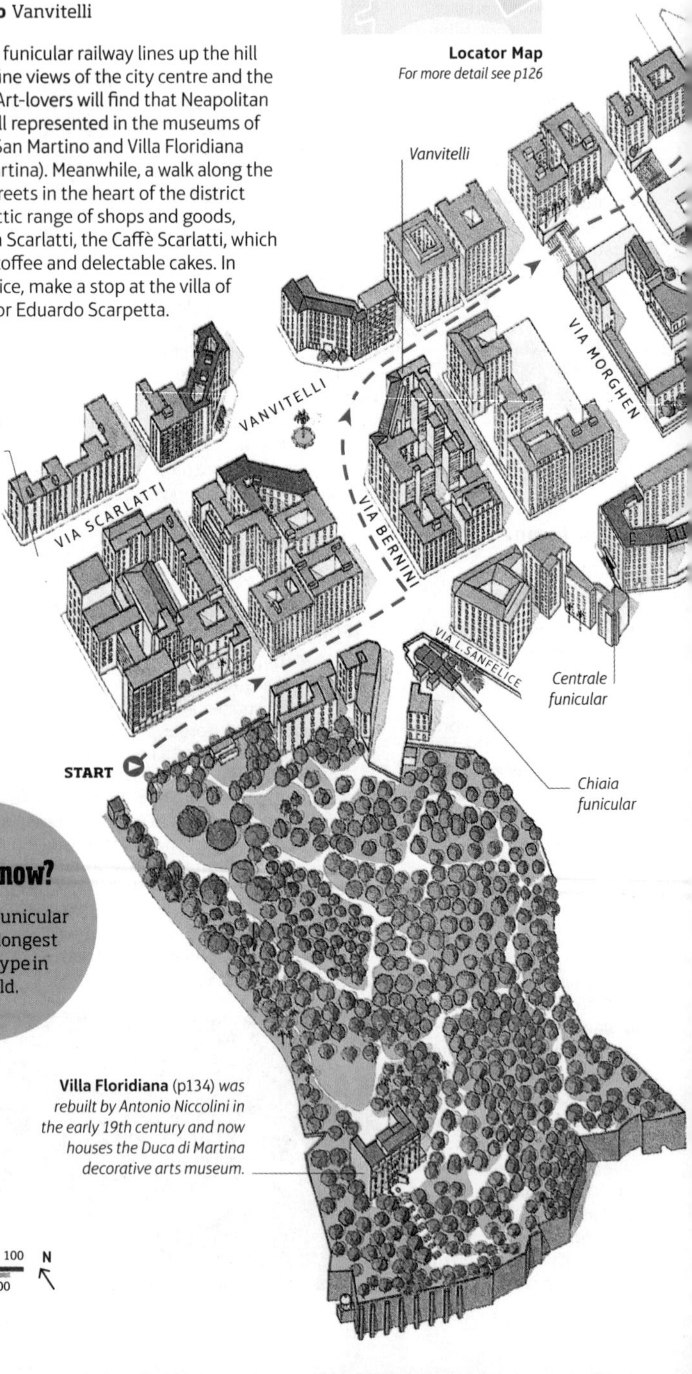

Vomero
VOMERO

Vanvitelli

VIA MORGHEN

Via Scarlatti
(p137) *is the main
thoroughfare
through Vomero.*

VANVITELLI

VIA SCARLATTI

VIA BERNINI

VIA L. SANFELICE

*Centrale
funicular*

START

*Chiaia
funicular*

Did You Know?

The Centrale funicular
is one of the longest
lines of its type in
the world.

Villa Floridiana (p134) *was
rebuilt by Antonio Niccolini in
the early 19th century and now
houses the Duca di Martina
decorative arts museum.*

0 metres   100   N
0 yards   100

VIA ANGELINI

FINISH

Montesanto funicular

Castel Sant'Elmo
(p135) *is a medieval fortress offering stunning views over the city.*

The Certosa di San Martino
(p130) *is an impressive complex built in the 14th century. It is now home to a museum focused on Neapolitan painting and sculpture of the 19th century.*

The Certosa di San Martino above the city and *(inset)* its sumptuous interior

CASTEL DELL'OVO AND CHIAIA

Dominated by the Castel dell'Ovo, the city's oldest castle, the Chiaia district has a long history. The area was originally home to a Roman patrician villa in the 1st century BC. About 500 years later, a monastery was founded here by a small community of monks. A castle was first built on the site by the Normans in the 12th century, but its importance only lasted until Castel Nuovo was built in the 13th century. The area was incorporated into the city under Spanish rule, and in the late 18th century the construction of the Villa Reale, now called the Villa Comunale, changed the face of this seafront stretch. In the meantime, the city was becoming popular with tourists and 8,000 visitors were reported per year by 1838 – a significant number for the time. In the second half of the 19th century the development of the Amedeo quarter, and the elegant streets that radiate from Piazza Amedeo, made this the favourite residential area of the upper middle classes. In 1869, the city began the construction of the curving seaside promenade known as the Lungomare, which, when completed, became instantly popular as a favoured spot for the evening *passeggiata* with residents and visitors alike – including 19th-century Grand Tour travellers and writers such as Mary Shelley and 20th-century visitors such as Henry James. It was pedestrianized in 2012 and a leisurely stroll here is still one of the city's defining experiences.

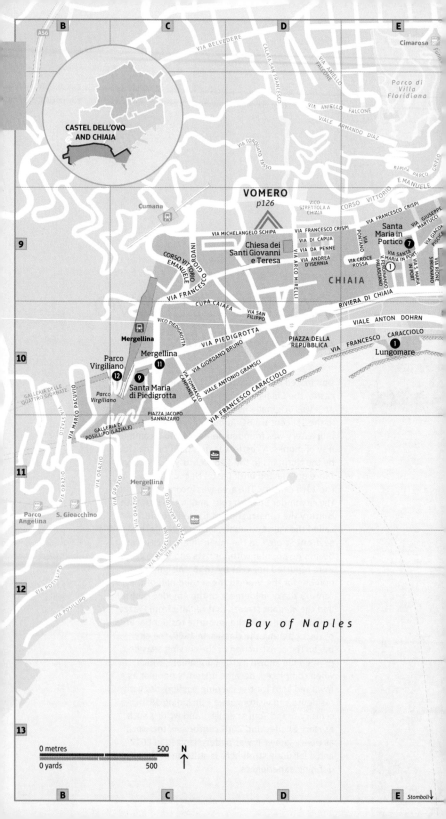

CASTEL DELL'OVO AND CHIAIA

A56

VIA BELVEDERE

Cimarosa

Parco di Villa Floridiana

VIA AMIELLO FALCONE

VIA ANIELLO FALCONE

VIALE ARMANDO DIAZ

CALATA SAN FRANCESCO

VIA TORQUATO TASSO

RAMPA PARCO GRIFEO

Cumana

VOMERO
p126

CORSO VITTORIO EMANUELE

VICO STRETTOLA A CHIAIA

VIA FRANCESCO CRISPI

VIA GIUSEPPE MARTUCCI

VIA FRANCESCO CRISPI

VIA MICHELANGELO SCHIPA

VIA DI CAPUA

VIA PONTANO

Santa Maria in Portico

VIA GIACOMO PISCICELLI

9

INDRIRIO GIORDANO

CORSO VITTORIO EMANUELE

Chiesa dei Santi Giovanni e Teresa

VIA DA PENNE

VIA ANDREA D'ISERNIA

VIA CROCE ROSSA

VIA SANTA MARIA IN PORT.

VIA FERDINANDO PALASCIANO

VIA S. MARIA IN PORT.

⑦

VIA ARCO MIRELLI

CHIAIA

VIA RIONE SIRIGNANO

①

VIA FRANCESCO

CUPA CAIAFA

VIA SAN FILIPPO

RIVIERA DI CHIAIA

VICO PIEDIGROTTA

VIALE ANTON DOHRN

Mergellina

VIA PIEDIGROTTA

PIAZZA DELLA REPUBBLICA

VIA FRANCESCO CARACCIOLO

10

Parco Virgiliano

Mergellina ⑪

VIA GIORDANO BRUNO

VIA FRANCESCO CARACCIOLO

Lungomare ①

GALLERIA DELLE QUATTRO GIORNATE

⑫

Parco Virgiliano

⑨

Santa Maria di Piedigrotta

VIA TOMMASO CAMPANELLA

VIALE ANTONIO GRAMSCI

VIA MARCO PACUVIO

GALLERIA DI POSILLIPO (LAZIALE)

PIAZZA JACOPO SANNAZARO

VIA ORAZIO

11

Parco Angelina

S. Gioacchino

Mergellina

VIA ORAZIO

VIA ORAZIO

VIA MERGELLINA

VIA FRANCE

VIA POSILLIPO

12

VIA POSILLIPO

Bay of Naples

13

0 metres   500

0 yards   500

N ↑

B   C   D   E   *Stromboli↓*

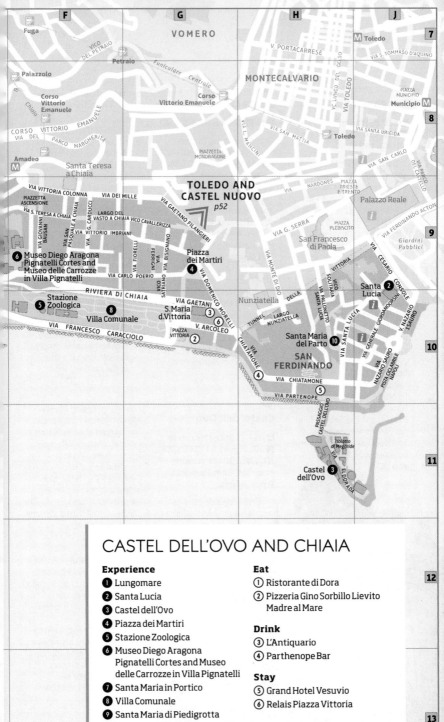

CASTEL DELL'OVO AND CHIAIA

Experience
1. Lungomare
2. Santa Lucia
3. Castel dell'Ovo
4. Piazza dei Martiri
5. Stazione Zoologica
6. Museo Diego Aragona Pignatelli Cortes and Museo delle Carrozze in Villa Pignatelli
7. Santa Maria in Portico
8. Villa Comunale
9. Santa Maria di Piedigrotta
10. Santa Maria del Parto
11. Mergellina
12. Parco Virgiliano

Eat
1. Ristorante di Dora
2. Pizzeria Gino Sorbillo Lievito Madre al Mare

Drink
3. L'Antiquario
4. Parthenope Bar

Stay
5. Grand Hotel Vesuvio
6. Relais Piazza Vittoria

EXPERIENCE

❶ Lungomare

📍E10 Ⓜ Mergellina
🚌C12, C16, C18, C20, C24, N1, N2, 140

In a city devoid of vast green spaces, the Lungomare serves as Naples' outdoor recreational hub. Stretching 3 km (2 miles) along the coast, it was created in the 19th century from reclaimed land, and by 2012 it became a pedestrian zone that welcomes cyclists, joggers and anyone looking for some of the city's best scenery. Castel dell'Ovo rises to the east, while the lights of Posillipo begin to twinkle to the west each evening. The ends of this long, pleasant seafront promenade are marked by two beautiful 17th-century fountains: the Immacolatella, built by sculptors Michelangelo Naccherino and Pietro Bernini in 1601, and the Sebeto fountain, which was the work of sculptor Cosimo Fanzago and built between 1635 and 1637.

❷ Santa Lucia

📍J9 🚌C25, E6, N1, 128, 140

One of the most famous streets in Naples, Santa Lucia exemplifies the city's striking contrasts. Luxury hotels that were built for the elite in the 19th century and imposing government buildings rub shoulders with the more modest neighbourhood of Pallonetto di Santa Lucia. This quarter is named after the church at the beginning of the street, Santa Lucia a Mare, the history of which goes back to the 9th century. Before reaching the seafront, visitors will see on the right the tall rocky face of the hill of Pizzofalcone, the site of the oldest part of Naples (p66).

❸ Castel dell'Ovo

📍H11 🏛 Borgo Marinaro
📞081 795 45 93 🚌C25, E6, N1, 128 🕐8am–sunset Mon–Sat, 9am–2pm Sun & public hols

Greek legends have it that the mythical Siren Parthenope was

THE LEGEND OF THE EGG

Opinion varies as to the origin of the curious name given to Castel dell'Ovo, or Castle of the Egg, which first appears in documents from the 14th century. According to legend, Virgil (p149) placed an egg in the building's foundations, warning that if it shattered, terrible things would befall Naples. For centuries, leaders had to reassure people that the egg was intact, earning Virgil status as protector of the city. A less fantastic theory is that the name simply derives from the shape of the castle.

washed ashore on the island where this fort now stands, having died after her songs failed to enchant Odysseus. Her tears are said to have filled the Bay of Naples. Today, Castel dell'Ovo is the city's oldest fortification, jutting dramatically from the sea. The site has transformed over the centuries, having hosted a Roman patrician villa that was later home to the exiled Romulus Augustulus, Rome's last emperor. By 492, a community of monks had founded the San Salvatore monastery, with only the church remaining today.

A castle first appeared by the 12th century, acting as a prison for numerous political convicts, but its present appearance is the result of rebuilding in the 1500s

←

The ornate Immacolatella fountain, which stands at one end of Lungomare

↑ Colourful boats moored outside Castel dell'Ovo at night

following sieges by the Spanish and French. A 19th-century fishing village sprung up at the base of the fortress. However, the castle itself soon fell into ruins and by the late 1800s it was earmarked for demolition. Fortunately these plans were never set in motion; thorough restoration work was begun in 1975, and succeeded in bringing the site back to life. It is now used for cultural events, and visitors can climb to the ramparts and observation deck for great views. Today the picturesque fishing village remains a popular place for visitors to the area, due to its excellent restaurants and cafés, lively atmosphere and unbeatable views of Vesuvius.

Sculpture of a lounging lion in the Piazza dei Martiri ↓

4 🖥️ 🏛️
Piazza dei Martiri

📍 **G9** 🚇 **Chiaia: Piazza Amedeo** 🚌 **C24, E6**

The Square of Martyrs is the heart of the city's chic commercial centre. Its focal point is the Monumento ai Martiri Napoletani, designed by architect Enrico Alvino in 1866–8, with four lions symbolizing the anti-Bourbon uprisings of 1799, 1820, 1848 and 1860. Palazzo Calabritto, built by architects Luigi and Carlo Vanvitelli, dominates the square on the south. Palazzo Portanna, built in the 18th century by Mario Gioffredo, was rebuilt by Antonio Niccolini for Lucia Migliaccio, Ferdinand IV's morganatic wife. Along the streets that radiate from the square, historic palazzos alternate with elegant shops and cafés.

Among the Neo-Renaissance buildings along Via Filangieri and Via dei Mille, Palazzo Mannajuolo (at No 36 Via Filangieri) is worth seeing for its beautiful inner staircase. In nearby Via Poerio and Via San Pasquale are the Lutheran and Anglican churches.

EAT

Ristorante di Dora
Head to this cosy spot, run by a family of fishermen, for good Neapolitan pasta and seafood options.

📍 **E9** 🏠 **Via Ferdinando Palasciano 30** 🚫 **Mon** 🌐 **ristorantedora.it**

€ € €

Pizzeria Gino Sorbillo Lievito Madre al Mare
The famed Sorbillo opened this seafront pizzeria, with views to match his amazing pizzas. Gluten-free options are available.

📍 **G10** 🏠 **Via Partenope 1** 🌐 **sorbillo.it**

€ € €

↑ The sun-dappled façade of the Stazione Zoologica, which lies within the Villa Comunale

6

Museo Diego Aragona Pignatelli Cortes and Museo delle Carrozze in Villa Pignatelli

♀ F9 **⌂** Riviera di Chiaia
200 **☎** 081 761 23 56
▨ Chiaia: Parco Margherita
🚌 C12, C18, C24, N1, 128,
140 **◷** 8:30am-4:30pm
Wed-Mon

The Neo-Classical villa was built in 1825 by Pietro Valente for the illustrious Acton family, whose English roots and pro-Italian political roles may have helped incite the French to invade southern Italy under Napoleon. The Rothschilds became the new owners 20 years later and changed the furnishings and interior. Prince Diego Aragona Pignatelli Cortes then bought the villa, which is now named after him, and in 1955 his granddaughter donated it to the Italian state. The loveliest rooms are the red hall in Louis XVI style, the smoking room with leather-lined walls and the ballroom with its large mirrors and magnificent chandeliers. Villa Pignatelli is used for temporary exhibitions, concerts and other cultural events. The adjacent Museo delle Carrozze (Carriage Museum) features a collection of 34 Italian, English and French coaches dating from the late 1800s to the early 1900s, collected by a marquis.

5

Stazione Zoologica

♀ F10 **⌂** Villa Comunale
🚌 C12, C18, C24, N1, 128, 140
◷ Mar-Oct: 9:30am-6:30pm
Tue-Sun; Nov-Feb: 9:30am-
5pm Tue-Sun **⊕** szn.it

Located within the Villa Comunale park, this institute, run by the Consiglio Nazionale delle Ricerche (National Research Council), is one of the oldest and best known of its kind in the world. It was established in 1872–4 by German scientist Anton Dohrn to study marine environments. The building, which was designed by German sculptor Adolf von Hildebrandt, contains research labs, a small exhibition and the oldest aquarium in Europe,

with specimens from the Bay of Naples. The frescoes depicting marine and rural scenes in the reading room of the library were painted by Hans von Marées in 1873, and can be viewed by appointment.

An interesting story is told about the institute and the Allied forces, who arrived to take control of Naples in 1943. Commander Clark, an American army captain, was due to dine with Italian counterparts and had suggested he enjoyed fish. Since boats were forbidden from leaving Naples at this time, the hosts improvised and served up a baby manatee from the aquarium. Not even the accompanying garlic sauce could convince their guests to eat the resulting dish.

7

Santa Maria in Portico

♀ E9 **⌂** Via Santa Maria in Portico 17 **☎** 081 66 92 94
Ⓜ Amedeo **▨** Chiaia: Parco Margherita **🚌** C12, C18, C24
◷ 8-11am & 4:30-7pm daily

In 1632 the Duchess of Gravina, Felice Maria Orsini,

> **Commander Clark had suggested he enjoyed fish. Since boats were forbidden from leaving Naples at this time, the hosts improvised and served up a baby manatee from the aquarium.**

→

Visitors wandering through the Villa Comunale, one of Naples' public parks

donated some of her property to the Padri Lucchesi della Madre di Dio congregation so they could build a monastery and church. For years the piperno stone façade was attributed to Cosimo Fanzago, but it is now known to be the work of architect Arcangelo Guglielminelli, who completed it in 1682. The interior has striking 18th-century canvases and stuccoes by late-Baroque artist Domenico Antonio Vaccaro (1678–1745), who was also responsible for designing the high altar.

A short walk down nearby Via Piscicelli takes you to the Chiesa dell'Ascensione a Chiaia, a 14th-century church that was rebuilt in the 1600s by Fanzago, with its dome reconstructed in 1767.

8 Villa Comunale

F10 **Via Carracciolo, Riviera di Chiaia** **C12, C18, C24, N1, 128, 140** **May-Oct: 7am-midnight daily; Nov-Apr: 7am-10pm daily**

The first design for this park area dates from 1697, but it was Ferdinand IV who, almost a century later, asked architect Carlo Vanvitelli and landscape gardener Felice Abate to lay out the Real Passeggio di Chiaia as a public park.

The Villa Reale, later the Villa Comunale, was built on reclaimed land and completed in 1781. Among the pine, palm, monkey puzzle and eucalyptus trees are 19th- and early 20th-century sculptures and fountains, including the *Paparelle*, which in 1825 replaced the famous *Farnese Bull* sculpture group, now in the Museo Archeologico (*p96*). The park is also home to the iron-and-glass kiosk known as the Cassa Armonica, designed in 1877 by architect Enrico Alvino. The site also hosts children's activities such as pony riding.

DRINK

L'Antiquario

A favourite hideaway for those looking to escape the city's hectic piazzas, this place offers a retro vibe and a fabulous selection of classic cocktails, all expertly prepared.

G10 **Via Vannella Gaetani 2** **081 764 53 90** **7:30pm-3am daily**

Parthenope Bar

Grab a seat at this waterfront bar for a morning coffee or head along in the evening for an aperitivo. It's an excellent spot for people-watching, as tourists and locals make their way to and from the Lungomare.

H10 **Via Partenope 13** **081 032 2461** **7:30am-3am daily**

STAY

Grand Hotel Vesuvio

Modern and elegant, this waterfront property is a staple of the city's hotel scene. Previous guests have included Hillary Clinton.

⑨H10 🚇Via Partenope 45 🌐vesuvio.it

€€€

Relais Piazza Vittoria

This boutique hotel has just six modern rooms decorated with splashes of vibrant colours.

⑨G10 🚇Via Giorgio Arcoleo 37 🌐relais piazzavittoria.com

€€€

---

⑨
Santa Maria di Piedigrotta

⑨C10 🚇Piazza Piedigrotta 24 🚇Mergellina 🚌C4, C16, C24 ⏰8am–7pm Mon–Sat, 8:30–10:30am & 12:30–7pm Sun & hols 🌐madonnadi piedigrotta.it

This church is mentioned in a letter written by Giovanni Boccaccio in 1339, in which he references the "Madonna de Pederotta". Much altered over the years, Santa Maria di Piedigrotta is thought to have been built in 1353 to replace a church founded by fishermen in Mergellina. In the mid-1500s, it was rebuilt again; this time the church – which had faced a cave (grotta) – was reoriented to face the city. The present façade is the result of 19th-century restoration by architect Enrico Alvino. Painter Gaetano Gigante decorated the vault. Inside hangs a

15th-century wooden panel, *Descent from the Cross*, by an unknown Neapolitan artist.

The great popularity of the church is linked to a beautiful 14th-century wooden sculpture of the *Madonna and Child*, which was made by the Siena School and dominates the interior. The worship of the Madonna culminates in the September feast (*p44*). In the past, even the royal family took part in the solemn procession. Worshippers, however, did not appreciate the statue's restoration in 1976 to its original state, because the Virgin's large blue mantle and luminous halo were removed.

---

⑩
Santa Maria del Parto

⑨H10 🚇Via Mergellina 96 📞081 66 46 27 🚇Mergellina 🚆Mergellina 🚌C16, C21, C24, 140 ⏰8:30am–7pm Mon–Sat, 9–10am & 11:30am–7pm Sun & hols (to 6:30pm daily in winter)

The history of the church of Santa Maria del Parto is closely linked to Jacopo Sannazaro (1458–1530), the famous Neapolitan humanist and poet of the Angevin court. Sannazaro began construction in the 1520s on land given by Frederick of Aragon and named it after one of his own works, *De Partu Virginis*. Behind the high altar is the tomb of the poet himself, a fine 1537 marble group by sculptors Giovanni Angelo Montorsoli and Francesco del Tadda. One of the side chapels houses a painting by Jan van Eyck, thought to be the first oil canvas in Italy. Another chapel features the "Mergellina devil", depicted in a wooden panel by 16th-century painter Leonardo da Pistoia on the

←

The wide nave and domed ceiling of Santa Maria di Piedigrotta

→ Panoramic view of Naples and the bay from the steps of Parco Virgiliano

> **Having begun life as a fishing village, Mergellina today is a significant harbour for pleasure and tourist boats, as well as an enjoyable place for a leisurely stroll.**

right-hand altar. The panel shows St Michael, who has just vanquished the devil. Curiously, the devil appears in the guise of a beautiful girl, a reference to a local woman who once – unsuccessfully – tempted a bishop and faced St Michael's sword.

---

⑪

Mergellina

📍C10 Ⓜ Mergellina 🚉Mergellina 🚌C16, C21, C24, N2, 140

Having begun life as a fishing village, Mergellina today is a significant harbour for pleasure and tourist boats, as well as an enjoyable place for a leisurely stroll. The numerous cafés, called *chalets* by the locals, offer excellent ice cream and fresh fruit.

The fishermen's quarter, which developed over the inlet at the foot of Posillipo hill and was hailed by poets and writers over the centuries for its beauty, was a popular place for pleasure trips from the Angevin age onwards. The harmony of the landscape was broken by 19th-century land reclamation that extended the coastline further into the sea.

> **VIRGIL**
>
> One of ancient Rome's leading poets, Virgil lived during the Augustan period (27 BC–AD 14). His epic, the *Aeneid*, has influenced Western culture for over 2,000 years. Virgil left an indelible mark on Naples, where he lived and worked, and where, in the 12th century, a belief developed that he possessed supernatural powers and the gift of divination (*p144*). In death too he is linked to the city - the verse on his tomb says "Mantua gave me life, the Calabrians took it away, Naples holds me now".

⑫

Parco Virgiliano

📍C10 Ⓐ Via Salita Grotta 20 Ⓜ Mergellina 🚌C16, C24, N2 🕘9am–1 hr before sunset daily

Those in search of Virgil climb the steps of this tiny park, but ultimately find little more than panoramic views over the bay. The park is of interest because, according to local legend, the famous poet is buried here. However, the so-called Tomb of Virgil is in fact an anonymous Roman funerary monument, with nothing to do with the great poet. Other memorials dot the park, including a monument to the poet Giacomo Leopardi erected in 1939, and two 17th-century stones listing the natural springs in the area and the illnesses they could cure.

Another legend involving Virgil is that with a single gesture he created the *Crypta Neapolitana*, a 700-m (2,300-ft) tunnel; but this too is belied by historical facts: it was built by the Roman architect Cocceius in the 1st century BC to connect Neapolis and Puteoli. In the 1920s the tunnel caved in and is now inaccessible, although its frescoed entrance can still be seen from the park.

A SHORT WALK
LUNGOMARE

Distance 2 km (1.5 miles) **Time** 30 minutes
Nearest Metro Napoli Piazza Amedeo

Besides being a pleasant way of spending the time, walking along the seafront is a tradition handed down over generations of Neapolitans. This is one of the city's most upscale districts, packed with five-star hotels and restaurants that were once frequented by A-list celebrities, such as Sophia Loren and Salvador Dalí.

Mary Shelley also visited in 1818, and Henry James lived here in 1887. The Lungomare is still a favourite spot for the evening *passeggiata* At the Villa Comunale, combine a walk in the park with a visit to Europe's oldest aquarium, the impressive Stazione Zoologica.

↑ Taking in the views from the seafront in Villa Comunale

Piazza dei Martiri (p145) *is a square adorned by a column flanked by four lion statues.*

Stazione Zoologica (p146) *was founded in 1872–4 as a centre for marine studies.*

Villa Pignatelli (p146) *is a house modelled on an ancient Pompeiian design. The sea-facing side consists of a loggia supported by Doric columns.*

VIA RIVIERA DI CHIAIA

PIAZZA DELLA VITTORIA

VIA FRANCESCO CARACCIOLO

START

Santa Maria in Portico (p146), *a church built on a Latin cross plan, has one nave and a dome covered with multicoloured tiles.*

Villa Comunale (p147) *is a splendid public park that was laid out in the 18th century.*

0 metres 200
0 yards 200

N

Locator Map
For more detail see p142

Boats in Borgo Marinaro's harbour, ↑
overlooked by Mount Vesuvius

Did You Know?

It is thought that Mary Shelley's *Frankenstein* was conceived during her walks along the Lungomare.

FINISH

VIA S. LUCIA

VIA CHIATAMONE

VIA PARTENOPE

Borgo Marinaro *is a lively area with a small harbour, cafés and trattorias.*

Castel dell'Ovo (p144), *a sturdy castle, dominates the surrounding area.*

←

The impressive stronghold of Castel dell'Ovo at dusk

A LONG WALK
CHIAIA

Distance 2 km (1 mile) **Time** 45 minutes
Nearest Metro Piazza Municipio

Naples is a city of contradictions: in the historic centre, labyrinthine streets are filled with revving scooters and pungent aromas, while in Chiaia, the wide avenues are lined with chic shops. This walk balances both sides of Neapolitan life, winding through the military district of Pizzofalcone to the elegant shopping streets of the Chiaia, offering a complete change of atmosphere with just the short ride down the Ponte di Chiaia lift.

Locator Map
For more detail see p54 and p142

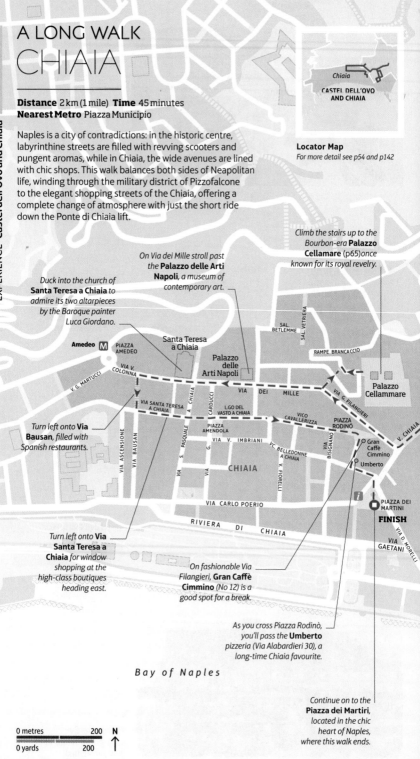

Climb the stairs up to the Bourbon-era **Palazzo Cellamare** (p65) once known for its royal revelry.

On Via dei Mille stroll past the **Palazzo delle Arti Napoli**, a museum of contemporary art.

Duck into the church of **Santa Teresa a Chiaia** to admire its two altarpieces by the Baroque painter Luca Giordano.

Turn left onto **Via Bausan**, filled with Spanish restaurants.

Turn left onto **Via Santa Teresa a Chiaia** for window shopping at the high-class boutiques heading east.

On fashionable Via Filangieri, **Gran Caffè Cimmino** (No 12) is a good spot for a break.

As you cross Piazza Rodinò, you'll pass the **Umberto** pizzeria (Via Alabardieri 30), a long-time Chiaia favourite.

Continue on to the **Piazza dei Martiri**, located in the chic heart of Naples, where this walk ends.

Bay of Naples

0 metres   200   N
0 yards   200

→ The Fontana del Carciofo in Piazza Trieste e Trento

You'll pass the 17th-century church of **Santa Maria della Mercede** *as you follow the curve of Via Santa Caterina.*

Take the lift back down, and head west along **Via Chiaia**.

At the Ponte di Chiaia, take the lift up to **Piazza Santa Maria degli Angeli** *where the Baroque church of the same name has frescoes by Beinaschi (p65).*

START

PIAZZA TRIESTE E TRENTO

Teatro San Carlo

VIA CHIAIA

VIA SERRA

Palazzo Reale

VIA F. ACTON

Begin this walk at **Piazza Trieste e Trento**, *near the glorious* **Palazzo Reale** *(p56), and head west on Via Chiaia.*

Ponte di Chiaia lift

Santa Maria degli Angeli

VIA EGIZIACA A PIZZOFALCONE

PIAZZA DEL PLEBISCITO

Basilica di San Francesco di Paola

VIA CESARIO CONSOLE

VIA SOLITARIA

VC. SOLITARIA

TUNNEL DELLA VITTORIA

Palazzo Serra di Cassano

VIA MONTE DI DIO

Walk south on Via Monte di Dio and pop into the **Palazzo Serra di Cassano** *(p66), one of the city's hidden architectural treasures, to peek at its spectacular staircase.*

Nunziatella

LARGO NUNZIATELLA

SAN FERDINANDO

VIA SANTA LUCIA

VIA CHIATAMONE

VIA CHIATAMONE

Bay of Naples

At the end of Via Monte di Dio, turn right to reach the **Nunziatella** *(p67), Italy's famous military academy.*

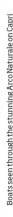
Boats seen through the stunning Arco Naturale on Capri

POMPEII AND THE AMALFI COAST

Coastal ruins bear out the fact that in Roman times a large settlement existed along the western edge of what is now the residential quarter of Posillipo. From the 17th century onwards Naples was an increasingly busy, crowded and often tormented metropolis, infested with plagues and invaders. In contrast, the countryside around the city retained its charm, attracting visitors who made Campania their home. Among these were the Spanish aristocracy, for whom it became a favourite holiday resort and who built luxurious seaside villas and palaces here, and travellers on the Grand Tour in the 1600s and early 1700s, who sought out the volcanic phenomena of the steaming Solfatara crater and the Phlegraean Fields. Only when the first archaeological digs in the 1750s unearthed the remains of Paestum and the buried Vesuvian cities – most famously Pompeii – did a tour of the ancient ruins become popular. Soon after, in the 19th century, the ethereal colour and light found on the islands of Capri and Ischia and the Sorrento peninsula began to bewitch landscape painters. The rest of the Amalfi Coast remained isolated until the mid-1960s, when it started to appeal to travellers in search of a remote lifestyle. Today, of course, this enchanting corner of Italy is one of its biggest draws.

POMPEII AND THE AMALFI COAST

Must Sees

1. Pompeii
2. Herculaneum
3. Mount Vesuvius
4. Posillipo
5. Paestum
6. Amalfi Coast
7. Sorrento
8. Capri
9. Ischia
10. Procida
11. Royal Palace of Caserta

Experience More

12. Caserta Vecchia
13. Ponti della Valle
14. Basilica Benedettina di San Michele Arcangelo
15. Belvedere Reale di San Leucio
16. Anfiteatro Campano
17. Pozzuoli
18. Baia
19. Bacoli
20. Cumae
21. Oasi Naturalistica di Montenuovo
22. Riserva Naturale Cratere degli Astroni
23. Portici and the Ville Vesuviane
24. Torre Annunziata
25. Torre del Greco

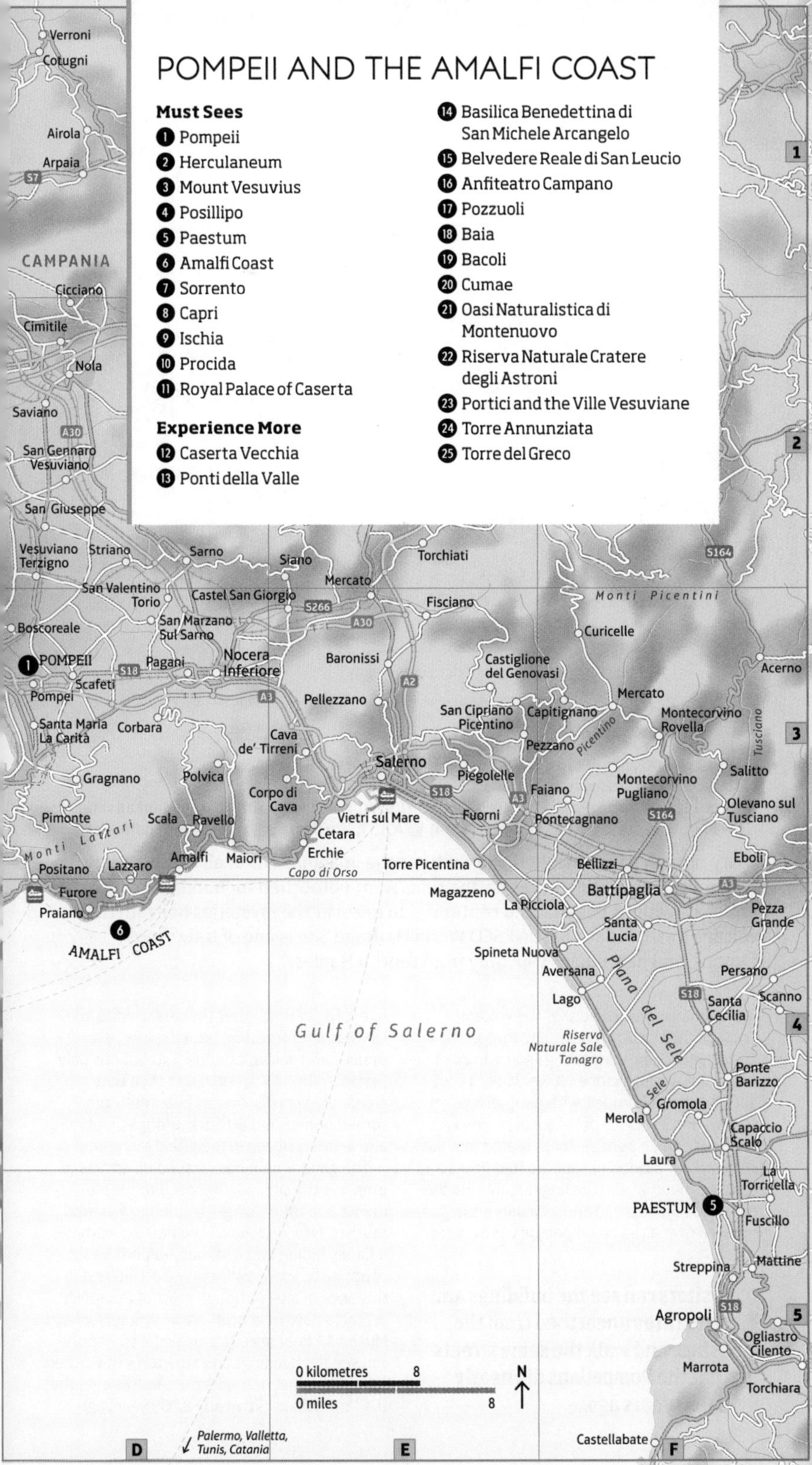

❶ 🛠 🍴 ☕

POMPEII

🅰D3 🚶25 km (15 miles) SE of Naples; entrances: Porta Marina, Piazza Anfiteatro, Piazza Esedra 🚉Pompei-Scavi 🚃Circumvesuviana: Pompei-Villa dei Misteri ⏰Apr-Oct: 8:30am-7:30pm (last adm 6pm); Nov-Mar: 8:30am-5pm (last adm 3:30pm) 🛈AAST, Via Sacra 1; www.pompeiisites.org

A city preserved in time, Pompeii captures the imaginations of all who walk down its streets. Fascinating yet eerie, the ruins went untouched for hundreds of years until excavations began – and continue – to uncover the mysteries beneath the volcano's ash. Today, this UNESCO World Heritage Site is one of Italy's most famous, and just a quick trip away from central Naples.

Historians long believed that the volcanic eruption that destroyed the city took place in August, AD 79, but discoveries made in 2018 suggest it was in October. It was likely a cool autumn day in Pompeii, with people in warm clothes and stalls full of seasonal produce. At about 1pm, Mount Vesuvius roared into life, spewing out a cloud of superheated gases and volcanic material and fuelling deadly pyroclastic flows. Panic spread and evacuations began, but well over a thousand people were unable to escape in time. After the catastrophe, the city was left forgotten, buried under ash, rock, pumice and volcanic debris. Excavations only began in the 1750s, and it was then that archaeologists discovered beautifully preserved homes and artworks alongside humans and animals frozen in their final moments.

The government has ramped up efforts to preserve the site, now exposed to the elements and other dangers, including careless tourists. New discoveries – a horse in harness, a family hiding and a sexually explicit fresco – continue to spark excitement and interest in this ancient site. Although most of Pompeii's artifacts have now been preserved at Naples' Museo Archeologico Nazionale *(p96)*, visitors can see the buildings and structures unearthed from the ashes, and walk the same streets that the Pompeiians did nearly 2,000 years ago.

> **Visitors can see the buildings and structures unearthed from the ashes, and walk the same streets that the Pompeiians did nearly 2,000 years ago.**

Did You Know?

Pyroclastic flows of up to 300° C (572° F) engulfed Pompeii – most victims were incinerated, not suffocated.

↑ The Forum, the focus of civic life, with Mount Vesuvius rising behind

← Scene from the famous fresco cycle in the Villa of the Mysteries

→ Rich wall decoration preserved in the House of the Vettii

THE PUBLIC SPACES OF POMPEII

The first Pompeii town plan (6th century BC) was irregular, but, from the 4th century BC on, building developed on a Greek-inspired grid plan. Slabs of old lava from Vesuvius were used to pave the roads. Large villas and houses of different periods and styles, made of brick, stone and cement and often richly decorated, offer an unparalleled view of ancient domestic architecture. The streets, workshops and public areas are in an excellent state of preservation. Finds such as furnishings, tools, jewellery and food and drink reveal how the people of Pompeii lived.

The Forum

The Forum, the centre of public life, is the oldest part of Pompeii. Arranged around it are important administrative and religious institutions. To the south is the Basilica, or law court, while opposite are the temples of Apollo, Jupiter and Vespasian, and the Sanctuary of the Lari. The Eumachia building was perhaps used by the wool merchants' guild or, more likely, for commercial transactions. On the other side of the Basilica is the site of the Temple of Venus, completely devastated by Vesuvius.

Forum Baths

These well-preserved baths, built after 80 BC, follow the traditional sequence, going from the dressing room to the *frigidarium* (cold room), then on to the *tepidarium* (warm room) and *calidarium* (hot room). Mythological figures decorate the vaults of the warm room, and the hot room contains a large marble basin.

Via Stabiana

This avenue, passing through the Porta di Stabia to the south, was a major thoroughfare used by carriages travelling between Pompeii and the port and coastal districts. On the west side of the avenue are the Stabian Baths. These are the most ancient in the city – the original structure dates from the 4th century BC. Near Porta Vesuvio are the remains of an aqueduct, which channelled water into three conduits that served both private homes and public fountains. The aqueduct fell into disuse after being damaged by the earthquake of AD 62. On the street parallel to Via Stabiana are the remains of the most organized of Pompeii's many brothels. While other such places were mostly single rooms, this *lupanare* features five rooms on the ground

> While other such places were mostly single rooms, this *lupanare* (brothel) features five rooms on the ground floor with masonry beds and erotic frescoes and graffiti.

> **INSIDER TIP**
> **Find Your Way**
>
> Pompeii is the world's largest archaeological and excavation site, covering about 66 ha (165 acres). Find your way around by downloading a free map from the official website.

←

Visitors pausing to rest among the well-preserved pillars of the Forum

The Great Theatre, built into the hollow of a hill for good acoustics ↑

floor with masonry beds, a latrine and erotic frescoes and graffiti lining the walls.

Amphitheatre and Great Gymnasium

The Amphitheatre (80 BC) and the Augustan-era Great Gymnasium, with a swimming pool, lie between the Nocera and Sarno gateways. The amphitheatre, the oldest of its kind in existence, was used for gladiatorial combat and could hold 20,000 people. The stone tiers were separated into different sections for the various social classes. A cloth canopy (*velarium*) shaded spectators from the sun.

Theatres

The 2nd-century-BC Great Theatre was rebuilt several times and in modern times has again been used as the venue for cultural events. It was built to seat about 5,000 people. The quadrangular portico behind the stage was turned into a barracks for the gladiators after AD 62. Next door is the indoor Small Theatre, used for music concerts. Behind this is the Temple of Isis, the goddess worshipped locally.

Via dell'Abbondanza

The excavations for this street end just to the left of the Amphitheatre. The buildings and their contents offer a vivid picture of everyday life, down to the cart tracks in the street. Well-preserved homes include those of the Ceii and Octavius Quartio (*p162*). You can visit the shop of Verecundus, who made felt and tanned hides; Stefano's well-preserved laundry, where urine was used as a cleaning agent; or the bakery run by Sotericus. The most famous *thermopolium* (fast-food shop) belonged to Asellina, whose obliging waitresses are depicted in graffiti on the wall. The inn still has the record of its income from that fateful autumn day in AD 79: 683 sesterces.

GARDEN OF THE FUGITIVES

Just outside the city to the northwest, along the Via dei Sepolcri, is a series of steps leading to an overlook of the city and into a villa with a large vineyard. Against a wall, behind glass, are the plaster casts of 13 people who were trying to flee the city when they were overcome by the final pyroclastic surge that swept across Pompeii. It was Giuseppe Fiorelli, excavation director from 1860 to 1875, who introduced the plaster cast method of preserving the bodies. Liquid plaster is poured into the cavity left in the bed of ashes by the gradual decomposition of the victim's body. As the plaster solidifies, it reproduces the body shape. This method is still used today.

THE HOUSES OF POMPEII

Many large houses of great historical value and architectural interest are concentrated in the area between Via di Mercurio (the most elegant *cardo*, reserved for pedestrians, in the northwest of Pompeii) and Via Stabiana, and along Via dell' Abbondanza. Wealthy residents had houses with courtyards, living rooms and gardens, often with decorated walls. A typical Pompeiian house was constructed around two open courts: the atrium, an Italic feature, and the colonnaded garden, a feature of Greek origin. The layout of suburban farmsteads was different; the Villa of the Mysteries is an example of this. Houses are occasionally closed; ask an official guide.

> A typical Pompeiian house was constructed around two open courts: the atrium, an Italic feature, and the colonnaded garden, a feature of Greek origin.

House of the Vettii

The owners of the House of the Vettii were freedmen who had become rich merchants. The interior walls are adorned with splendid paintings and friezes featuring mythological themes. In the atrium of the more rustic part of the house is the altar of the Lares – the house's guardian deities. This depicts the ancestral spirit of the paterfamilias with two Lares and, below, a serpent. On the house's north side is a kitchen, with a small room decorated with erotic scenes, murals and tapestries.

House of the Tragic Poet

The house's entrance has a mosaic of a dog with a "beware of the dog" inscription, but many of its frescoes are in the Museo Archeologico Nazionale (*p96*). The house's name derives from a mosaic showing a drama rehearsal.

House of Venus

This house is named after the goddess of love because of a fresco discovered there in 1952. Located on the back wall of the garden, it portrays Venus with two cherubs in a pink seashell. The atrium of the house was badly damaged by the bombardment on Pompeii in 1943.

House of the Ceii

The façade of this house bears a series of inscriptions that seem to indicate an electoral campaign programme. One of the messages is signed L Ceius Secundus, who is thought to have been the owner of the house at the time of the eruption. Behind the atrium, a richly decorated garden features a back wall frescoed with hunting scenes and fountains, giving the impression of a wider space. The sides are decorated with landscapes with an Egyptian flavour, a common style in the final years of Pompeii.

House of Octavius Quartio

This house belonged to a man who had made his fortune thanks to the two *cauponae* (restaurants) at the front of the building. The atrium has a marble impluvium (a pool used to collect rainwater) flanked by flower beds. Beyond the atrium is a garden that imitates an aristocratic country residence. A canal, whose borders are decorated with statuary, runs the length of the garden, interrupted only by a small temple in the middle. At one end of the garden is a frescoed nook with a double bed, probably used for outdoor dining.

Villa of the Mysteries

This large villa outside the city walls on Via dei Sepolcri was built in the early 2nd century BC. It was converted from an

←

Fresco portaying Venus, on a wall in the garden of the House of Venus

urban dwelling into an elegant country house. The architecture and paintings make it one of the most famous houses in Pompeii. It contains a fresco cycle of 29 brightly coloured life-size figures set against a red background; these represent a bride's initiation to the Dionysian mysteries or a postulant's initiation to the Orphic mysteries. Some scholars suggest this subject was depicted because the owner was a priestess of the Dionysian cult that was widespread in southern Italy.

House of the Faun

The name comes from a bronze statue of a dancing faun in the middle of the impluvium in one of the atria. The original is in the Museo Archeologico Nazionale, as are many of the mosaics, including the famous *Battle of Alexander (p99)*. Still here are the geometric patterned marble floors as well as some wall decorations. Built in the 2nd century BC, the dwelling once covered an entire *insula* (city block).

Thermopolium

Ancient Romans mostly ate lunch outside the home, in a *thermopolium*. These fast-food shops usually had a long counter on the street side with embedded *dolia* (terra-cotta jars for food storage), and benches for diners. A colourful fresco adorns the back wall of this shop, which belonged to Vetuvius Placidus and is one of the best examples of a business owner's house annexed to the workplace. It has an interesting garden triclinium, the room where Romans would eat lying down on beds. This triclinium is decorated with a fresco of *The Rape of Europa*,

← A bronze statue set in the courtyard pond of the House of the Faun

↑ The House of the Faun, one of Pompeii's largest private dwellings

where Jupiter appears as a bull. Across the street is the House of the Chaste Lovers, which had a bakery with an annexed dining and living room. The structure also contains the fossilized bodies of the mules that were used to drive the millstone for grinding wheat.

Enchanted Garden

Italy has made huge strides to protect Pompeii, keeping it off UNESCO's list of endangered heritages. Increased preservation has led to more discoveries, including a man found with a block on his head. Likely killed by volcanic gases and not the block, he was still a remarkable find in the increasingly excavated Regio V portion of Pompeii, where nearly a third of the city remains untouched. A resplendent *lararium*, a shrine to the family's Lares, was also discovered, dubbed the Enchanted Garden due to its pool, garden, and rich frescoes, sparking renewed interest in the ancient site.

2 🚶 🚭

HERCULANEUM

🅐C3 🏠 Corso Resina, rcolano, 14 km (9 miles) SE of Naples 🚆 Portici-Ercolano
🚉 Circumvesuviana: Ercolano-Scavi 🕐 Apr-Oct: 8:30am-7:30pm daily; Nov-Mar:
8:30am-5pm daily (Villa dei Papiri currently closed to the public) 🌐 pompeiisites.org

Named after Hercules, the ancient Roman town of Herculaneum was destroyed
in AD 79 by the same eruption of Vesuvius that engulfed Pompeii. As a result of
being entombed in mud and ash, Herculaneum is the best-preserved Roman town
in Italy, drawing in visitors with the surprising completeness of its buildings, the
depth of its details, and the stark evidence that people lived – and died – here.

Around the 5th century BC, Herculaneum fell
under Greek influence; just a century later, it
came to be dominated by the Samnites, a
group of tribes from southcentral Italy. In
89 BC it became a *municipium* and resort of
the Roman empire. After its destruction in
AD 79, Herculaneum lay forgotten until excavations began in the 18th century, uncovering
houses built on a grid plan, as well as artworks,
foodstuffs, plants, wood, textiles and other
perishable materials. Highlights include the
frescoes of the Villa dei Papiri, named for the
fine library of papyrus scrolls discovered here;
the frescoes in the College of the Augustales;
the exquisite glass-paste mosaics in the House
of Neptune and Amphitrite; the mosaics and
the changing rooms of the City Baths; the two-
storeyed Trellis House; the peristyle of the
House of Argus; the House with the Mosaic
Atrium; and the House of the Stags. Look out

↑ The Neptune and Amphitrite mosaic
in the house to which it gave its name

for the remains of a wooden boat in the Boat
House, and for terracotta amphorae set into
marble counters in the *thermopolia*, or fast-
food shops. Many of the town's best-preserved
sculptures and frescoes are now on display
in the Museo Archeologico Nazionale (*p96*).

←
Aerial view of the ancient
town of Herculaneum,
still under excavation

→
Sculpture of a stag harried by
hunting dogs, discovered in the
courtyard of the House of the Stags

Did You Know?

After the eruption, Herculaneum was buried under up to 25 m (82 ft) of mud and volcanic material.

The large peristyle, or porticoed inner courtyard, of the House of Argus ↑

MOUNT VESUVIUS

🅰 C2 🅰 22 km (14 miles) E of Naples 🚌 Autobus EAV: every 50 min from Pompeii (8am–3:30pm) & twice a day from Mergellina, eavsrl.it; Busvia del Vesuvio: hourly tours from Pompeii-Villa dei Misteri station (9am-3pm), busviadelvesuvio.com; Vesuvio Express: every 40 min from Ercolano railway station (9:45am-4pm), vesuvioexpress.info

Looming over Naples and the surrounding region, sometimes hiding in the clouds, sometimes spectacularly capped in a rare winter snowfall, Mount Vesuvius has decided the fate of people around Naples for centuries, most famously in AD 79, when it destroyed Pompeii, and most recently in 1944, when it last erupted.

In ancient times Vesuvius was simply "the mountain", covered with vegetation and vines. It had wiped away settlements in the Bronze Age long before the Romans called it Vesuvius, associating it with the god Jupiter. The first person to understand its volcanic nature was the Greek geographer Strabo (64 BC–AD 24), who suggested that its rocks had been burned by fire. In AD 62 the area was hit by a strong earthquake, and people had begun to leave. Seneca the Younger, advisor to the emperor Nero, tried to persuade them to stay, arguing "who can promise… that this or that piece of ground stands on better foundations?". He was to be proved wrong just a few years later. In AD 79 a deadly eruption led to volcanic ash falls and pyroclastic flows that destroyed Herculaneum and Pompeii on the volcano's foothills and greatly altered the surrounding landscape. Roman lawyer and writer Pliny the Younger recorded the cloud of black smoke that rose "like an umbrella pine" from the mountain as he watched his uncle, writer and military commander Pliny the Elder, head towards the disaster to save friends, never to return – he was suffocated by the gaseous vapours that engulfed the area. Since then, Mount Vesuvius has erupted several times, although never as catastrophically. Today, this dormant volcano inspires both fear and fascination and is constantly monitored for activity by a dedicated observatory.

Timeline

79
One of the volcano's most famous and catastrophic eruptions takes place, destroying Pompeii and Herculaneum.

1944
▽ The volcano's last active period ends with the March 1944 eruption, which also destroys the funicular.

1631
An eruption claims 600 victims. Naples is saved and thanks San Gennaro by building the Guglia *(p104)*.

1880
△ The funicular opens to the public.

1906
△ Another major eruption widens the crater by 300 m (985 ft).

← Hiking the trail around the rim of Mount Vesuvius

VOLCANIC MYTHS

Associated with both creation and destruction myths, volcanoes have fascinated civilizations around the world. In this geologically volatile area, natural volcanic phenomena were attributed to the supernatural. Vesuvius itself was regarded as a divinity by the Romans, who also believed that the smouldering supervolcano nearby, the Phlegraean Fields *(p199)*, was once the home of giants as well as the entrance to the underworld. Here, the Solfatara crater was believed to be the chimney of the forge of the divine blacksmith Hephaestus, who was called Vulcan by the Romans and gave his name to volcanoes.

← Mighty Mount Vesuvius and the beautiful Bay of Naples seen from Castel Sant'Elmo

4

POSILLIPO

🅰B3 📍12 km (7 miles) SW of Naples 🚉To Mergellina, then bus 🚌C27, C31, N2, 140 ℹvisitnaples.eu

The peninsula that juts into the sea, separating the Bay of Naples from Pozzuoli, was called Pausilypon ("respite from pain") by the ancient Greeks, because of the great beauty of the site. As attested to by the ruins along the coast, in Roman times a huge settlement grew up along the westernmost edge of what is now called Posillipo, and was connected to the neighbouring Phlegraean Fields. The area became the favourite holiday resort of the Spanish aristocracy in the 17th century, when luxurious palaces were built here. Despite later periods of economic decline and unregulated property development, Posillipo's historic villas and rambling gardens can still be enjoyed today.

①
Palazzo Donn'Anna
🏠Largo Donn'Anna 9
🚫To the public

In 1637 the Spanish viceroy Ramiro Guzman, Duke of Medina, married princess Anna Carafa of Naples. To celebrate, Don Ramiro asked the architect Cosimo Fanzago to build the large Palazzo Donn'Anna at the water's edge. Construction began in 1642, but the building was never completed or used by the couple. The viceroy returned to Spain in 1644, and Anna died soon after. The palazzo was damaged during the 1647 uprising and again in the 1688 earthquake. It was partly restored in the 1700s but decades later it was still being described as a building in a state of total neglect. Its air of mystery gave rise to the rumour that in its past the palace had been used by Queen Joan II of Naples (1371–1435) for secret assignations with her lovers. Popular belief has it that after these men had served their purpose, they were thrown into the sea below the palace.

Palazzo Donn'Anna suffered further damage in the early 19th century, when part of the façade was demolished to build the Via Posillipo. In 1870 attempts were made to turn it into a hotel, but the idea was abandoned. Despite its tormented history and the damage wrought by time and neglect, the massive tufa palace with its cavernous vaults is still one of the city's celebrated sights.

Did You Know?

Anna Carafa's niece, who mysteriously disappeared one night, is said to haunt the Palazzo Donn'Anna.

← Posillipo's colourful coastline, lined with palazzos, viewed from the sea

building in 1883 as a tomb for his brother Marco. The monument was purchased and finished in 1923 by the Naples city council in order to house the remains of soldiers who had died in World War I.

③ Santa Maria del Faro

🏛 Via Marechiaro 96a
📞 081 769 1439 🕐 During services

This church was probably built over the remains of an ancient Roman lighthouse (*faro* in Italian). It was restored by Sanfelice in the 18th century, but the façade dates from the 19th century.

④ Capo Posillipo

🏛 Via Ferdinando Russo

The main attraction at the bay of Capo Posillipo is Villa Volpicelli (*p171*), which gives the impression of a castle floating on the sea. Originally known as Candia e Santacroce villa, it was built in the 17th century. In 1881, the villa was bought by Raffaele Volpicelli,

② World War I Memorial

🏛 Via Belsito 🕐 7am-noon Tue-Sun

The War Memorial, or Ara Votiva, is situated in a small park beyond the Piazza San Luigi. The middle of the park is dominated by the large Egyptian-style mausoleum that Matteo Schilizzi began

who restored it and added romantic details such as the crenellated towers. The locals call the surrounding area the Riva Fiorita, or flowered shore. In the summer months, the little harbour and the cliff area opposite hum with life.

EAT

Il Miracolo dei Pesci
A no-frills dining room with rustic seafood dishes is the ideal local experience in Posillipo.

🏛 Largo Sermoneta 17
📞 081 769 0778 🕐 Mon

€€€

Ristorante Reginella
Dine on fresh seafood and pizza with views of the coast and central Naples.

🏛 Via Posillipo 45a 🌐 ristorante reginella.com

€€€

Map

Il Miracolo dei Pesci 2 km (1 mile) →
Palazzo Donna Anna 2 km (1 mile) ① → Ristorante Reginella

POSILLIPO

PARCO DELLO SPORT

VIA PETRARCA

VIA ALESSANDRO MANZONI

Collettore Arena Sant'Antonio

CUPA ANGARA

VIA TORRE RANIERI

VIA BELSITO

② World War I Memorial

COROGLIO

VIA GIOVANNI PASCOLI

PIAZZA CAPO POSILLIPO

VIA COROGLIO

VIA PASQUALE LEONARDI CATTOLICA

DISCESA COROGLIO

VIALE VIRGILIO

DISCESA COROGLIO

VIA MARECHIARO

VIA SANTO STRATO

VIA FERDINANDO RUSSO

VIA POSILLIPO

Villa Volpicelli

VIA TITO LUCREZIO CARO

VIA FRANCO ALFANO

STRADA PRIVATA VILLA MAISSO

Parco Residenziale di Villa Rosebery

④ Capo Posillipo

VIA NUOVA DI NISIDA

Grotta di Seiano ⑥

DISCESA COROGLIO

Grotta di Seiano

⑤ Parco Virgiliano

Villa Rosebery

Isola di Nisida 500 m (550 yd)

Cala di Trentaremi

MARECHIARO

⑦ Marechiaro

Punta Cavallo

Marinella Beach

Area Marina Protetta Parco Sommerso di Gaiola

③ Santa Maria del Faro

Palazzo degli Spiriti

Bay of Naples

Isola la Gaiola

0 metres 600
0 yards 600

N ↑

DRINK

Miranapoli
This little local bar features a delicious range of drinks and a view that's worth stopping for.

🅰 Via Francesco Petrarca 62 📞 081 769 0943

Ke' Bar Manzill
Indulge in plenty of nibbles with your drink at this bustling piazza bar.

🅰 Piazza S Luigi 📞 081 575 56 51

⑤

Parco Virgiliano
🅰 Viale Virgilio

Beautiful Parco Virgiliano, also known as Parco della Rimembranza, occupies the top of a hill overlooking the sea. It offers spectacular views across the Bay of Naples to Mount Vesuvius and the Sorrento peninsula on one side, and the Bay of Pozzuoli and the Phlegraean Fields on

→

Fishing boats moored at the quaint town of Marechiaro, a great spot for fresh seafood

the other. Below the park is the little island of Nisida, which was formed from an ancient volcanic crater. The remains of the old ILVA steelworks can also be viewed. At sunset, the sweeping views towards Ischia *(p190)* are particularly stunning.

⑥

Grotta di Seiano
🕐 By appt only, call 081 575 44 65

In Roman times, a 770-m- (0.5-mile-) long tunnel gave access to a vast villa, home of Publius Vedius Pollio, friend of Emperor Augustus. Known as Pausylipon, the villa included a 2,000-seat amphitheatre and thermal baths. In the 1700s, the Bourbon kings discovered and repaired the tunnel and it was later used as a World War II air raid shelter.

⑦

Marechiaro
A famous song by Neapolitan artist Salvatore di Giacomo

(p43) says that this coastline is so romantic that even the fish make love in the moonlight. Going down Via Marechiaro, visitors will see elegant villas surrounded by greenery and beautiful panoramic views of the countryside. Towards the sea is a small square with the remains of a Roman column from the so-called Temple of Fortune. Further down, in the laid-back fishing village of Marechiaro *(p173)*, there are a few bars, cafés and restaurants overlooking the water. Local fishermen often bring their catch straight to the restaurants to serve.

The romantic sunset view from the coastal lookout point at Parco Virgiliano ↓

↑ The ruins of Palazzo Donn' Anna, framed by purple bougainvillea flowers

THE VILLAS OF POSILLIPO

The Romans set the trend, building grandiose getaways along the Posillipo coast, and Spanish and Italian nobility followed centuries later with ornate villas jutting out over the sea. Most are privately owned, while Villa Doria d'Angri is part of a university, but all the residences recall a high point in Naples' achitectural history.

PALAZZO DONN'ANNA

A landmark of Posillipo, Palazzo Donn'Anna (p168) continues to crumble on the edge of the coast. Dark stories echo around its unfinished halls, and the palace remains cloaked in mystery.

VILLA VOLPICELLI

Adjacent to Villa Rosebery, and skirting the edge of the harbour, is the private Villa Volpicelli (p169). The romantic castle-like building is where the popular soap opera *Un posta al sol (A Place in the Sun)* is filmed. Homeating *(www.homeating.com)* organize private dinners here.

↑ The cylindrical towers of the imposing Villa Volpicelli

VILLA ROSEBERY

Villa Rosebery is the Neapolitan residence of the President of the Italian Republic. It was here that King Vittorio Emanuele II abdicated. Guided tours must be booked in advance *(www.palazzo.quirinale.it)*.

VILLA DORIA D'ANGRI

The northern stretch of Via Posillipo is dominated by Villa Doria D'Angri, built in 1833 by Bartolomeo Grasso for Prince D'Angri and now part of the Parthenope University of Naples. The villa is generally closed to the public.

↑ Villa Roseberry's attractive tiled terrace area

VILLA D'ABRO

Villa d'Abro (No 46) was named after the nobleman Aslan d'Abro, who bought it in 1870 and had it restored in Neo-Romantic style. The villa is a private residence.

VILLA ROCCAROMANA

This pagoda-shaped villa, which was built in 1814 for Prince Caracciolo, is best admired from the water.

↑ Villa Roccaromana, rising from the craggy cliff edge

POSILLIPO ON THE WATER

One of the best ways to admire the Bay of Naples is from the water. To the west of the city, from Castel dell'Ovo as far as the Phlegraean Fields, Posillipo's historic coast is dotted with grottoes and inlets. Beyond the headland of Posillipo, the fishing village of Marechiaro, ancient Roman ruins and the little islands of Gaiola and Nisida await. Bars and bathing beaches lure visitors here in summer, and in winter the dramatic coastline can be enjoyed from a hydrofoil or ferry on an excursion to Procida and Ischia.

ISOLA DI NISIDA

The ancients knew this volcanic islet as Nesis, or "little island". It was here that Brutus and Cassius plotted to kill Caesar in 44 BC. The Angevin building that dominates the island became a prison under the Bourbons.

CALA DI TRENTAREMI

The striking tufa cliffs of Cala di Trentaremi are reflected in the sea, which gleams blue and green. This cove is particularly sheltered and is a favourite with bathers.

ISOLA LA GAIOLA

The presence of ancient ruined buildings between the tufa island of Gaiola and the village of Marechiaro has led scholars to suggest that a complete Roman city once existed here. The Gaiola Underwater Park offers snorkelling, diving and glass-bottom boat tours to catch a glimpse of the submerged ruins.

PARCO VIRGILIANO

A well-equipped sports centre is one of the attractions in the park of Posillipo, on the Coroglio summit.

POSILLIPO'S BATHING SPOTS

If sightseeing in central Naples in midsummer gets too much, take a break at a *stabilimento balneare*. At these bathing spots along the Posillipo coast, you can rent a deckchair and an umbrella and swim in the sea or a natural seawater lido. This Neapolitan pastime emerged during the 19th century at the Bagno Elena, a sandy beach resort, which first opened in 1838. For those who prefer cliffs to sand, there is the Villa Fattorusso, with two seawater pools; Bagno Marechiaro, with its restaurant overlooking the waters of the bay; and the elegant Villa Imperiale.

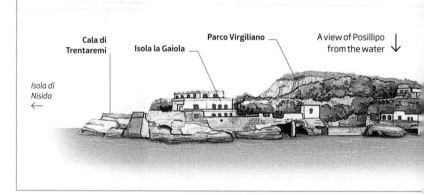

Isola di Nisida ←

Cala di Trentaremi

Isola la Gaiola

Parco Virgiliano

A view of Posillipo from the water ↓

Looking out over the rugged cliffs at Cala di Trentaremi

MARINELLA BEACH

With its parks and lido, this is one of the area's most popular resorts.

PALAZZO DEGLI SPIRITI

The ruins of the mysterious Roman "palace of the spirits" are visible only from the sea.

MARECHIARO

The original name for the water by this fishing village was Mare planum ("calm sea"), which was translated to Marepiano in Italian, which over time became Marechiaro *(p170)*.

↑ Kayaking along the Posillipo coast at sunset

Harbour of Gaiola

Marinella Beach

Palazzo degli Spiriti

Marechiaro →

EAT

Casa Coloni
Enjoy innovative Italian cuisine and attentive service after visiting the temples.

📍 Via Tavernelle 86, Paestum 🕔 Mon
🌐 tenutaduca marigliano.it

€€€

Mareluna Ristorante
Head towards the beach after the temples and stop for a quick pizza at this local joint just off the main route.

📍 Via Torre di Mare 2, Licinella-Torre di Paestum 📞 0828 199 53 98

€€€

5

PAESTUM

🗺 F5 📍 Via Magna Grecia, Paestum, 95 km (59 miles SE of Naples) 🚉 Paestum station on the Napoli–Salerno line 🕔 Site: 8:30am–7:30pm daily; museum: 8:30am–7:30pm Tue-Sun 🚫 1 Jan, 25 Dec ℹ AAST, Via Magna Grecia 887; infopaestum.it, paestumsites.it

This atmospheric site recalls the days when the Greeks governed this region, a rich colony they called Magna Graecia. The beautifully preserved Doric temples here have stood for over 2,000 years, a majestic testament to the people that built them.

The seaside town of Poseidonia was founded around 600 BC by Greek colonists. Although the Romans conquered it in 273 BC, renaming it Paestum, the three temples that stand today are the work of the Greeks. Dating back to 550-450 BC and now part of a UNESCO World Heritage Site, these structures are among the most complete Greek ruins in all of Italy.

> King Charles III even proposed – unsuccessfully – using the imposing columns of the temples in the new palace he was having built at Capodimonte.

Rediscovered in the 18th century after the ruins of Pompeii and Herculaneum had been found, the temples sparked off an interest in Greek Revival architecture. King Charles III even proposed – unsuccessfully – using the imposing columns of the temples in the new palace he was having built at Capodimonte (p114). The temples served as Red Cross shelters for the Allied forces during World War II, since neither side would bomb the ruins.

Paestum is also known for its painted tombs, the most famous of which is the Tomb of the Diver, dating to around 480 BC. It is named after the enigmatic fresco on the covering slab showing a young man diving into a stream of water, symbolizing the passage to the afterlife.

↑ The impressive ruins of the Temple of "Poseidon", the largest of Paestum's temples

↑ The fluted columns of the Temple of Hera, the oldest of the temples

↑ The Temple of Athena, the smallest of the site's three temples

PAESTUM'S THREE TEMPLES

The Temple of Hera (c 550 BC) has nine front columns, 18 columns on each side and two aisles divided by a row of columns. The Temple of Athena (c 500 BC), once thought to be dedicated to Ceres, has six columns at the front, 13 on each side and an undivided cella (sanctum). The largest temple (c 450 BC) was once believed to be sacred to Poseidon, but scholars now argue for Zeus or Apollo. It has six front columns, 14 on the sides and a cella divided into three aisles by two rows of two-tier columns.

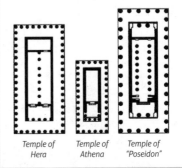

Temple of Hera   Temple of Athena   Temple of "Poseidon"

AMALFI COAST

D4 🚌 🚢🚢 Regular ferry & hydrofoil services in the summer ℹ️ Corso delle Repubbliche Marinare 27, Amalfi; www.amalfituristoffice.it

With its colourful cliff-hanging towns and serene limestone islands bathed in a sunny glow, the Amalfi Coast enchants travellers and artists alike. Seemingly suspended between sea, sky and earth, State Road 163 twists and turns along the full length of the "divine coast" and offers stunning views at every corner.

① Nerano

C4 🚗 67 km (42 miles) SE of Naples 🚌 Sita

The first stop on the Amalfi coast road is Nerano. The track to this quiet village goes upwards from Sorrento and cuts across the end of the peninsula near the village of Termini. Nerano is perched on a ridge; below is the beach and the town of Marina del Cantone, popular mostly because of its small seafront restaurants, some supported by stilts. Walkers can descend on foot among the olive trees to the Bay of Ieranto.

② Positano

D3 🚗 62 km (39 miles) SE of Naples 🚌 Sita 🚢🚢 From Capri, Naples, Salerno, Amalfi & Sorrento ℹ️ AAST, Via del Saracino 4; www.positano.com

In 1953 John Steinbeck wrote that Positano "is a dream place that isn't quite real when you are there and becomes beckoningly real after you have gone". The town climbs the hill, with the oldest houses at the top, faded red and pink, and decorated with Baroque stuccoes. The street down to the sea, Via Pasitea, penetrates

the heart of town with its houses featuring tiny gardens that defy the rock. Near the beach is the church of Santa Maria dell'Assunta, whose cupola is covered with yellow, blue and green majolica tiles.

> 🔍 HIDDEN GEM
> **Nocelle**
>
> Positano can get busy with day-trippers. To escape the crowds and stretch your legs, make the steep ascent to Montepertuso, from where a scenic path leads to the quiet mountain village of Nocelle.

↓ A dusty pink light suffusing the picturesque town of Positano

The descent ends at Marina Grande, a beach lined with bars and restaurants. Boats are available here to inlets inaccessible by land, or to the islands of Li Galli. If you prefer to go on foot, you can swim at Ciumicello, Arienzo or take the path to Fornillo beach, with its two watchtowers. There are also craggy grottoes in the inlets, including La Porta, where there are Palaeolithic and Mesolithic ruins.

③
Praiano

🏠 D4 🚗 69 km (43 miles) SE of Naples 🚌 Sita

This fishing village is perched on the ridge of Monte Sant' Angelo and stretches towards Capo Sottile. The church of San Luca, with paintings by Giovan Bernardo Lama, lies in the upper part. On the road from Positano there are many delightful beaches; just before Praiano is Vettica Maggiore and, further on, Conca dei Marini. The views are splendid from the square of Vettica Maggiore, by the church of San Gennaro. Before you reach Amalfi, the road widens into an open space, where you can go down by lift to **Grotta dello Smeraldo**, where stalagmites and stalactites merge to form columns in the emerald water.

Grotta dello Smeraldo
🚶 🚗 6 km (4 miles) E of Praiano, State Road 163, Km 264 (via lift or stairs) 🚌 From Amalfi or Praiano 🕐 Daily (weather permitting)

④
Vietri sul Mare

🏠 E3 🚗 56 km (35 miles) SE of Naples 🚌 Sita 🛈 Pro Loco, Via O Costabile 4; www. prolocovietrisulmare.it

The majolica-decorated dome and bell tower of San Giovanni Battista have almost come to symbolize this town overlooking the Bay of Salerno. Vietri sul Mare is famous as a seaside resort and especially for its ceramics. Plates, vases and tiles have been made here since the 1400s. In the mid-18th century, Vietri became known as the majolica-makers' district. The most original items made were the tiles painted with religious subjects; you can still see these tiles throughout the town. The donkey used as the logo on pieces by local artisans is a relatively recent invention, inspired by the German artist Richard Doelker in 1922. The **Museo della Ceramica** (Ceramics Museum) features local items from the 1600s to the present.

Museo della Ceramica
🏠 Raito di Vietri sul Mare ☎ 089 21 18 35 🕐 Jun-Sep: 9am-6pm Tue-Sun; Oct-May: 9am-3pm Tue-Sun

EAT

Chez Black
Feast on seafood steps away from the water at this Hollywood-style spot.

🏠 Via del Brigantino 19, Positano 🌐 chezblack.it

€€€€

Da Teresa
This relaxed fish restaurant on the beach has its own free boat service from Amalfi.

🏠 Spiaggia di Santa Croce 🌐 ristorante dateresa.it/amalfi

€€€€

⑤
Amalfi

D3 🚗 66 km (41 miles) SE of Naples 🚌 Sita 🚢🚢 From Capri, Naples, Sorrento 🚉 AAST, Corso Repubbliche Marinare 27; www.amalfitouristoffice.it

Tucked ibetween mountains and sea, Amalfi is a perennial favourite for its scenic beauty and original architecture. The town was once a powerful maritime republic – in the 11th century it rivalled the ports of Venice and Genoa – but little remains to show for this colourful trading history.

Amalfi's cathedral, the **Duomo di Sant'Andrea**, was founded in the 9th century but rebuilt in Romanesque style in the 11th century. The façade and atrium date from the late 1800s, but the bronze doors were cast around the year 1000 in Constantinople. The garden features fragments of historic sculptures and is surrounded by a colonnade.

Inland from Amalfi, you can visit the Valle dei Mulini (Valley of the Mills), famous for its traditional paper production and the **Museo della Carta**, or the Museum of Paper.

Duomo di Sant'Andrea
📍 Piazza Duomo 🕐 Mar-Oct: 7:30am-7pm daily; Nov-Feb: 9-11:30am & 4:30-7pm daily

---

PAPERMAKING
Papermaking reached Italy from the East via Amalfi's ports, and by 1220 King Ferdinand II required all official documents to be printed on the new product. Amalfi developed paper factories in the Valle dei Mulini, attracting customers such as Mozart and the pope. Visitors can hike through the valley to the Museum of Paper, set in a 13th-century paper mill.

Museo della Carta
📍 Via delle Cartiere 🕐 Mar-Oct: 10am-6:30pm Tue-Sun; Nov-Feb: 10:30am-3:30pm Tue, Wed & Fri-Sun 🌐 museodellacarta.it

---

⑥
Ravello

D3 🚗 60 km (37 miles) SE of Naples 🚌 Sita 🚉 AAST, Via Roma 18 bis; www.ravellotime.it

Ravello's history is entwined with that of Amalfi: the former became part of the Duchy of Amalfi in the 9th century. Just off the beaten track, Ravello is an ideal retreat for peace and quiet. However, it does liven up for the Ravello Festival hosted during July and August. Walking around the town, Moorish details are evident in buildings, courtyards and gardens, and the narrow streets offer occasional coastal views.

The **Duomo** is dedicated to San Pantaleone, Ravello's patron saint. The church dates from 1086 and its great bronze doors from 1179. Two of the town's other architectural highlights are Villa Rufolo and Villa Cimbrone, the latter now a luxury hotel. **Villa Rufolo**, originally built for the Rufolo family, is a mixture of 13th- and 14th-century styles. It was remodelled in the 19th century by a Scottish enthusiast, who preserved the Arabic elements. The villa is famed for its tropical gardens, which inspired Wagner's Parsifal – the annual Ravello Festival stages concerts here. On Via San Francesco, which takes you to Villa Cimbrone, are the churches of San Francesco and Santa Chiara, the only one on the coast that has retained its gynaeceum (women's gallery).

Did You Know?
The blood of the patron saint of Ravello, San Pantaleone, is said to be kept in the town's Duomo.

Duomo

⌂ Piazza Duomo ☎ 089 858311 ⌚ 9am–noon & 5:30–7pm daily

Villa Rufolo

♿ ⌂ Piazza Duomo ⌚ Apr–Oct: 9am–8pm daily; Nov–Mar: 9am–4pm daily 🖥 villarufolo.it

---

⑦

Maiori, Minori and Cetara

⌂ D3–E3 ⌂ 71 km (44 miles) SE of Naples 🚌 Sita 🛈 Maiori: AAST, Corso Regina 73, www.aziendaturismomaiori.it; Cetara: Pro Loco, Corso Garibaldi 15, www.prolococetara.it

Ancient Reginna Minori and Maiori are now popular seaside resorts with noble histories. Minori, where the Amalfi Maritime Republic arsenals were situated, dates back to Roman times. Near the seafront is the basilica of Santa Trofimena, built in the 12th–13th centuries. The church houses the relics of the ancient patron saint of the town, Santa Trofimena, in the crypt.

Founded in the 9th century Maiori is now a modern town, rebuilt after a flood in 1954. The beautiful beaches and good bathing facilities have made it one of the most visited towns on this part of the coast.

East of Maiori is Cetara, which was once a stronghold for Arab pirates, who moored their ships at Cala di Fuenti cove. The name perhaps derives from the Latin *cetaria*, or tuna fishing net; the fish, salted and sold in ceramic pots, is a typical local product.

---

⑧

Cava de' Tirreni

⌂ E3 ⌂ 51 km (32 miles) SE of Naples 🚌 Sita

Lying in a valley, Cava de' Tirreni is the only town in southern Italy to have streets lined with porticoes. The old Scacciaventi quarter has winding streets that block the wind (*scacciaventi* means "windchaser").

Must See

STAY

Casa Privata
This luxury seaside getaway offers a secluded escape from the tourists along the coast.

⌂ Via Rezzola 41, Praiano 🖥 casaprivata.it

€€€

Hotel Villa Cimbrone
Perched atop the town of Ravello, this graceful hotel has idyllic views along the coast, a pool, a Michelin-starred restaurant and frescoed rooms that once hosted Greta Garbo, Gore Vidal, and D H Lawrence.

⌂ Via Santa Chiara 26, Ravello 🖥 hotelvillacimbrone.com

€€€

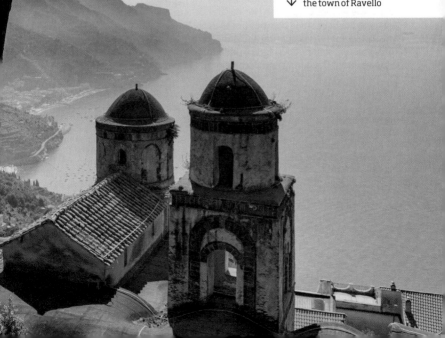

The historic towers of Villa Rufolo, located in ↓ the town of Ravello

↑ Sun-drenched Sorrento, looking out to the tantalizing clear blue sea

7

SORRENTO

🅰 C4 🚗 54 km (34 miles) SE of Naples 🚉 Circumvesuviana: Sorrento 🚌 Sita 🚢 From & to Naples and Capri
ℹ️ Azienda Autonoma di Soggiorno Sorrento-Sant'Agnello, Via de Maio 35; www.sorrentotourism.com

Located on the cliffs at the southern end of the Bay of Naples, Sorrento has been a popular resort town since the 1700s. The town had ancient beginnings and the original Greek town plan can still be seen in the centre. Down at the water's edge, both Marina Grande and Marina Piccola have small beaches but the coast primarily caters for ferries arriving and departing for Naples and the islands. Local lemons dominate in the area as both flavouring and decoration.

① Piazza Tasso

The hub of Sorrento, Piazza Tasso is also the most attractive part of town, with narrow streets following the layout of Roman Surrentum. The statue here is of Torquato Tasso, the great 16th-century Renaissance poet who was born in the town. The atmospheric piazza is also the popular starting and finishing place for the ritual evening *passeggiata*, or stroll, around the streets of Sorrento.

② Duomo

🏠 Corso Italia 📞 081 878 22 48 🕐 8am–12:30pm & 4:30–9pm daily

The Duomo is of ancient origin and was rebuilt in the 1400s and then remodelled several times. Its façade was reconstructed in the early 20th century. Inside the cathedral is the archbishop's marble throne, sculpted in 1537, and fine intarsia (inlaid wood) decorated choir stalls.

③

Sedile Dominova

🏠 Via P R Giuliani
🕐 To the public

The Sedile Dominova, in the piazza of the same name, is a 16th-century building once used as an assembly hall for the nobility. Its external faded frescoes, including the coats of arms of local families, can still be seen in its arches, though the building is now used as a working men's club.

---

④

Museo Bottega della Tarsialignea

🏠 Palazzo Pomarici Santomasi, Via San Nicola 28 🕐 Apr–Oct: 10am–6:30pm daily; Nov–Mar: 10am–5pm daily 🕐 Public hols 🌐 museomuta.it

Sorrento's long tradition of inlaying wood, instances of which can be seen in its cathedral, is on display at this private museum, which is housed in an 18th-century palace. The collection includes plenty of fine and unusual examples of the art, including ornate furniture and natural and stained wooden objects from the 17th to the 20th century. Don't miss the impressive decorated ceilings in two of the rooms on the second floor. The museum also traces the history of the coastal town through prints and paintings.

⑤

San Francesco

🏠 Piazza San Francesco 8-9
🕐 8:30am–8pm daily

Bougainvillea flowers tumble down around the peaceful 14th-century cloisters of the church of San Francesco. The architecture is a vibrant mixture of styles and periods.

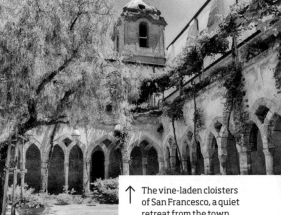

↑ The vine-laden cloisters of San Francesco, a quiet retreat from the town

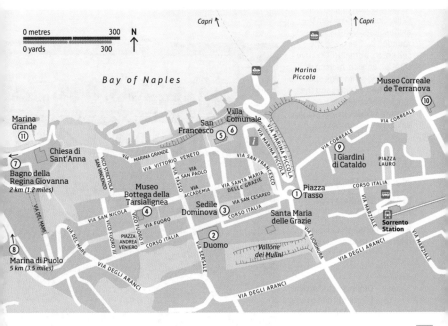

⑥
Villa Comunale

🏠 Via San Francesco
🕐 Sunrise-sunset

One of Sorrento's most tranquil spots, the Villa Comunale is a thin stretch of tree-lined park overlooking Marina Piccola and the Bay of Naples beyond. The views are especially spectacular when the colours change at sunset, and it is easy to while away the time watching the comings and goings far below. There are steps that lead from the park down to the sea.

⑦
Bagno della Regina Giovanna

🏠 Punta del Capo descent (Calata), 3 km (2 miles) NW of Piazza Tasso

Northwest of the town, a cobbled lane leads from Capo di Sorrento down to Punta del Capo, where you can visit the Bagno della Regina Giovanna, Roman ruins of what was probably the home of a wealthy citizen called Pollius Felix. Close to the water, the archaeological site is surrounded by trees, and the sea enters a small, rocky cove through an arch, making it a sheltered swimming spot. Above, Roman walls and the remains of an underfloor heating system are all that is left of the ancient villa.

⑧
Marina di Puolo

🏠 4 km (2.5 miles) W of Piazza Tasso

Beyond Punta del Capo, a path and a road descend to Marina di Puolo, a small, secluded cove and one of the best beaches in the area. Sunbathers share the sand and pebbles with small boats and pretty fishermen's cottages lining the beach.

⑨
I Giardini di Cataldo

🏠 Via Correale 27 🕐 9am-7pm daily 🌐 igiardinidicataldo.it

Lemons are everywhere in Sorrento: the distinctively large, thick-skinned fruit hang outside shops, decorate ceramics and flavour the local tipple, *limoncello*. In the centre of town is a traditional citrus grove typical of the kind found all over the region. The Agruminato is owned by the town council and run by a local farm. Visitors can wander

HAVE A LITTLE BITTER LEMON!

Whether the peel is seeped in grappa to make *limoncello* or a slice is simply dusted with sugar and eaten directly, Sorrento lemons are legendary. A thick rind and few seeds make them ideal for cooking. Probably brought to Campania by Jewish migrants two millennia ago, the lemon is clearly depicted in frescoes in Pompeii.

Diners seated on the twinkling pier of the Marina Grande

around the orchard and buy a variety of lemon-based products, as well as a range of other liqueurs, including mandarin and liquorice.

---

⑩

Museo Correale di Terranova

📍 Via Correale 50 🕐 Apr-Oct: 9:30am-6:30pm Tue-Sat, 9:30am-1:30pm Sun; Nov-Mar: 9:30am-1:30pm Tue-Sun 🖥 museo correale.it

The Museo Correale di Terranova is Sorrento's most important museum. Housed in an ancient villa, the museum's collections consist of fascinating 17th–19th-century objets d'art including furnishings, china, ceramics, glassware and paintings by a range of well-known Neapolitan and international artists as well as some local archaeological finds.

---

⑪

Marina Grande

📍 Via del Mare

Fishing boats bob gently in the calm water at the picturesque Marina Grande, northwest of the town centre. The colourful, though slightly faded, houses that face the waterfront add to the charm of this area. Nearby, the deep waters at Marina Piccola have led to the development of a hectic port. Boats leave here for Naples, Capri, and, in the summer months, for the Amalfi Coast. Both of the harbours have small stretches of sand – visitors must generally pay a small fee to access these.

DRINK

Sorrento Limoncello
A standard in Sorrento for the lemony liqueur.

📍 Via Padre Giuliani 64 🖥 sorrentolimoncello. com

I Giardini di Cataldo
Offers factory tours and *limoncello* tastings.

📍 Via Correale 27 🕐 8am-9pm daily 🖥 igiardinidicataldo.it

Sapori e Colori Sorrento
This family-run shop has *limoncello* and other digestives.

📍 Via S Cesareo 57 🕐 9am-11pm daily 🖥 saporiecolori sorrento.com

A DRIVING TOUR
ALONG THE
SORRENTO COAST

Length 40 km (25 miles) **Stopping-off points** Sorrento, Marina di Massa Lubrense **Terrain** Roads are winding, narrow and steep

The Sorrento peninsula forms a natural boundary between the bays of Naples and Salerno. Its northern side has been inhabited for centuries, and is dotted with Roman as well as modern villas. The coast between Vico Equense and Sorrento is especially built up, and affords spectacular views across the Bay of Naples. Further south, the rugged coastline becomes gradually wilder and more precipitous – Punta della Campanella was almost inaccessible by land until the 19th century. Today, scenic coast roads snake around the headland, winding through fishing villages perched on hillsides, past ancient watch-towers, olive groves and isolated beaches.

↑ Enjoying refreshments in Sorrento's busy Piazza Tasso

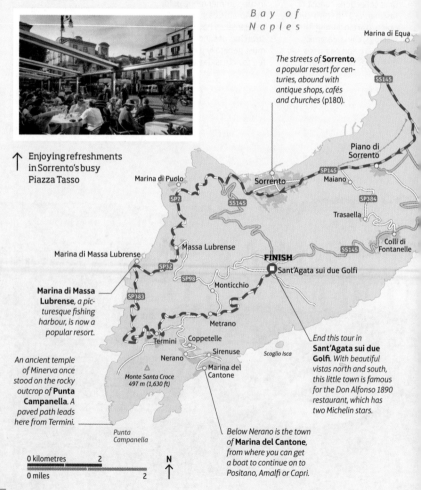

Bay of Naples

The streets of **Sorrento**, a popular resort for centuries, abound with antique shops, cafés and churches (p180).

Marina di Equa

SS145

Piano di Sorrento

Marina di Puolo

SP7

SS145

Sorrento

SP145

Maiano

SP384

Trasaella

Colli di Fontanelle

SS145

Massa Lubrense

FINISH
Sant'Agata sui due Golfi

Marina di Massa Lubrense

SP32

SP98

Monticchio

Marina di Massa Lubrense, *a picturesque fishing harbour, is now a popular resort.*

SP383

Metrano

Termini   Coppetelle

Sirenuse   *Scoglio Isca*

Nerano

Marina del Cantone

Monte Santa Croce 497 m (1,630 ft)

An ancient temple of Minerva once stood on the rocky outcrop of **Punta Campanella**. *A paved path leads here from Termini.*

End this tour in **Sant'Agata sui due Golfi**. *With beautiful vistas north and south, this little town is famous for the Don Alfonso 1890 restaurant, which has two Michelin stars.*

Punta Campanella

Below Nerano is the town of **Marina del Cantone**, *from where you can get a boat to continue on to Positano, Amalfi or Capri.*

0 kilometres   2
0 miles   2

N ↑

Villa di Arianna on the Varano hill, is the town's oldest villa, dating back to the 1st century BC.

Begin this tour in **Castellammare di Stabia**. It was built on the ruins of ancient Stabiae, once home to Pliny the Elder and destroyed in the AD 79 eruption of Vesuvius.

The Eutruscan town of **Vico Equense**, once famous for its wine, is now a popular tourist resort.

POMPEII AND THE AMALFI COAST

Along the Sorrento Coast

Locator Map
For more detail see p156

Castellammare di Stabia
START

Villa Arianna

Villa San Marco

Gragnano   SS366

Villa San Marco has the remnants of a Roman swimming pool.

Bagni di Pozzano

SS145

Monte Pezzulli
412 m (1,352 ft)

Monte Faito
1,131 m
(3,710 ft)

The wooded slopes of **Monte Faito** are accessible by cable car from Castellammare de Stabia railway station.

SS145

SP269

Villaggio Monte Faito

Vico Equense   Massaquano

Seiano

SP269

Moiano

Monte Cerasuolo
1,124 m (3,687 ft)

Colle Garofalo
1,052 m (3,451 ft)   SS366

Fornacelle

Ticciano

Monte S.Michele
(Molare)
1,444 m (4,737 ft)

Alberi

Preazzano

Santa Maria del Castello

Agerola

Arola

Monte Comune
877 m (2,877 ft)

SP425   Montepertuso

Bomerano

SS163

Monte Vico Alvano
642 m (2,106 ft)

Positano

Nocelle

Monte Tre Calli
1,122 m (3,681 ft)

Arienzo

SS163

Positano (p176) clings to the steep slopes of Monte Sant'Angelo a tre Pizzi and Monte Comune.

SS163

Praiano

Gulf of Salerno

La Castelliccia

Gallo Lungo

La Rotonda

→ The pastel-coloured houses of Positano overlooking the sea

8

CAPRI

A B4 · **car** 42 km (26 miles) S of Naples · **boat** From Naples & Sorrento all year, from Amalfi, Ischia & Positano in summer · **i** AAST, Capri Town; www.capritourism.com

Set at the southern end of the Bay of Naples, this small, rugged island has a long history of attracting well-heeled visitors. Roman emperors Augustus and Tiberius enjoyed lengthy stays here, with the latter ruling for the last decade of his life from his luxurious Capri villa. In the 19th century, Capri became popular with Grand Tour travellers, foreign politicians, artists and intellectuals. It remains a tourist mecca, and while it can swell with crowds of day-trippers, its charm and stunning natural beauty make it well worth a visit.

EXPERIENCE Pompeii and the Amalfi Coast

> **INSIDER TIP**
> **Sole Satisfying**
>
> The path from Anacapri to Monte Solaro (589 m/ 1,930 ft) is delightful, with a great view and a detour halfway up to the 14th-century Santa Maria di Cetrella monastery on Marina Piccola. Experienced walkers come back down via the Passetiello path to Capri; this includes a stretch directly above the sea.

① Capri Town

Straddling the eastern part of the island, the town of Capri is where most excursions around the island begin. Visitors usually arrive by boat into the main harbour, Marina Grande, a couple of kilometres to the north. From the harbour, a short funicular ride leads to the heart of Capri's old town, which is focused around Piazza Umberto I.

Commonly known as the "Piazzetta", this famous square is the town's popular outdoor living room, crowded day and night. A top people-watching venue, it is full of café tables buzzing with gossip and animated conversations. The picturesque dome of the Baroque Santo Stefano church overlooks the bustling scene. The narrow alleys around the piazza are also a delight to explore. Take a stroll along Via Camerelle, the island's answer to New York's Fifth Avenue, for some luxury brand shopping.

② Anacapri

A 4 km (2.5 miles) W of Capri Town · **i** AAST, Via Orlandi 59; www.capritourism.com

On the lower slopes of Monte Solaro lies the island's second town, Anacapri, with its relatively quiet lanes and piazzas making a refreshing contrast to Capri town. The bus from Capri stops at Piazza Vittoria,

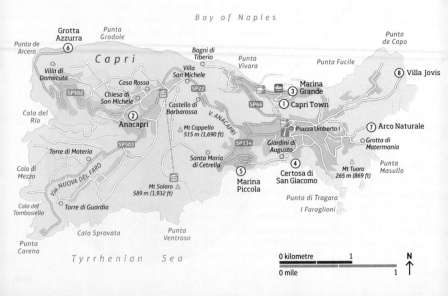

Amalfi, Positano Sorrento, Naples ↗

Bay of Naples

Tyrrhenian Sea

↑ The hills of Capri encircling Marina Grande, with its colourful houses and boats

just below the chairlift to Monte Solaro, whose summit offers an excellent vantage point for taking in the entire island. Piazza Vittoria also marks the beginning of Via Giuseppe Orlandi, a long lane that is home to artisanal workshops and the **Casa Rossa**, which contains the original Roman statues from the Grotta Azzurra *(p188)*. Opposite the piazza is **Villa San Michele**, a museum set in the remarkable former home of Swedish physician Axel Munthe. Also worth a visit are the church of San Michele and the excavations at Emperor Tiberius's Villa Damecuta.

Casa Rossa

⊗ 🏠 Via Giuseppe Orlandi 78 📞 081 838 21 93 🕐 Apr & May: 10am–5pm Tue–Sun; Jun–Sep: 10am–1:30pm, 5:30–8pm Tue–Sun; Oct: 10am–4pm Tue–Sun

Villa San Michele

⊗ 🏠 Viale Axel Munthe 34 📞 081 837 14 01 🕐 Mar: 9am–4:30pm daily; Apr & Oct: 9am–5pm daily; May–Sep: 9am–6pm daily; Nov–Feb: 9am–3:30pm daily

③

Marina Grande

🏠 2.5 km (1.5 miles) N of Capri Town 🛈 AAST, Banchina del Porto; www.capritourism.com

Curving around a picturesque bay dotted with yachts, Marina Grande – a colourful village of shops, bars and cafés – is Capri's main harbour and the arrival point for ferries and hydrofoils from the mainland. Many visitors to the island pass through without stopping, hopping on the old funicular to Capri Town. But aside from being a launching point, Marina Grande has several offerings of its own: excellent seafood restaurants, Roman and Byzantine ruins and the island's largest public beach. From the harbour, near the hydrofoil ticket office, a shuttle boat transfers visitors to Bagni di Tiberio, a private beach beside the scattered ruins of Palazzo a Mare. Built by the first emperor of the Roman empire, Augustus, and modified by his successor Tiberius, this was once one of Capri's largest imperial villas.

EAT

Da Paolino
Dine under the famed lemon trees of this Capri institution.

🏠 Via Palazzo a Mare 3, Marina Grande Ⓦ paolinocapri.com

€€€

Lido del Faro
The food here is worth every penny. Try the homemade ravioli.

🏠 Localita Punta Carena, Anacapri 📞 089 837 17 98

€€€

L'Olivio
A Michelin-starred study in masterful Mediterranean cuisine.

🏠 Via Capodimonte 14, Anacapri 🕐 Oct–mid-Apr Ⓦ capripalace.com

€€€

④

Certosa di San Giacomo

🏛 Viale della Certosa, 400 m (437 yd) S of Capri Town
📞 081 837 62 18 (AACST)
🕐 Summer: 9am–2pm & 5–8pm Tue–Sun; winter: 9am–2pm Tue–Sun

The Certosa di San Giacomo monastery is the island's most impressive medieval complex. Founded in 1371, it was expanded by Certosini monks throughout the 16th and 17th centuries and later converted into a prison and barracks. It is now partly occupied by the Karl Wilhelm Diefenbach Museum, in which the German painter's representations of Capri are displayed along with other historical objects.

⑤

Marina Piccola

🏛 2.5 km (1.5 miles) SW of Capri Town

Occupying a picturesque bay dotted with yachts, the laid-back Marina Piccola has bars and restaurants pressed along the water and a few spits of sand wedged between rocky outcrops. It's a great spot for swimming and sunbathing, with views of I Faraglioni, the rock formations soaring up to 109 m (360 ft) out of the sea. Via Mulo, winding down the slope from Capri's Via Roma, offers a shortcut to the town.

The famous Via Krupp, built by German industrialist Alfred Krupp in 1902, offers a spectacular route from Capri to

Did You Know?

Emperor Augustus decided to build villas on Capri after he saw a dead tree miraculously sprout here.

Marina Piccola, in a series of hairpin bends that make a vertiginous descent to the sea. Even if the path is closed for renovations, it is worth glimpsing from the **Giardini di Augusto**, terraced gardens set up by Krupp and named after Emperor Augustus.

Giardini di Augusto

 🏛 Via Matteotti 🕐 Mar–Nov: 9am–5:30pm daily; Dec–Feb: 9am–7:30pm daily

⑥ 🅼

Grotta Azzurra

🚤 Boat tours from Marina Grande

The Grotta Azzurra or the Blue Grotto is one of the island's most popular sights. This large sea cave is illuminated by an incredible, otherworldly blue light, created by the sunlight that streams through the small entrance and is then reflected from the bottom of

the sea. During Tiberius's reign, the grotto was decorated with several statues, now displayed in Anacapri's Casa Rossa (p186). Check the weather before you visit, as the grotto can be closed during high tides or rough seas.

⑦ 🚴

Arco Naturale

🏛 2 km (1.5 miles) E of Capri Town

The beauty of Capri is on full display at this magnificent natural arch. Walking trails wind through stunning landscapes to this awe-inspiring structure, the remains of a collapsed grotto dating from Paleolithic times, soaring 18 m (59 ft) above the sapphire seas below. Further down the cliff is the Grotta di Matermania, said to have once been the site of pagan rituals relating to the Mithraic mysteries or the mother goddess Cybele.

↑ The stunning switchbacks of Via Krupp leading down to the turquoise waters below

 ⑧

Villa Jovis

📍 Via Tiberio, 2.5 km (1.5 miles) NE of Capri Town ⏰ 9am–1 hr before sunset daily

The retreat built by Emperor Tiberius stands proudly on the mountain named after him, its dramatic setting chosen for its seclusion. Excavations at the site have unearthed cisterns, baths, apartments and "Tiberius's Drop", from which the emperor's victims were supposedly thrown to their deaths into the sea. The ruins also include the remains of a tower once used to communicate with the mainland.

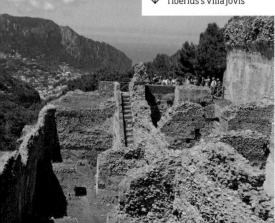

↓ Visitors exploring the ruins of Emperor Tiberius's Villa Jovis

DRINK

La Capannina
A popular wine bar offering the ideal place to relax, with majolica-tiled floors, soft lighting and comfy sofas.

📍 Vico S Tommaso 1, Capri Town ⏰ Wed 🖥 capanninacapri.it/en/winebar

---

Capri Rooftop
Venture outside the town centre to enjoy tipples and nibbles next door to the Giardini di Augusto with a view of Capri's dramatic sea stacks, I Faraglioni.

📍 Via Matteotti 7, Capri Town 🖥 caprirooftop.com

↑ The Castello Aragonese rising above the colourful streets of Ischia Town

⑨

ISCHIA

Ⓐ A3 **Ⓒ 52 km (32 miles) SE of Naples** **🚢🚢 From Naples, Pozzuoli, Procida & Capri**

The green and rugged volcanic island of Ischia, centred around the dormant volcano of Mount Epomeo, abounds with natural charm. Visitors will discover something different on each coast, from beaches to craggy cliffs, busy nightlife to quiet seclusion. With more than 100 hot springs, the island has also given rise to a thriving wellness industry.

①

Ischia Town

ⓘ AAST, Via Sogliuzzo 72, Ischia Porto; www.infoischiaprocida.it

Ischia's largest and busiest town serves as the main port for ferries and hydrofoils. Although the town is roughly divided into Ischia Porto and Ischia Ponte, locals know both parts of the town simply as "Ischia". Beyond the port, Ischia Porto has luxury hotels and an upscale shopping district along Corso Vittorio Colonna, while Ischia Ponte contains the bulk of the town's attractions. These include a charming main street along the harbour, perfect for the *passeggiata* (evening stroll), the 16th–17th-century Roman-style Pilastri aqueduct and, just across a 15th-century causeway, the medieval Castello Aragonese.

②

Castello Aragonese

Ⓠ Ischia Ponte **Ⓣ 9am–sunset daily** **Ⓦ castello-aragoneseischia.com**

This island castle is an iconic landmark, towering over the pretty bay of Cartaromana. The fortress traces its history back to the Greeks, although many others have left their mark, including the Bourbon kings who used it as a prison. Connected to Ischia Ponte by a bridge, within the fortified walls are gardens, frescoed catacombs and cathedrals. Many architectural styles are represented, from the Angevin cathedral of the Assunta to the hexagonal church of San Pietro a Pantaniello.

③

Forio

Ⓠ 10 km (6 miles) W of Ischia Town

Set on the west coast of Ischia, Forio is the island's second largest town, known for its tropical gardens and iconic church, the Santa Maria del Soccorso. The English composer Sir William Walton lived to the north of the town at the **Giardini la Mortella** (Mortella Gardens). The lush gardens contain a dazzling array of exotic flora. Nearby, there are a number of excellent thermal spa options.

Did You Know?

Forio's many towers, such as the Torre Torrone, were built to defend the city against pirates.

Giardini la Mortella

🅐 Via F Calise 39 🕒 Apr-Nov: 9am-2 hrs before sunset Tue, Thu, Sat & Sun

④
Sant'Angelo

🅐 16 km (10 miles) SW of Ischia Town

Sant'Angelo's small marina and pleasantly pedestrianized centre spread beneath vertical cliffs. Originally a fishing village, it is now known for its thermal parks and coastal views. Several beaches in both directions offer pretty views of the town, the most famous among them being Maronti beach, with access along a steep and winding road from Sant'Angelo. From here, as well as the town, taxi boats can be hired to take visitors to coves otherwise inaccessible by land. Between Maronti and Sant'-Angelo is a smaller beach, Le Fumarole, featuring volcanic steam jets that warm the sand.

⑤
Casamicciola Terme

🅐 6 km (4 miles) NW of Ischia Town 🚌🚢 From Naples, Pozzuoli & Procida

The spa town of Casamicciola Terme has attracted visitors since Roman times. While an earthquake in 1883 caused considerable damage to the town, it has retained some of its Art Nouveau architecture, and today the atmosphere is decidedly chic, with plenty of glamorous villas, gardens and yachts around the marina. The town's adjacent port connects it to Naples and Pozzuoli.

⑥
Lacco Ameno

🅐 7 km (4 miles) NW of Ischia Town

The smallest of Ischia's main towns, Lacco Ameno has a charming main square named after the town's patron saint, Santa Restituta. There are several good beaches and thermal spas around the town, most notably San Montano beach, with shallow water in a protected cove. Near the beach is the **Negombo Giardini Termali** (Negombo Thermal Gardens). Off the main pier from the centre of town is the Fungo di Lacco Ameno, a prominent mushroom-shaped rock that reportedly marks where Greek colonists first landed. The town has several museums, including the **Museo di Pithecusae**, where items from the Greek settlement are displayed, and the **Museo di Santa Restituta**, which illustrates island life as it was in Greek and Roman times.

Negombo Giardini Termali

🅐 San Montano Bay 🕒 Apr-mid-Oct: 8:30am-7pm daily

Museo di Pithecusae

🅐 Corso A Rizzoli 📞 081 996 103 🕒 9am-6:30pm Tue-Sun

Museo di Santa Restituta

🅐 Piazza Santa Restituta 🕒 Summer: 9:30am-12:30pm & 5-7pm daily; winter: 9:30am-12:30pm & 4-6pm daily 🚫 Sun afternoon

---

THERMAL SPAS

Geothermal energy fuels Ischia's many hot springs. These springs have attracted celebrities such as Elizabeth Taylor, but today, spas like Poseidon (*www. giardiniposeidonterme. com*) and Casamicciola are open to the public without Hollywood-style fees. Alternating dips between hot and cool pools - a practice enjoyed by the ancient Greeks - can be therapeutic, if not relaxing.

10

PROCIDA

A3 From Naples & Pozzuoli **i** Pro Loco, Piazza S Antonio 6; www.prolocodiprocida.it

Much smaller than Capri and Ischia and less affected by tourism, the third island in the Bay of Naples is a favourite with those who love the simplicity and traditions of the local culture. This is the enchanting world that author Elsa Morante, recollecting her many visits here, evoked in *L'isola di Arturo* (Arthur's Island), her 1957 novel about a young motherless boy growing up on Procida.

PICTURE PERFECT
Pigment of Your Imagination

Fight gravity up Salita Castello to the Palazzo d'Avalos, set on Terra Murata, the highest point on Procida. From outside this old prison, you can look down on the fishing village of Marina Corricella below. If the light is right, the pastel-shaded houses make a vibrant image.

The multicoloured houses built against tufa rock make Procida's architecture one of the most charming in the region. Its unique vaulted buildings were originally built as winter boat shelters and later enlarged, acquiring long external staircases, loggias, terraces and arches that frame the doors and windows. Spend a morning exploring these buildings in Marina Grande and at the small, popular Chiaiolella port on the other side of the island.

The Abbazia di San Michele Arcangelo, dominating the majestic walled citadel on Terra Murata, dates back to 1026, although it has since been rebuilt. A Benedictine abbey originally dedicated to St Angelo, it was named after St Michael the Archangel in the 15th century. Tours are offered daily between Easter and December. At the foot of Terra Murata,

delightful Marina Corricella has remained virtually untouched by time. With its colourful houses, steep hidden stairways and winding alleys, the village is a lovely place to explore.

Alongside its medieval buildings, quiet groves of lemon trees, and appealing little villages clinging to the rocks, Procida has a magnificent coast with splendid beaches, including Ciraccio in the west, Chiaiolella in the southeast, and, in the northwest, Pozzo Vecchio, made famous by the 1994 movie *Il Postino*, which was filmed there.

Deeply rooted local traditions are evident in Procida's various festivals, including the Good Friday procession that descends from Terra Murata to Marina Grande and the processions held by the abbey in May and September in honour of St Michael.

1 On Good Friday, a church procession makes its way through the island.

2 The strategically located promontory of Terra Murata was the first inhabited part of the island, with imposing defensive walls and towers to protect against pirate raids.

3 Marina Sancio Cattolico, more commonly known as Marina Grande, is the island's main port and has a range of shops and cafés.

Did You Know?

The houses were said to be different colours so that fishermen could spot their homes from sea.

↑ The array of brightly painted houses lining Marina Corricella

❶ ⟨🗡⟩ ⟨M3⟩

ROYAL PALACE
OF CASERTA

🔺C1 🏠Via Douhet 22 🕒Apartments: 8:30am–7:30pm Wed–Mon; park: 8:30am–
1 hr before sunset Wed–Mon 🌐reggiadicaserta.beniculturali.it

With its sweeping carved staircases and monumental frescoed rooms, this
royal palace outshines most of its European counterparts. As one of the world's
largest royal residences and a UNESCO World Heritage Site, it demands a visit
from all who pass through Naples to experience its grandeur inside and out.

In his memoirs, the architect Luigi Vanvitelli
says it was the king who designed the Royal
Palace. This may have been adulation, or
perhaps Charles of Bourbon knew what he
wanted – to emulate his favourite models, the
Buen Retiro in Madrid and Versailles in France.
Vanvitelli drew inspiration from the former
for this quadrangular, 1,200-room structure,
which was completed only in 1845, 72 years
after his death. The lower ground floor holds
a museum, with photos and exhibits relating
to the palace and Caserta culture. The ground
floor also houses the glittering Court Theatre.
On the upper floor, the Halberdiers Hall, its
ceiling adorned with Domenico Mondo's fresco
The Triumph of the Bourbon Arms (1785), connects the vestibule and the 18th-century Royal
Apartments. The 19th-century Throne Room,
decorated in 1844–5, was once filled with elegant French furniture, while in the Art Gallery
you can see a portrait of Queen Maria Carolina.

Vanvitelli also designed the palace's park,
one of the last examples of a formal Baroque
garden. The 3-km- (2-mile-) long central canal
descends several levels punctuated by ornamented pools and fountains, creating a remarkable effect. The play of flowing water culminates
in the Grande Cascata, almost 80 m (260 ft)
high, also known as the Fountain of Diana and
Actaeon. Next to this is the informal English
Garden, perhaps the first of its kind in Italy.
It was suggested to Maria Carolina by Lord
Hamilton, the British ambassador; landscaping
was begun by Luigi's son Carlo in 1786.

Did You Know?

The rear of the Court
Theatre's stage could
be opened to the air,
creating a natural
backdrop.

1 The grand staircase is set to one side so that it doesn't ruin the park view from the main doorway.

2 The Baroque Palatine Chapel shimmers in gold.

3 The Fountain of Diana and Actaeon is located beside a cascading waterfall in the park.

Pools, fountains and waterfalls ↓ cutting through the park laid out in front of the Royal Palace of Caserta

←
A narrow street in the well-preserved medieval town of Caserta Vecchia

EXPERIENCE MORE

12

Caserta Vecchia

🅰C1 🏠45 km (29 miles) N of Naples 🚆Caserta 🚌ATC 🅸Palazzo Reale; www.casertavecchia.net

The fascination of Caserta Vecchia, which is set 10 km (6 miles) along a winding road northeast of the modern agricultural town of Caserta, does not lie in individual monuments but in the town itself, which has a remarkably well-preserved medieval character. This small hilltop town was probably founded by the Lombards in the 8th century, before coming under Norman rule. When Charles III built his new palace (p194), activity in this lively community moved into the new town in the plains. Today, life in Caserta Vecchia still revolves around the main square, where the **Duomo di San Michele Arcangelo** stands.

The construction of the cathedral was completed in 1153. Its faded yellow and grey tufa façade is simple, with three marble portals. Columns on the triangular tympanum above the middle portal are supported by lions. The 14th-century dome has the interlaced Arabic arches often seen on Romanesque buildings in southern Italy. The interior of the church is lined with irregular columns and stunning majolica tiles. A starlit sky is represented in the dome, with grey stone for the night and white marble stars. To the right of the cathedral stands the dark

stone bell tower, added a century later, with an archway over the road.

Near the cathedral is the Gothic church of Annunziata, which has a marble portal opening onto a 17th-century portico. On the eastern side of the village are the ruins of a 13th-century castle, which is dominated by a towering 30-m (98-ft) turret.

Duomo di San Michele Arcangelo

🏠Piazza del Vescovado 1 📞0823 371318 🕐9am–1pm & 3:30–6pm daily (to 10:30pm in summer)

13

Ponti della Valle

🅰C1 🏠21 km (13 miles) SE of Caserta Vecchia

This section of the Caroline Aqueduct, bridging the Valle di Maddaloni, is a UNESCO World Heritage Site. Modelled on ancient Roman aqueducts, the 529-m- (1,735-ft-) long section consists of three imposing rows of arches. It was built between 1753 and 1762 by Luigi Vanvitelli, technical adviser at the Vatican, to bring water to the Royal Palace at Caserta (p194).

14

Basilica Benedettina di San Michele Arcangelo

🅰B1 🏠Via Luigi Baia, 18 km (11 miles) NW of Caserta Vecchia 📞0823 32 24 93 🕐9am–5pm Mon–Fri, 9am–12:30pm & 3–6pm Sat & Sun by appt

This small Romanesque church was originally built on the ruins of an ancient temple

> The interior of the Duomo is lined with stunning majolica tiles. A starlit sky is represented in the dome, with grey stone for the night and white marble stars.

to Diana, Roman goddess of the forest, and reconstructed in 1073. Many features of the temple were incorporated into the church, such as the delicate Corinthian columns on the portico and the church floor. Inside, a cycle of 11th-century frescoes, painted in Byzantine style by artists of the School of Montecassino, depict stories from the Bible.

15

Belvedere Reale di San Leucio

🄰C1 🄰10 km (6 miles) NW of Caserta Vecchia 🄲9:30am-6pm Wed-Mon by appt; three tours each on Sat & Sun 🄦sanleucio.it

This area near Caserta was purchased by Charles III in 1750. Five years later, his son Ferdinand IV built a royal lodge here, the Casino di Belvedere. In 1789, Ferdinand ordered an existing building be made into a silk factory to be used by the local artisans. All that remains of the ambitious project are the workmen's dwellings and the royal lodge, which was also the residence of the managers of the silk factory.

16

Anfiteatro Campano

🄰B1 🄰Santa Maria Capua Vetere, 17 km (10 miles) W of Caserta Vecchia 🄲0823 79 88 64 🄲9am-1 hr before sunset Tue-Sun

The amphitheatre at Santa Maria Capua Vetere dates from the 1st century BC. Second in size only to the Colosseum in Rome, it once had four storeys as well as a warren of subterranean passageways where wild animals were kept in cages. Today, a museum at the site houses artifacts and a life-size reproduction of the gladiatorial fights. A short drive from the amphitheatre is an underground sanctuary dedicated to the god Mithras. It features a 1st-century BC fresco of Mithras slaying a bull.

> **THE IDEAL VILLAGE OF SAN LEUCIO**
>
> San Leucio was founded in 1789 by Ferdinand IV as a village for workers at the local silk factory. The aim of this social experiment was to create a community dedicated to the pursuit of happiness instead of personal profit. The community had its own laws, attributed to the king but in fact written by musicologist and scholar Antonio Planelli. Based on reason and morality, these included compulsory education; equal inheritance rights for men and women (although all members did have to marry within the community); the abolition of dowry; and medical assistance for the aged and disabled. The 1799 revolution brought about the end of the most ambitious project of the founders, the creation of a model city, Ferdinandopoli, although the city plans survive. San Leucio is famous for its silk manufacture and the upscale articles produced here are still very much in demand.

↓ The ruins of the Roman amphitheatre at Santa Maria Capua Vetere

EAT

Trattoria da Rita

Honest home cooking at this buzzing local favourite.

B2 Via Miliscola 402, Pozzuoli 081 866 52 71 Wed

€€€

Baia Marinella

An upscale eatery with sweeping sea views and first-rate seafood.

B2 Via Napoli 4, Pozzuoli baia marinella.it

€€€

17

Pozzuoli

B2 20 km (12 miles) W of Naples Cumana: Pozzuoli M Pozzuoli Garibaldi: M1B i Via G Matteotti 1/A; www. infocampiflegrei.it

Around the 7th century BC, the Greek colony of Dicearchia was founded on this site overlooking the port. By 194 BC Roman Puteoli was a flourishing trade centre with luxurious villas. The town later became the Rione Terra quarter.

Evacuated in 1970 due to volcanic activity and neglected for decades, the area has since received a great deal of archaeological attention, most notably in the Roman temple complex under **La Cattedrale San Procolo Martire**.

The **Anfiteatro Flavio**, the third-largest amphitheatre of the Roman world, had a seating capacity of 40,000. The underground area housed caged animals, as well as a sophisticated drainage system to collect rainwater.

The so-called **Temple of Serapis** (2nd century AD), actually the *macellum*, or food market, is all that remains of the ancient port district. At some point in its history the temple was under the sea, as the building is covered with traces of sea molluscs.

A dormant volcano, the **Solfatara** features a mud lake bubbling at 160° C (320° F) and two fumaroles. Vulcan, the Roman god of fire, was thought to have his workshop here, and the Solfatara is also believed to have inspired Virgil's description of the underworld in the *Aeneid*. The Romans harnessed the therapeutic waters of this area and created mineral baths. Today hi-tech equipment monitors the earth's crust.

↑ The remains of a Roman temple in Pozzuoli, which is an area of great archaeological interest

La Cattedrale San Procolo Martire

Largo Sedile di Porto Sat & Sun cattedrale pozzuoli.it

Anfiteatro Flavio

Corso Terracciano 75 848 800 288 07 9am–1 hr before sunset Wed–Mon

Temple of Serapis

Piazza Serapide

Solfatara

Via Solfatara 161 Temporarily closed, check website before visiting volcanosolfatara.it

---

18

Baia

B3 23 km (14 miles) W of Naples Cumana: Lucrino, Fusaro

On the coast between Pozzuoli and Capo Miseno, Baia has sumptuous Roman villas with terraces overlooking the sea, famous therapeutic springs and an Aragonese castle, now an archaeological museum.

In 1794 Carlo Vanvitelli built the **Casina Vanvitelliana del Fusaro**, a hunting lodge for Ferdinand IV on an island in Lake Fusaro. This is the only non-volcanic lake in the area.

The Castello di Baia was once an Aragonese fortress. It was totally rebuilt in the 1600s and now houses the **Museo Archeologico dei Campi Flegrei**, with finds from the Phlegraean Fields. Also on display are Roman plaster casts of Greek statues found in Baia. From the northwest tower you can see the rebuilt Sacello degli Augustali, used for worship of the emperor and found near Miseno's Forum.

Casina Vanvitelliana del Fusaro

Via Fusaro 162 Cumana: Fusaro Summer: 10am–8pm Sat & Sun parco vanvitelliano.it

→ People kayaking past the Casina Vanvitelliana del Fusaro in Baia

Museo Archeologico dei Campi Flegrei

⊗ 🏠 Via Castello 39 📞 081 523 37 97 🚉 Cumana: Fusaro ⏰ May-Sep: 9am-7pm Tue-Sun; Oct-Apr: 9am-2:30pm Tue-Sun

---

⑲

Bacoli

🅰 B3 🏠 27 km (17 miles) SW of Naples 🚉 Cumana: Lucrino, Fusaro

Bacoli lies along the coast and runs into the modern town of Miseno, which developed over the site of the Roman town of Bauli. The port was planned so as to avoid silting from volcanic movement, and replaced Porto Giulio, the headquarters of the Roman navy. The Arco Felice, which in the 1st century AD was the gateway to Cumae (p200), stands on the peninsula protecting the Bay of Pozzuoli. Beaches and clubs make this area a summer favourite.

The large domes at the **Parco Archeologio di Baia** are the remains of a spa that included baths named after Venus and Mercury and the so-called Temple of Diana.

This monumental complex was built from the late 2nd century to the early 1st century BC, over two levels, with terraced land descending to the sea. Some of the park lies underwater, but guided dives are available. The site is now used to exhibit finds from the Phlegraean Fields area.

Nearby, the **Piscina Mirabilis** is an enormous reservoir, divided into five sections supported by pillars. It collected water from the River Serino via the Roman aqueduct to supply to the fleet at Miseno.

A windy, narrow stretch of road leads through a dark tunnel to the dramatic peak of Capo Miseno. Pliny the Younger watched the Vesuvius eruption from this hill. This is also where the Roman Imperial Navy had its headquarters. Visitors can park here and hike up a trail leading to some stunning views of Naples.

Parco Archeologico di Baia

⊗ 🏠 Via Sella di Baia 22 📞 081 868 75 92 🚉 Cumana: Fusaro ⏰ 9am-1 hr before sunset Tue-Sun

Piscina Mirabilis

🏠 Via Piscina Mirabile 63 📞 081 523 31 99 ⏰ Noon-7pm Mon-Sat, 10:30am-7pm Sun (call ahead for appt)

> ### THE PHLEGRAEAN FIELDS
>
> The wide arc of land around the bay of Pozzuoli has been known for centuries as the Campi Flegrei, or "burning fields", because of its constant volcanic activity. Mud still bubbles from the clay bed of the Solfatara and in places the ground is still hot. Over time some of the Phlegraean craters have become lakes. Lake Averno, once thought to be the entrance to hell, owes its name (a-ornon in Greek: "without birds") to the once-suffocating vapours that have been harnessed medicinally. Volcanic activity in the fields even created the Monte Nuovo (p201), which claims the unusual title of Europe's youngest mountain. Visitors can explore the park, although they should make sure to approach it with appropriate caution.

20

Cumae

🅰A2 🏠23 km (14 miles) W of Naples 🚇Cumana: Fusaro 🚌Autobus EAV: from Piazza Garibaldi, from Fusaro (10 mins to Cumae)

Founded in the 8th century BC, probably by Greeks stationed on Ischia, Cumae is one of the oldest colonies of Magna Graecia. A powerful port for centuries, Cumae resisted the Etruscans but succumbed to the Romans in the 3rd century BC. A village grew up over the ruins of the upper city in the 5th–6th centuries but was utterly destroyed by the Arab pirates in 915, and the ancient settlement has not yet been completely excavated.

The best known areas of this **Archaeological Park** are the acropolis on the rise to the northwest and the necropolis on the plain. The acropolis walls, partly rebuilt, and two huge temples are well preserved. The Temple of Apollo lies on the lower terrace, the Temple of Jupiter on the upper one; both were rebuilt in the age of Augustus and the pre-Christian era. Most of the finds from the Temple of Apollo date from the Roman era, when a terrace overlooking the city was added. In the early Christian period the temple was turned into a basilica and burial pits were hewn out of the ancient foundations. The Temple of Jupiter, meanwhile, is an ancient sanctuary that became an early Christian church, with the remains of the altar and baptistry still visible.

At the foot of the acropolis is the entrance to the so-called Sibyl's Cave. According to myth, this was the place to find the Cumaean Sibyl, the oracle consulted by Aeneas. The tufa passageway, trapezoid in section, is illuminated by narrow fissures and ends in a vaulted chamber. Despite its undoubted fascination, there is no proof of the tunnel ever having had a religious function. It seems more likely that the tunnel was part of a network of underground routes used for military purposes. The complex system includes the Roman crypt and the Grotto of Cocceius, which connected Cumae to Lake Averno. The crypt has only one part that is visible; it is the last stretch of a long tunnel that begins at Via Sacra and goes through the hill of Cumae.

The site's lower city, inhabited at a later period, is still being excavated and studied. There is a forum, baths and an amphitheatre. There are also the remains of different epochs: the Samnite-

THE SIBYL OF CUMAE

Something of a rock star in her day, Sibyl of Cumae was one of ten sibyls - priestesses at oracles and temples working as prophetesses. At Apollo's temple in Cumae, this old woman shared her wisdom with those who came seeking it. Her greatest claim to fame, however, was appearing in Virgil's *Aeneid*. In the story, she helps the protagonist find his way to the underworld, the entrance of which was nearby, to meet his dead father.

Did You Know?

Greek geographer Strabo thought Cumae was named for the *kumata* or high waves on its beach.

age forum conceals the more ancient agora, or Greek city centre. A sanctuary dedicated to the Egyptian goddess Isis – revered throughout the Roman empire – has also been discovered in the port area; it had been destroyed with the rise of Christianity.

Archaeological Park
🏛 Via Acropoli 📞 081 804 04 30 🕒 9am–sunset Tue–Sun

㉑

Oasi Naturalistica di Montenuovo

🅰 B2 📍 21 km (13 miles) W of Naples 📞 081 804 14 62 🕒 9am–1 hr before sunset

After a 1538 eruption in the Phlegraean Fields supervolcano destroyed the village of Tripergole, a new mountain was left behind: Monte Nuovo. The slopes of Europe's youngest mountain were eventually covered in flora and fauna and, today, the area is a designated natural reserve that welcomes visitors looking for a break from urban life. There are plenty of paths across the site, all of which are well signposted, and breath-taking views on each side. A hike up the hill reveals fumaroles where hot sulphurous gas escapes the ground; medieval relics from nearly 500 years ago can also be seen. The hike from the crater to the saddle gets a little bit higher each year since, due to ongoing volcanic activity in the area, the mountain is still growing. Hikes are best undertaken on days with good visibility, and all visitors are advised to wear sturdy footwear for walking.

㉒

Riserva Naturale Cratere Degli Astroni

🅰 B2 📍 16 km (10 miles) W of Naples 🕒 Hours vary, check website 🌐 cratere degliastroni.org

Located in one of the 30 craters of the Phlegraean Fields, this natural reserve includes some 15 km (9 miles) of trails and pathways. This is a haven for wildlife, especially birds, and it's not unusual to spot owls, buzzards and falcons soaring overhead. The diversity of wildlife in the area made it a favourite hunting location for Alfonso I of Aragon, and later – after a brief period of ownership by the Jesuits – for the Bourbon royalty. The nature reserve officially opened to the public in 1992, and the site's educational centre encourages everyone to learn about the area's biodiversity. Visitors can explore the various themed footpaths through the forests inside this extinct volcano.

STAY

Resort Cala Moresca
Take a break from the city in this hotel and spa, which offers a range of rooms with unbeatable sea views.

🅰 B2 🏠 Via Tripergola 62, Pozzuoli 🌐 calamoresca.it

€€€

The ruins of the Temple of Jupiter at Cumae's ↓ Archaeological Park

㉓

Portici and the Ville Vesuviane

🅰C2 🅐11 km (7 miles) E of Naples 🅵🅂 🅷Circumvesuviana: Via Libertà, Bellavista, Miglio d'Oro 🚌 🕒10am-1pm Tue-Sun (also 3-8pm in spring & summer) 🛈 Villa Campolieto, Corso Resina 283, Ercolano; www.villevesuviane.net

The coast east of the city, up to the foot of Mount Vesuvius, has always been dotted with rural estates, owned by the nobility but used for agriculture as much as rural retreats. The luxurious villas now known as the Ville Vesuviane were built in the early 1700s, when the value of land in the area rose due to the interest in local archaeological excavations. A few decades later, after the building of the Royal Palace at Portici, these villas grew in number, and the road between Resina and Torre del Greco became known as the Miglio d'Oro, or Golden Mile.

The presence of the Bourbon palace and the well-located villas made this area a popular resort among the aristocracy.

There are 122 villas in all, but only a few can be visited. The **Reggia di Portici** (Royal Palace) was built between 1738 and 1742 in the centre of a splendid park at the foothills of Vesuvius and overlooking the sea. On the site are botanical gardens and the Herculanense Museum, which houses copies of sculptures found in Herculaneum; the originals are in the museum at Capodimonte (p114). The palace did not have a mooring, so the sovereigns bought the Villa d'Elboeuf, which was designed by Ferdinando Sanfelice, for this purpose. In 1873, the palace and its park became the home of the Faculty of Agriculture of the University of Naples.

Also worth a visit is nearby **Villa Campolieto**. Built in 1755–75 first by architect Mario Gioffredo and then by architect Luigi Vanvitelli, this is the only Vesuvian villa that

> The luxurious villas now known as the Ville Vesuviane were built in the early 1700s, when the value of land in the area rose due to the interest in local archaeological excavations.

DRINK

Baraonda Café
Come here to sit by the harbour, sip an aperitivo, and watch the sun set.

🅰C3 🅐Via Calastro 15, Torre del Greco
📞081 341 35 33

Fuori Bottega
Popular with locals, this hip little bar offers flaming shots and a fabulous cocktail menu.

🅰C3 🅐Corso Umberto I 202, Torre Annunziata
📞342 158 75 08

has been completely restored. Vanvitelli's elegant portico hosts the Festival delle Ville Vesuviane each summer, and the villa stages events.

Villa Favorita, set in an extensive park, was designed by Ferdinando Fuga in 1768 as a royal residence. Ferdinand IV decorated it with paintings, silk from San Leucio (p197) and a mosaic removed from the Villa Jovis (p189) in Capri.

Built in the first half of the 18th century, **Villa Ruggiero** has been owned by the family of the same name since 1863. It was occupied all year round, not just in the summer, as the rich agricultural land shows.

Reggia di Portici
♿♿ 🅐Via Università 100, Portici 🕒3-6:30pm Thu, 9:30am-6:30pm Fri-Sun
🅦centromusa.it

Villa Campolieto
♿ 🅐Corso Resina 283, Ercolano 📞081 732 21 34
🕒10am-1pm Tue-Sun

←

The richly decorated interior of Villa Campolieto, a restored 18th-century villa

→ Boats moored in the harbour by Torre del Greco at sunset

Villa Favorita

🏠 Corso Resina 291, Ercolano 📞 081 739 39 61 🕐 10am–1pm Tue–Sun (park only)

Villa Ruggiero

🏠 Via Alessandro Rossi 40, Ercolano 📞 081 732 21 34 🕐 10am–1pm Tue–Sun

---

㉔

Torre Annunziata

🅰 C3 🏠 22 km (14 miles) SE of Naples 🚆 🚉 Circumvesuviana: Torre Annunziata 🛈 Via Sepolcri 16; 081 862 31 63

This town was built over the ruins of Oplontis, destroyed in the AD 79 Vesuvius eruption. Its name comes from a watchtower *(torre)*, built to warn of Arab pirate raids, and a chapel consecrated to the Annunziata (the Virgin Mary), around which the town grew.

In the late 1700s and early 1800s Torre Annunziata became a centre for pasta production, and there are still many factories in the town today. Towards the sea are the spas, Terme Vesuviane Nunziante, named after the general who discovered the ruins of a Roman baths complex here in 1831.

The site of the **Oplontis Excavations** includes the villas of Craxus and Poppaea, which were buried during the AD 79 eruption. Brought to light in 1964, the complex reflects the owners' elegant taste. As well as gardens and porticoes, the house's baths can also be seen, complete with *calidarium* (hot room) and *tepidarium* (warm room), and a swimming pool. Also interesting are the ancient wall paintings, which depict still lifes or scenes combining architecture and figures.

Oplontis Excavations

♿ 🏠 Via Sepolcri 1 🕐 Apr–Oct: 8:30am–7:30pm daily; Nov–Mar: 8:30am–5pm daily 🚫 1 Jan, 1 May, 25 Dec 🌐 pompeiisites.org

---

㉕

Torre del Greco

🅰 C3 🏠 15 km (9 miles) SE of Naples 🚆 🚉 Circumvesuviana: Torre del Greco 🛈 Via Procida 2a; 081 881 46 76

Though its name derives from the local vineyards that produce wine from a grape variety called Greco, Torre del Greco is mainly known for its fine coral manufacture. The old town lines the coast; don't miss Palazzo Vallelonga in Via Vittorio Emanuele and the Camaldoli alla Torre monastery, both 18th-century buildings. The poet Giacomo Leopardi lived in the Villa delle Ginestre and wrote his last poems there, including *La Ginestra (The Broom)*.

> **RED GOLD**
>
> By the 15th century the main trade in Torre del Greco was coral fishing. The first factories were established during the 1800s; the Bourbon rulers then set up their own. Designs were initially inspired by Classical models, and later by Art Nouveau. As well as coral, there are mother-of-pearl, turtle shell and ivory pieces. The coralline collection boats have been modernized and re-equipped, but today most of the raw material comes from Japan. Admirers of "red gold" can visit the numerous workshops in town or the Coral Museum *(Piazza Palomba 6; open 9am–1pm Mon–Sat)*.

NEED TO KNOW

BEFORE
YOU GO

Forward planning is essential to any successful trip. Be prepared for all eventualities by considering the following points before you travel.

AT A GLANCE

CURRENCY
Euro

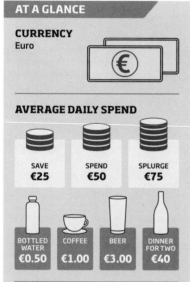

AVERAGE DAILY SPEND

SAVE	SPEND	SPLURGE
€25	**€50**	**€75**

BOTTLED WATER	COFFEE	BEER	DINNER FOR TWO
€0.50	**€1.00**	**€3.00**	**€40**

ESSENTIAL PHRASES

Hello	Buon giorno
Goodbye	Arrivederci
Please	Per favore
Thank you	Grazie
Do you speak English?	Parla inglese?
I don't understand	Non capisco

ELECTRICITY SUPPLY

Power sockets are type F and L, fitting two- and three-pronged plugs. Standard voltage is 220–230 volts.

Passports and Visas

EU nationals and citizens of the UK, US, Canada, Australia and New Zealand do not need visas for tourist visits of up to three months. Check the **Ministry of Foreign Affairs** or **Polizia di Stato** websites, or contact the nearest Italian embassy.
Ministry of Foreign Affairs
W esteri.it
Polizia di Stato
W poliziadistato.it

Travel Safety Advice

Visitors can get up-to-date travel safety information from the **UK Foreign and Commonwealth Office**, the **US Department of State** and the **Australian Department of Foreign Affairs and Trade**.
Australia
W smartraveller.gov.au
UK
W gov.uk/foreign-travel-advice
US
W travel.state.gov

Customs Information

An individual is permitted to carry the following within the EU for personal use:
Tobacco products 800 cigarettes, 400 cigarillos, 200 cigars or 1 kg of smoking tobacco.
Alcohol 10 litres of alcoholic beverages above 22 per cent strength, 20 litres of alcoholic beverages below 22 per cent strength, 90 litres of wine (60 litres of which can be sparkling wine) and 110 litres of beer.
Cash If you plan to enter or leave the EU with €10,000 or more in cash (or equivalent in other currencies) you must declare it to the customs authorities prior to departure.
Limits vary if travelling outside the EU, so always check restrictions before travelling.

Insurance

It is wise to take out an insurance policy covering theft, loss of belongings, medical problems,

cancellations and delays. EU and Australian citizens are eligible for free emergency medical care if they have a valid **EHIC** (European Health Insurance Card) or **Medicare** card respectively.

EHIC
W gov.uk/european-health-insurance-card

Medicare
W humanservices.gov.au/individuals/medicare

Vaccinations

No vaccinations are needed for Italy, but mosquito repellent is useful in summer.

Money

Goods and services are cheaper in Naples than in the Amalfi Coast and the islands. Most establishments accept major credit, debit and pre-paid currency cards, but carry cash for smaller items and street markets. Minimum amounts are often needed to use cards without extraneous fees. ATMs *(bancomat)* are available outside most banks, which are plentiful in Naples although less so in smaller villages.

Booking Accommodation

Naples and and the Amalfi Coast offer a huge range of accommodation, from farm stays *(agriturismi)* to luxury hotels. In the summer accommodation fills up quickly, and prices are often inflated, so book in advance. Hotels will often charge an additional city tax on top of the room price, even if it is a private rental on Airbnb. By law, hotels are required to register guests at police headquarters and issue a receipt of payment *(ricevuta fiscale)*, which you must keep until you leave Italy.

Travellers with Specific Needs

Naples and the Amalfi Coast can be a challenge for travellers with specific needs. Cobbled streets, steep staircases and a lack of elevators are all common hurdles. Renting a car and planning in advance will help, but most attractions and establishments do not offer easy access. The islands tend to be a bit easier to navigate than the city, though transport should be organized in advance. **Sage Traveling** and **WheelchairTraveling** are useful resources.

Sage Traveling
W www.sagetraveling.com/naples-accessible-travel

WheelchairTraveling
W wheelchairtraveling.com/naples-italy-wheelchair-accessible-travel-tips/

Language

While Neapolitans speak Italian, the local dialect will seem unfamiliar even to native speakers of the language. Other dialects in the region and around the islands further complicate communication. Do not expect English in every establishment, although tourist sights and ticket offices are generally staffed by those who can manage basic communication in English.

Closures

Lunchtime Businesses may be closed for a few hours in the afternoon.

Monday Several museums and cafés are closed on Monday, so always check first.

Sunday Shops and restaurants are generally open along Via Toledo and other major commercial areas, but public transport has reduced services. Churches and cathedrals forbid tourists from visiting during Mass.

Public holidays Most small businesses and some restaurants either close early or for the entire day; transport services are reduced.

PUBLIC HOLIDAYS

1 Jan	New Year's Day
6 Jan	Epiphany
Early Apr	Easter Sunday
Early Apr	Easter Monday
25 Apr	Liberation Day
1 May	Labour Day
2 Jun	Republic Day
15 Aug	Ferragosto
1 Nov	All Saints' Day
8 Dec	Feast of the Immaculate Conception
25 Dec	Christmas Day
26 Dec	St Stephen's Day

GETTING
AROUND

Whether you are visiting for a short city break or rural country retreat, discover how best to reach your destination and travel like a pro.

AT A GLANCE

PUBLIC TRANSPORT COSTS

NAPLES

€1.50

Single journey
Naples Metro

CIRCUMVESUVIANA

€4.00

Single journey
Naples to Sorrento

AMALFI COAST

€10.00

24 hours unlimited
SITA bus trips

TOP TIP
Be sure to validate your bus or train ticket at the machine before you travel.

SPEED LIMIT

MOTORWAY

130 km/h
(80 mph)

DUAL CARRIAGEWAY

110 km/h
(68 mph)

SECONDARY ROAD

90 km/h
(56 mph)

URBAN AREA

50 km/h
(30 mph)

Arriving by Air

Naples International Airport is the main airport for flights to Naples, the Amalfi Coast and the general Campania region. Non-stop service from major hubs like London and New York are available, while many more airlines offer a layover in Rome first. European budget airlines fly to Naples at very reasonable prices. In general, the airport is easy to navigate, although it gets busy in the summer months with the inflow of high-season travellers. For outbound travellers, there are plenty of shopping and dining facilities once through security at the terminal.

There is no train or metro the airport, which is only 5 km (3 miles) from the city centre. The cheapest and easiest option to get to town is the Alibus service operating between the airport and downtown Naples, with stops at the Naples railway station and the port for ferries to the islands. These buses are usually parked a block or two past the airport's exit; walk through the parking lots to where the buses are stationed kerbside. Tickets are available on board, but be sure to have cash handy, preferably coins or small bills. Taxis are also available, but agree on the fixed rate before committing to a drive to avoid any surprises.

Naples International Airport
W aeroportodinapoli.it/en

Train Travel

International Train Travel
Regular high-speed international trains (both direct and with changes) link Naples to several towns and cities across Europe. These include London, Paris, Nice, Berlin, Munich, Amsterdam, Vienna, Lisbon, Geneva, Brussels, Barcelona, Budapest, Warsaw and Ljubljana. **Eurail** and **Interrail** sell passes (to European non-residents and residents respectively) for international trips lasting from five days up to three months. Journeys should be reserved in advance.

Eurail
W eurail.com
Interrail
W interrail.eu

TRAVEL BETWEEN KEY DESTINATIONS

From	To	Distance	Transport	Time	Price
Naples airport	Railway station	5 km (3 miles)	Alibus	20 mins	€5
Naples airport	Railway station	5 km (3 miles)	Taxi	15 mins	from €15
Naples	Sorrento	47 km (29 miles)	Train	45–75 mins	€4
Naples	Sorrento	47 km (29 miles)	Ferry	35–55 mins	€18.50–19.50
Naples	Capri	45 km (28 miles)	Ferry	45 mins	€28.50
Naples	Procida	35 km (22 miles)	Ferry	40 mins	from €21.50
Naples	Ischia	56 km (35 miles)	Ferry	90 mins	from €16.50
Sorrento	Positano	16 km (10 miles)	SITA bus	50 mins	€10
Sorrento	Praiano	23 km (14 miles)	SITA bus	70 mins	€10
Sorrento	Amalfi	31 km (19 miles)	SITA bus	110 mins	€10
Sorrento	Ravello	38 km (24 miles)	SITA bus	120 mins	€10
Sorrento	Salerno	56 km (35 miles)	SITA bus	120 mins	€10

RAILWAY CONNECTIONS AROUND NAPLES

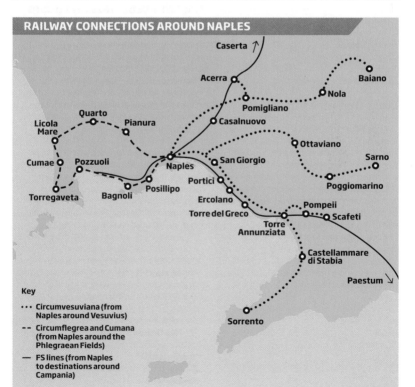

Key

··· Circumvesuviana (from Naples around Vesuvius)

–– Circumflegrea and Cumana (from Naples around the Phlegraean Fields)

— FS lines (from Naples to destinations around Campania)

Domestic Train Travel

Naples is also well connected to other main towns and cities within Italy. Both **Trenitalia**, the main train operator within Italy, and **Italo Treno** (NTV) offer a high-speed service between major railway stations throughout the country. Making reservations for these services is essential and tickets are booked up quickly, so try to buy as far ahead as possible. Trips usually require a change in Rome, which is under 90 minutes away by high-speed train from the main railway station in Naples, **Napoli Centrale**.

Most towns and sights along the Amalfi Coast are accessible from Naples by train in under 90 minutes. The L1 line and air-conditioned Campania Express operated by **Ente Autonomo Volturno** (EAV) link Naples to Sorrento, with stops at Herculaneum and Pompeii, allowing easy access to those who wish to visit the Roman ruins.

All train tickets must be validated before boarding by stamping them in machines at the entrance to platforms. If you're using a pass, check that your pass is valid before boarding. You will incur on-the-spot fines if caught with an unvalidated ticket.

Ente Autonomo Volturno
W eavsrl.it

Italo Treno
W italotreno.it

Napoli Centrale
W napolicentrale.it/en

Trenitalia
W trenitalia.com

Long-Distance Buses

Outside Naples, the **SITA** bus service connects towns on the Amalfi Coast between Sorrento and Salerno, with changes required for some destinations. Tickets generally need to be purchased at a local tobacconist *(tabaccheria)* before boarding and seats cannot be reserved. Those suffering from motion sickness should be prepared for a twisting ride through the hills of the Amalfi Coast.

Capri, **Ischia** and **Procida** all have local bus services around the islands, although service is infrequent. Be sure to check the schedules and arrive well before the scheduled departure of the bus you want to take.

Capri
W capri.com/en/getting-around#section-getting-around-02

Ischia
W ischia.it

Procida
W procidareview.com/procida-buses.html

SITA
W sitasudtrasporti.it

Ferries and Hydrofoils

One of the easiest, but more expensive ways to get around the region is by the ferries that connect Naples, the Amalfi Coast and the islands further afield. There are several ferry companies to choose from. From Naples to Ischia, for example, there are nearly 35 choices per day, with cheaper ferries and the more expensive but faster hydrofoils leaving from the main port all day. Trips generally range between 50 and 90 minutes depending on the destination. Nearly 20 ferries shuttle between Naples and Capri and between Naples and Procida each day. Ferries also link Naples to Sorrento, where visitors can change to another boat going up the coast to Positano and Amalfi. The **Naples Bay Ferry** website is a comprehensive resource for planning.

Tickets are usually readily available until a few minutes before departure at the ticket windows at the port. Prices range between €12 and €25 for a one-way fare. Be sure to give yourself plenty of time to purchase tickets. Note that services are reduced on Sundays and holidays.

Naples Bay Ferry
W naplesbayferry.com/en/index

Metro, Funiculars and Buses

Naples Metro has a fairly straightforward system with Linea 1, Linea 2, Linea 6 (currently closed) and the Napoli-Aversa line. Single tickets cost €1.50 from ticket windows or machines, and can be used for 90 minutes after being validated. Art aficionados may want to explore Linea 1, known as the Metro dell'Arte for the contemporary works of art by local and international artists that have been installed in many of its stations.

More important for visitors are the many funiculars that transport people up and down the hills in Naples and beyond – a welcome alternative to walking up steep staircases. Naples has four funiculars linking the centre to Vomero and Posillipo, while Capri town has one. Buy tickets directly before boarding.

Buses are the best way to get to the airport, around the Amalfi Coast and around the islands. Due to traffic congestion within the city of Naples, however, they are not always the fastest way to get around – walking or taking the metro or funiculars will be often faster. If you are heading further afield, or if mobility is an issue, the public bus system may well be more helpful. The **Hop On Hop Off** buses are a good option for an overview of the city's main sights.

Hop On Hop Off
W hop-on-hop-off-bus.com

Naples Metro
W anm.it

Taxis

Naples has a reputation for taxi scams, but it is an easy thing to avoid. Licensed taxis have a menu of fares posted in the car that you can ask to see, and fares are determined based on the starting point and destination as marked on it. While most drivers are honest, tourists may sometimes be charged double unless the fare was clearly defined before the trip. If a driver tries to suggest that it is a holiday or that the fares do not apply, do not board the taxi. Avoid drivers who seem too eager to pick you up. Visit **Napoli Unplugged** for useful taxi information. Private services like Uber are not available.

Napoli Unplugged
w napoliunplugged.com/naples-taxi-services

Driving

Car Rental

To rent a car in Italy you must be over 21 and have held a valid driver's licence for at least a year. Some companies may allow drivers to rent at the age of 18 if they have held their licence for at least one year. Most apply young driver surcharges for under 25s.

Driving licences issued by any of the EU member states are valid in Italy. If visiting from outside the EU, you may need to apply for an International Driving Permit (IDP). Check with your local automobile association. Most rental agencies in Naples operate near the main train station, allowing drivers to avoid the traffic of the central areas of town.

Driving to Naples

While driving within Naples is challenging, a car can be an easy way to get to and around the region. If you bring your own foreign-registered car into the country, you must carry a Green Card, the vehicle's registration documents and a valid driver's licence with you when driving.Main towns and cities often enforce a ZTL (Limited Traffic Zone). To avoid fines, consult the **Urban Access Regulations in Europe** website.

Toll fees are payable on most motorways (*autostrade*), and payment is made at the end of the journey by cash, credit card or pre-paid magnetic VIA cards. These are available from tobacconists and the **ACI** (Automobile Club d'Italia). You can avoid tolls by using the national roads (*strade nazionali*) or secondary state roads (*strade statali*). Although less direct, they are often more scenic, allowing you to stop at viewpoints, towns and places of interest en route. One of the most famous, the Amalfi Drive (State Road 163) connects Amalfi Coast towns through a winding but very scenic route.

Drivers should note that roads known as white roads (*strade bianche*) have only a gravel surface. These are often narrow and steep, but are usually passable to cars. However, always check your route before travelling.

ACI
w aci.it
Urban Access Regulations in Europe
w urbanaccessregulations.eu

Rules of the Road

Make sure you are familiar with the rules of the road and have all your documentation, as traffic police (*carabinieri*) carry out routine checks. Drive on the right, use the left lane only for passing, and yield to traffic from the right. Seat belts are required for all passengers in the front and back, and heavy fines are levied for using a mobile phone while driving. Dipped headlights are compulsory during the day on motorways, dual carriageways and on all out-of-town roads.

A red warning triangle, fluorescent vests and spare tyre must be carried at all times for use in an emergency. If you have an accident or break-down, switch on your hazard warning lights and place the triangle 50 m (55 yd) behind your vehicle. For breakdowns call the ACI (116) or the emergency services (112 or 113). The ACI will tow any foreign-registered vehicle to the nearest affiliated garage free of charge.

Italy has a strict limit of 0.5 mg BAC (blood alcohol content) for drivers. This means that you cannot drink more than one small beer or a small glass of wine if you plan to drive. For drivers with less than three years of driving experience the limit is 0.

Bicycles and Motorbikes

It is not advisable to try riding motorbikes, scooters or bicycles within Naples. Traffic is difficult to navigate and cobbled streets and tangled alleys make it harder and less enjoyable than simply walking or taking public transport. However, all three are excellent options on the islands, where traffic is less dense and the hills not very daunting. E-bikes are also a popular option in Procida.

Walking

Walking is the most agreeable way to explore Naples and other towns, but always pay close attention to the traffic. On the Amalfi Coast and the islands, cross-country walks can be a peaceful and even exciting adventure for those who are reasonably fit, although reliable maps can be hard to come by. The famed Sentiero degli Dei, or Path of the Gods, which stretches 7.6 km (4.7 miles) between Praiano and Positano, offers breathtaking views of the Amalfi Coast and is a popular hike. Walking on larger roads or highways is not recommended anywhere.

PRACTICAL
INFORMATION

A little local know-how goes a long way in Naples and the Amalfi Coast. Here you will find all the essential information you will need during your stay.

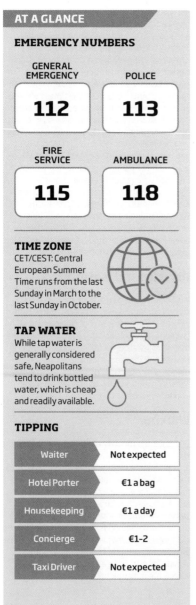

AT A GLANCE

EMERGENCY NUMBERS

GENERAL EMERGENCY	POLICE
112	**113**

FIRE SERVICE	AMBULANCE
115	**118**

TIME ZONE
CET/CEST: Central European Summer Time runs from the last Sunday in March to the last Sunday in October.

TAP WATER
While tap water is generally considered safe, Neapolitans tend to drink bottled water, which is cheap and readily available.

TIPPING

Waiter	Not expected
Hotel Porter	€1 a bag
Housekeeping	€1 a day
Concierge	€1-2
Taxi Driver	Not expected

Personal Security

Naples is a generally safe city, but be wary of pickpockets on public transport and in crowded areas, especially around markets. While stereotypes about organized crime still prevail, the reality is that visitors are usually not affected by this. Most areas of Naples feel safe during the day, but, as in any city, general caution should be exercised in certain areas at night. Wandering into residential areas may attract attention from locals, but this should not be interpreted as threatening. If you have anything stolen, report the crime to the nearest police station within 24 hours; take ID with you if possible. If you need to make an insurance claim, get a copy of the crime report (denuncia). Contact your embassy if you have your passport stolen, or in the event of a serious crime or accident. During big football matches or celebrations, piazzas can get a bit rowdy, with outdoor drinking and fireworks.

Health

If you fall sick, pharmacies (farmacie) are a good source of advice – they can diagnose minor ailments, suggest appropriate treatment and supply medicines. You can find details of the nearest 24-hour service on all pharmacy doors. The **UK Foreign and Commonwealth Office** publishes a list of English-speaking doctors.

Emergency medical care is free for all EU and Australian citizens if you have an **EHIC** or **Medicare** card (p207). Citizens of other countries have to pay for medical expenses, so it is important to arrange insurance before your trip (p206).
UK Foreign and Commonwealth Office
W assets.publishing.service.gov.uk/government/uploads/system/uploads/attachment_data/file/687019/Italy_List_of_Medical_Practitioners.pdf

Smoking, Alcohol and Drugs

Smoking is banned in enclosed public places, though some locals do not adhere strictly to these rules. The possession of illegal drugs is prohibited and could result in a prison sentence.

ID

By law you must carry identification at all times in Italy. A photocopy of your passport photo page (and visa if applicable) should suffice. If you are stopped by the police you may be asked to present the original within 12 hours.

Bar and Café Culture

In Italy, establishments called "bars" are not just for alcoholic drinks but also for coffee. Often you'll pay for your coffee at a till and present the receipt to the bartender who will serve a glass of water and espresso while you're standing at the bar. At outdoor tables, waiters will usually come to newly seated patrons. It is normal to ask for the bill afterwards if the server does not bring it to the table immediately, and a simple raised hand and eye contact should do the trick.

LGBT+ Travel

Homosexuality is legal in Italy, but the southern regions, including Naples, are less open about non-traditional relationships or sexualities. While overt displays of affection may receive glances from locals, LGBT+ travellers should not feel unsafe, especially in the more touristy parts of the city, the Amalfi Coast and Capri. There are few recognized gay bars or districts, although there is a Pride Parade in June.

Visiting Churches and Cathedrals

Entrance to many churches is free, although there may be entry fees for the more famous monuments. Strict dress codes apply: cover your torso and upper arms, and ensure shorts and skirts cover your knees.

Mobile Phones and Wi-Fi

Wi-Fi is generally widely available throughout the region, and cafés and restaurants will usually give you the password for their Wi-Fi if you make a purchase. Visitors travelling to Italy with EU tariffs are able to use their devices without being affected by roaming charges – they will pay the same rates for data, SMS and voice calls as they would pay at home.

Post

Stamps (francobolli) are sold at tobacconists (tabaccherie) – look for a blue sign with a white T. Although the state post can be slow, the private postal services with yellow letterboxes at shops and stalls cost more and usually take longer.

Taxes and Refunds

VAT (called IVA in Italy) is usually 22 per cent, with a reduced rate of 4–10 per cent on some items. Non-EU citizens can claim an IVA rebate subject to certain conditions. It is easier to claim before you buy; you will need to show your passport to the shop assistant and complete a form. If claiming retrospectively, present a customs officer with your purchases and receipts at the airport. Receipts will be stamped and sent back to the vendor to issue a refund.

Discount Cards

The **Naples Pass** offers discounts on entry to some main sights, city tours, routes to Procida and Ischia and at well-known restaurants. Many variations of the pass are available, with some including use of public transport. The **Campania Artecard** covers an astonishingly long list of sights across the region. Again, there are several variations, so look at the website to decide which suits your itinerary best.

Campania Artecard
W www.campaniartecard.it
Naples Pass
W naplespass.eu/en

INDEX

Page numbers in **bold** refer to main entries.

E

F

G

H

PHRASE BOOK

IN AN EMERGENCY

Help!	Aiuto!	eye-**yoo**-toh
Stop!	Ferma!	fair-**mah**
Call a doctor	Chiama un medico	kee-**ah**-mah oon **meh**-dee-koh
Call an ambulance	Chiama un' ambulanza	kee-**ah**-mah oon am-boo-**lan**-tsa
Call the police	Chiama la polizia	kee-**ah**-mah lah pol-ee-**tsee**-ah
Call the fire brigade	Chiama i pompieri	kee-**ah**-mah ee pom-pee-**air**-ee
Where is the telephone?	Dov'è il telefono?	dov-**eh**eel teh-**leh**-foh-noh?
The nearest hospital?	L'ospedale più vicino?	loss-peh-**dah**-leh pee-**oo**vee-**chee**-noh?

COMMUNICATION ESSENTIALS

Yes/No	Sì/No	see/noh
Please	Per favore	pair fah-**vor**-eh
Thank you	Grazie	**grah**-tsee-eh
Excuse me	Mi scusi	mee **skoo**-zee
Hello	Buon giorno	bwon **jor**-noh
Goodbye	Arrivederci	ah-ree-veh-**dair**-chee
Good evening	Buona sera	**bwon**-ah **sair**-ah
morning	la mattina	lah mah-**tee**-nah
afternoon	il pomeriggio	eel poh-meh-**ree**-joh
evening	la sera	luh **sair**-ah
yesterday	ieri	ee-**air**-ee
today	oggi	**oh**-jee
tomorrow	domani	doh-**mah**-nee
here	qui	kwee
there	la	lah
What?	Quale?	**kwah**-leh?
When?	Quando?	**kwan**-doh?
Why?	Perchè?	pair-**keh**?
Where?	Dove?	**doh**-veh

USEFUL PHRASES

How are you?	Come sta?	**koh**-meh stah?
Very well, thank you.	Molto bene, grazie	**moll**-toh **beh**-neh **grah**-tsee-eh
Pleased to meet you.	Piacere di conoscerla.	pee-ah-**chair**-eh dee coh-**noh**-shair-lah
See you soon.	A più tardi.	ah pee-**oo** tar-dee
That's fine.	Va bene.	va **beh**-neh
Where is/are ...?	Dov'è/Dove sono...?	dov-**eh**/doveh **soh**noh?
How long does it take to get to ...?	Quanto tempo ci vuole per andare a ...?	**kwan**-toh **tem**-poh chee voo-oh-leh pair an-**dar**-eh ah...?
How do I get to ...?	Come faccio per arrivare a ...?	koh-meh **fah**-choh pair arri-**var**-eh ah...?
Do you speak English?	Parla inglese?	par-lah een-**gleh**-zeh?
I don't understand.	Non capisco.	non ka-**pee**-skoh
Could you speak more slowly, please?	Può parlare più lentamente, per favore?	pwoh par-**lah**-reh pee-**oo** len-ta-**men**-teh pair fah-**vor**-eh?
I'm sorry.	Mi dispiace.	mee dee-spee-**ah**-cheh

USEFUL WORDS

big	grande	**gran**-deh
small	piccolo	**pee**-koh-loh
hot	caldo	**kal**-doh
cold	freddo	**fred**-doh
good	buono	**bwoh**-noh
bad	cattivo	kat-**tee**-voh
enough	basta	**bas**-tah
well	bene	**beh**-neh
open	aperto	ah-**pair**-toh
closed	chiuso	kee-**oo**-zoh
left	a sinistra	ah see-**nee**-strah
right	a destra	ah **dess**-trah
straight on	sempre dritto	**sem**-preh **dree**-toh
near	vicino	vee-**chee**-noh
far	lontano	lon-**tah**-noh
up	su	soo
down	giù	joo
early	presto	**press**-toh
late	tardi	**tar**-dee
entrance	entrata	en-**trah**-tah
exit	uscita	oo-**shee**-ta
toilet	il gabinetto	eel gah-bee-**net**-toh
free, unoccupied	libero	**lee**-bair-oh
free, no charge	gratuito	grah-**too**-ee-toh

MAKING A TELEPHONE CALL

I'd like to place a long-distance call.	Vorrei fare una interurbana.	vor-**ray** far-eh oona in-tair-oor-**bah**-nah.
I'd like to make a reverse-charge call.	Vorrei fare una telefonata a carico del destinatario.	vor-**ray** far-eh oona teh-leh-fon-**ah**-tah ah kar-ee-koh dell dess-tee-nah-**tar**-ree-oh.
Could I speak to...?	Potrei parlare con...?	po-tray par-lah-reh con?
I'll try again later.	Ritelefono più tardi.	ree-teh-**leh**-foh-noh pee-oo tar-dee.
Can I leave a message?	Posso lasciare un messaggio?	**poss**-oh lash-**ah**-reh oon mess-**sah**-joh?
Hold on	Un attimo, per favore	oon **ah**-tee-moh, pair fah-**vor**-eh
Could you speak up a little please?	Può parlare più forte, per favore?	pwoh par-**lah**-reh pee-**oo** for-teh, pair fah-**vor**-eh?
local call	la telefonata locale	lah teh-leh-fon-**ah**-ta loh-**kah**-leh

SHOPPING

How much does this cost?	Quant'è, per favore?	kwan-**teh**, pair fah-**vor**-eh?
I would like ...	Vorrei ...	vor-**ray**...
Do you have ...?	Avete ...?	ah-**veh**-teh...?
I'm just looking.	Sto soltanto guardando	stoh sol-**tan**-toh gwar-**dan**-doh
Do you take credit cards?	Accettate carte di credito?	ah-chet-**tah**-teh **kar**-teh dee creh-dee-toh?
What time do you open/close?	A che ora apre/ chiude?	ah keh or-ah **ah**-preh/kee-**oo**-deh?
this one	questo	**kweh**-stoh
that one	quello	**kwell**-oh
expensive	caro	**kar**-oh
cheap	a buon prezzo	ah bwon **pret**-soh
size, clothes	la taglia	lah **tah**-lee-ah
size, shoes	il numero	eel **noo**-mair-oh
white	bianco	bee-**ang**-koh
black	nero	**neh**-roh
red	rosso	**ross**-oh
blue	blu	bloo
green	verde	**vair**-deh
yellow	giallo	**jal**-loh

TYPES OF SHOP

antique dealer	l'antiquario	lan-tee-**kwah**-ree-oh
bakery	la panetteria	lah pah-net-tair-**ree**-ah
bank	la banca	lah **bang**-kah
bookshop	la libreria	lah lee-breh-**ree**-ah
butcher's	la macelleria	lah mah-chell-eh-**ree**-ah
cake shop	la pasticceria	lah pas-tee-chair-**ee**-ah
chemist's	la farmacia	lah far-mah-**chee**-ah
department store	il grande magazzino	eel **gran**-deh mag-gad-**zee**-noh
delicatessen	la salumeria	lah sah-loo-meh-**ree**-ah
fishmonger's	la pescheria	lah pess-keh-**ree**-ah
florist	il fioraio	eel fee-or-**eye**-oh
greengrocer	il fruttivendolo	eel froo-tee-**ven**-doh-loh
grocery	alimentari	ah-lee-men-**tah**-ree
hairdresser	il parrucchiere	eel par-oo-kee-**air**-eh
ice cream parlour	la gelateria	lah jel-lah-tair-**ee**-ah
market	il mercato	eel mair-**kah**-toh
news-stand	l'edicola	leh-**dee**-koh-lah
post office	l'ufficio postale	loo-**fee**-choh pos-**tah**-leh
shoe shop	il negozio di scarpe	eel neh-**goh**-tsioh dee **skar**-peh
supermarket	il supermercato	eel su-pair-mair-**kah**-toh
tobacconist	la tabaccheria	lah tah-ba-kair-**ree**-ah
travel agency	l'agenzia di viaggi	lah-jen-**tsee**-ah dee vee-**ad**-jee

SIGHTSEEING

art gallery	la pinacoteca	lahpeena-koh-**teh**-kah
bus stop	la fermata dell'autobus	lah fair-**mah**-tah dell **ow**-toh-booss
church	la chiesa la basilica	lah kee-**eh**-zah lah bah-**seel**-i-kah
garden	il giardino	eel jar-**dee**-no
library	la biblioteca	lah beeb-lee-oh-**teh**-kah

221

museum	il museo	eel moo-zeh-oh
railway station	la stazione	lah stah-tsee-oh-neh
tourist	l'ufficio	loo-fee-choh
information	turistico	too-ree-stee-koh
closed for the	chiuso per la	kee-oo-zoh pair lah
public holiday	festa	fess-tah

STAYING IN A HOTEL

Do you have any	Avete camere	ah-veh-teh kah-mair
vacant rooms?	libere?	-eh lee-bair-eh?
double room	una camera	oona kah-mair-ah
	doppia	doh-pee-ah
with double bed	con letto	kon let-toh mah-tree-
	matrimoniale	moh-nee-ah-leh
twin room	una camera	oona kah-mair-ah
	con due letti	kon doo-eh let-tee
single room	una camera	oona kah-mair-ah
	singola	sing-goh-lah
room with a	una camera	oona kah-mair-ah
bath, shower	con bagno,	kon ban-yoh,
	con doccia	kon dot-chah
porter	il facchino	eel fah-kee-noh
key	la chiave	lah kee-ah-veh
I have a	Ho fatto una	oh fat-toh oona preh-
reservation.	prenotazione.	noh-tah-tsee-oh-neh

EATING OUT

Have you got	Avete un tavolo	ah-veh-teh oon
a table for ...?	per ... ?	tah-voh-loh pair ...?
I'd like to	Vorrei riservare	vor-ray ree-sair-vah-
reserve a table.	un tavolo.	reh oon tah-voh-loh
breakfast	colazione	koh-lah-tsee-oh-neh
lunch	pranzo	pran-tsoh
dinner	cena	cheh-nah
The bill, please.	Il conto, per	eel kon-toh pair
	favore.	fah-vor-eh
I am a vegetarian.	Sono	soh-noh veh-jeh-tar
	vegetariano/a.	ee-ah-noh/nah
waitress	cameriera	kah-mair-ee-air-ah
waiter	cameriere	kah-mair-ee-air-eh
fixed price	il menù a	eel meh-noo ah
menu	prezzo fisso	pret-soh fee-soh
dish of the day	piatto del giorno	pee-ah-toh dell jor-no
starter	antipasto	an-tee-pass-toh
first course	il primo	eel pree-moh
main course	il secondo	eel seh-kon-doh
vegetables	il contorno	eel kon-tor-noh
dessert	il dolce	eel doll-che
cover charge	il coperto	eel koh-pair-toh
wine list	la lista dei	lah lee-stah day
	vini	vee-nee
rare	al sangue	al sang-gweh
medium	a puntino	a poon-tee-noh
well done	ben cotto	ben kot-toh
glass	il bicchiere	eel bee-kee-air-eh
bottle	la bottiglia	lah bot-teel-yah
knife	il coltello	eel kol-tell-oh
fork	la forchetta	lah for-ket-tah
spoon	il cucchiaio	eel koo-kee-eye-oh

MENU DECODER

apple	la mela	lah meh-lah
artichoke	il carciofo	eel kar-choff-oh
aubergine	la melanzana	lah meh-lan-tsah-nah
baked	al forno	al for-noh
beans	i fagioli	ee fah-joh-lee
beef	il manzo	eel man-tsoh
beer	la birra	lah beer-rah
boiled	lesso	less-oh
bread	il pane	eel pah-neh
butter	il burro	eel boor-oh
cake	la torta	lah tor-tah
cheese	il formaggio	eel for-mad-joh
chicken	il pollo	eel poll-oh
chips	patatine fritte	pah-tah-teen-eh
		free-teh
baby clams	le vongole	leh von-goh-leh
coffee	il caffè	eel kah-feh
courgettes	gli zucchini	lyee dzoo-kee-nee
dry	secco	sek-koh
duck	l'anatra	lah-nah-trah
egg	l'uovo	loo-oh-voh
fish	il pesce	eel pesh-eh
fresh fruit	frutta fresca	froo-tah fress-kah
garlic	l'aglio	lahl-yoh
grapes	l'uva	loo-vah
grilled	alla griglia	ah-lah greel-yah
ham	il prosciutto	eel pro-shoo-toh
cooked/cured	cotto/crudo	kot-toh/kroo-doh
ice cream	il gelato	eel jel-lah-toh

lamb	l'abbacchio	lah-back-kee-oh
lobster	l'aragosta	lah-rah-goss-tah
meat	la carne	la kar-neh
milk	il latte	eel laht-teh
mineral water	l'acqua minerale	lah-kwah mee-nair-
fizzy/still	gasata/naturale	ah-leh gah-zah-tah/
		nah-too-rah-leh
mushrooms	i funghi	ee foon-gee
oil	l'olio	loll-yoh
olive	l'oliva	loh-lee-vah
onion	la cipolla	lah chee-poll-ah
orange	l'arancia	lah-ran-chah
orange/lemon	succo d'arancia/	soo-kohdah-ran-chah/
juice	di limone	dee lee-moh-neh
peach	la pesca	lah pess-kah
pepper	il pepe	eel peh-peh
pork	carne di maiale	kar-neh dee
		mah-yah-leh
potatoes	le patate	leh pah-tah-teh
prawns	i gamberi	ee gam-bair-ee
rice	il riso	eel ree-zoh
roast	arrosto	ar-ross-toh
roll	il panino	eel pah-nee-noh
salad	l'insalata	leen-sah-lah-tah
salt	il sale	eel sah-leh
sausage	la salsiccia	lah sal-see-chah
seafood	frutti di mare	froo-tee-dee-mah-reh
soup	la zuppa,	lah tsoo-pah,
	la minestra	lah mee-ness-trah
steak	la bistecca	lah bee-stek-kah
strawberries	le fragole	leh frah-goh-leh
sugar	lo zucchero	loh zoo-kair-oh
tea	il tè	eel teh
herb tea	la tisana	lah tee-zah-nah
tomato	il pomodoro	eel poh-moh-dor-oh
tuna	il tonno	eel ton-noh
veal	il vitello	eel vee-tell-oh
vegetables	i legumi	ee leh-goo-mee
vinegar	l'aceto	lah-cheh-toh
water	l'acqua	lah-kwah
red wine	vino rosso	vee-noh ross-oh
white wine	vino bianco	vee-noh bee-ang-koh

NUMBERS

1	uno	oo-noh
2	due	doo-eh
3	tre	treh
4	quattro	kwat-roh
5	cinque	ching-kweh
6	sei	say-ee
7	sette	set-teh
8	otto	ot-toh
9	nove	noh-veh
10	dieci	dee-eh-chee
11	undici	oon-dee-chee
12	dodici	doh-dee-chee
13	tredici	treh-dee-chee
14	quattordici	kwat-tor-dee-chee
15	quindici	kwin-dee-chee
16	sedici	say-dee-chee
17	diciassette	dee-chah-set-teh
18	diciotto	dee-chot-toh
19	diciannove	dee-chah-noh-veh
20	venti	ven-tee
30	trenta	tren-tah
40	quaranta	kwah-ran-tah
50	cinquanta	ching-kwan-tah
60	sessanta	sess-an-tah
70	settanta	set-tan-tah
80	ottanta	ot-tan-tah
90	novanta	noh-van-tah
100	cento	chen-toh
1,000	mille	mee-leh
2,000	duemila	doo-eh mee-lah
5,000	cinquemila	ching-kweh mee-lah
1,000,000	un milione	oon meel-yoh-neh

TIME

one minute	un minuto	oon mee-noo-toh
one hour	un'ora	oon or-ah
half an hour	mezz'ora	medz-or-ah
a day	un giorno	oon jor-noh
a week	una settimana	oona set-tee-mah-nah
Monday	lunedì	loo-neh-dee
Tuesday	martedì	mar-teh-dee
Wednesday	mercoledì	mair-koh-leh-dee
Thursday	giovedì	joh-veh-dee
Friday	venerdì	ven-air-dee
Saturday	sabato	sah-bah-toh
Sunday	domenica	doh-meh-nee-kah

ACKNOWLEDGMENTS

The publisher would like to thank the following for their kind permission to reproduce their photographs:

Key: a-above; b-below/bottom; c-centre; f-far; l-left; r-right; t-top

123RF.com: evrenkalinbacak 77cra; Eddy Galeotti 145bl.

4Corners: Guido Baviera 195cra; Susanne Kremer 151tl.

Alamy Stock Photo: Adam Eastland Art + Architecture 59bl, 97; age fotostock / Christian Goupi 106-7b, / Danuta Hyniewska 84-5t, / Carlo Morucchio 200-1b, / Jose Peral 13t, 25tl, / Angela Sorrentino 43cl, 67bl; AGF Srl / Hermes Images 196tl, / Giuseppe Masci 17br, 29tc, 110-1, 139clb; Archive Farms Inc / Burton Holmes Historical Collection 167tr; Arco Images GmbH / B. Bönsch 27c, 56bl, 56-7, 87b, 153tr, / Joko 190t; aroundtheworld.photography 26bl; AWP 118bl; Bailey-Cooper Photography 28-9t, 69tl; Mark Bassett 16br, 72-3; Laura Di Biase 29br; Bildagentur-online / Joko 16cl, 52-3, 62b, 108bl; Stuart Black 182-3b; Bogomyako 33br; George Brice 165; Michael Brooks 11br, 64tl; Massimo Buonaiuto 132bl; Frank Chmura 193; Roy Conchie 160bl; Ian Dagnall 80b, 167ca; Design Pics Inc / Axiom / Keith Levit 22crb; Andrew Duke 11cr, 94bl; Adam Eastland 13br, 104t, 119t, 120-1t, 125tl; Peter Eastland 36-7t, 39tl, 70; eFesenko 86tl, 100bl, 187t; Richard Ellis 33cl; federikk 122-3b, 123tr, 125br,133tr; funkyfood London - Paul Williams 12clb, 195cla; Gibon Art 117tr; Giovanni Guarino Photo 78b; Antonio Gravante 39cr; Richard Hart 10clb; hemis.fr / Patrice Hauser 68bl, 114-5t, / Herve Hughes 30bl, / Ludovic Maisant 56clb; Heritage Image Partnership Ltd / © Fine Art Images 77cla, 133bl; Historic Images 130bc; Peter Horree 31crb, 35crb, 147b; imageBROKER / BAO 130br, / Helmut Corneli 87crb, / Moritz Wolf 95cra; incamerastock / ICP 117br; Independent Photo Agency Srl 44clb; Peppe Iovino 170b; David Jackson 150cla; Inge Johnsson 25tr, 27br, 176b; Evren Kalinbacak 82b; Keystone Press / USA 31cl; Ton Koene 63tr; Lavernicvs 109tl; Lazyllama 39br; Domingo Leiva 58-9t; Look / Sabine Lubenow 12t, 34bl; Francesco Lorenzetti 202bl; Carlo Maggio 96crb; MARKA / touring club italiano 96clb,167tc; Giuseppe Masci 132t; Andrea Matone 88br; mauritius images GmbH / ClickAlps 170tr; MB_Photo 115bc, 116-7b; Annapurna Mellor 35cl; MiraMira 34-5t; Nikreates 146tl; Pacific Press Agency / Salvatore Esposito 44cr; Photononstop / Benoit Bacou 40-1t; Pictorial Press Ltd 48cr; The Picture Art Collection 96cb; Pictures Now 99cb; Enrico Della Pietra 18tr, 79crb,126-7; Premium Stock Photography GmbH / Scattolin 131tr; Anna Quaglia 77br, 135b; Alex Ramsay 12-3b; Realy Easy Star / Salvatore Pipia 105br; REDA & CO srl / Alfio Giannotti 82tl, 171br, 173t, / Giuseppe Greco 148bl, / Vittorio Sciosia 44crb, 192clb; John Reveley 19t, 154-5; robertharding / Eleanor Scriven 50-1, 61br; Paolo Romiti 10ca; Alexandre Rotenberg 151bl; Shalom Rufeisen 41b; Francesca Sciarra 121br, 164clb; Vittorio Sciosia 32tl, 32-3b,102tl; Douglas Scott 137br; steven gillis hd9 imaging 182tr; David Sutherland 163t; Tetra Images 145t; Jane Tregelles 192bl; Ivan Vdovin 47tr, 77tc, 95tl, 115clb; Christine Webb 116t; Westend61 GmbH / Lisa und Wilfried Bahnmüller 189bl; Susan Wright 172cra; Z2A Collection 42-3b; ZUMA Press; Inc. / Fabio Sasso 83t.

© Archivio Museo Cappella Sansevero: Marco Ghidelli 81tr.

AWL Images: ClickAlps 2-3; Michele Falzone 184cl; Francesco Iacobelli 178-9b; Montico Lionel 38b.

Bridgeman Images: 47cb; Marcello Mencarini 48br; Luisa Ricciarini / *Plan of Naples* (Neapolis), Italy from Civitates Orbis Terrarum (Atlas of World Cities) by Georg Braun (1541-1622) and Franz Hogenberg (1540-1590) 46t.

Culinary Backstreets www.culinarybackstreets.com: Gianni Cipriano 37crb.

Dreamstime.com: Alexirina27000 20t; Alkan2011 40bl; Leonid Andronov 20crb, 197b; Ivan Bastien 45cl; Bographics 164cra; Claudio Camilli 49tr; Digoarpi 8clb; Eddygaleotti 18bl, 140-1; Elenaphotos 101cla; Iannone Gerardo 22cr; Ruslans Golenkovs 117cla; Antonio Gravante 13cr, 24-5ca; Laszlo Konya 85br; Vladimir Korostyshevskiy 59br; Laudibi 66-7t, 136, 144bl; Lucamato 44cra; Rosario Manzo 134tl; Marcorubino 181cra; Massimobuonaiuto 171crb; Minnystock 166-7b; Danilo Mongiello 44cl; Roberto Nencini 194-5b; Massimo Parisi 195t; Simona Pavan 139b; Phanompai 37cla; Photogolfer 42-3t; Enrico Della Pietra 56ca, 98-9b, 115cb,199t; Barbara Pinto 171cr; Dzianis Rabtsevich 158-9t; Floriano Rescigno 11t, 174-5t, 175clb, 175bl; Rudi1976 6-7, 185br; Scaliger 24tl; Victoria Schaal 168-9t; Jacek Sopotnicki 38tl; Tanialerro 203t; Daria Trefilova 44cla; Xantana 30-1t.

Getty Images: Bettmann 43crb, 49clb; Giorgio Cosulich 163bl; De Agostini Picture Library / DEA 102bc, 134br, / A. Dagli Orti 46br, 47bl, 117cb / G. Dagli Orti 33tr, 48tl, 48bc, / Archivo J. Lange 46bc, / MUST 47cra, / G. Nimatallah 98tr, / L. Romano 59tr, 59ca, 159bc, 162bl; Hulton Fine Art Collection / Mondadori Portfolio 47tl; The LIFE Picture Collection / Alfred Eisenstaedt 48-9t, / George Rodger 167cra; LightRocket / KONTROLAB 45tr, 45cr, 49bc, 101t, 149t, 173cr; Lonely Planet Images / Richard I'Anson 26-7t; Moment / Francesco Riccardo Iacomino 22t; NurPhoto / Paolo Manzo 45tl; Photolibrary / Eri Morita 192crb, / Maremagnum 24tr; Stockbyte / Atlantide Phototravel / Massimo Borchi 65b.

iStockphoto.com: Angelafoto 8cl, 45crb, 89tl, 103b, 198bl; cnicbc 161t; drferry 45clb; E+ / spooh 188-9t, / THEPALMER 180t; giorgiogalano 204-5; Eric Hameister 36b; holgs 79tr; MaRabelo 10-1b; mathess 20cr; mikolajn 8-9b, 22bl; Philippe Paternolli 4; peeterv 60t; Planetix 20bl.

Museo MADRE, Naples: Amedeo Benestante / *Lavoro in situ* by Daniel Buren, Axer / Désaxer. (2015) Courtesy l'artista, © DB-ADAGP Paris and DACS, London 2019 17tl, 28br, 90-1t.

Regina Isabella – Resort SPA Restaurant: 40tc.

Robert Harding Picture Library: Christian Goupi 164br, 171t; Carlo Moruchio 159clb.

SuperStock: Funkystock / age Fotostock 99tr.

Front flap
Alamy Stock Photo: age Fotostock / Jose Peral cra; Stuart Black br; Domingo Leiva t; **Dreamstime.com:** Floriano Rescigno bl; **Getty Images:** Photolibrary / Eri Morita cla; **iStockphoto.com:** ; E+ / spooh cb.

Sheet Map cover
Getty Images: Francesco Riccardo Iacomino.

Cover images:
Front and Spine: **Getty Images:** Francesco Riccardo Iacomino.
Back: **4Corners:** Susanne Kremer tr; **Alamy Stock Photo:** AGF Srl cla, Richard Hart c; **Getty Images:** Francesco Riccardo Iacomino b.

For further information see: www.dkimages.com

Published for the first time in Italy in 1997, under the title Guida Mondadori: Napoli e Dintorni.
© Fabio Ratti Editoria, Milan 1997
© Dorling Kindersley Ltd, London 1997

Main Contributers Bryan Pirolli, Ros Belford,
Patrizia Antignani, Mariella Barone,
Sima Belmar, Ciro Cacciola, Angela Catello,
Judy Edelhoff, Daniela Lepore, Julius Honnor,
Leonie Loudon, Emilia Marchi, Kirsi Viglione,
Beatrice Vitelli, Barbara Zaragoza

Senior Editor Ankita Awasthi Tröger

Senior Designer Tania Da Silva Gomes

Designers Jordan Lambley, Bharti Karakoti,
Stuti Tiwari Bhatia, Priyanka Thakur

Factchecker Alessandra Pugliese

Editors Emma Grundy Haigh,
Alison McGill, Lucy Sara-Kelly,
Lucy Sienkowska, Jackie Staddon,
Rachel Thompson

Proofreader Clare Peel

Indexer Helen Peters

Senior Picture Researcher Ellen Root

Picture Research Sophie Basilevitch,
Manpreet Kaur, Sumita Khatwani,
Vagisha Pushp, Rituraj Singh

Illustrators Giorgia Boli,
Paola Spampinato, Nadia Viganò

Senior Cartographic Editor James Macdonald

Cartography Rajesh Chhibber,
Subhashree Bharati, Simonetta Giori

Jacket Designers Tania Da Silva Gomes,
Maxine Pedliham

Jacket Picture Research Susie Watters

Senior DTP Designer Jason Little

DTP Rohit Rojal

Producer Rebecca Parton

MIX
Paper from
responsible sources
FSC™ C018179
www.fsc.org

A CIP catalog record for this book
is available from the British Library.

A catalog record for this book is available
from the Library of Congress.

ISSN: 1542 1554
ISBN: 978 0 2414 0800 1

Printed and bound in China.

www.dk.com